ATROCITY
EXHIBITION

ATROCITY EXHIBITION

Life in the Age of Total Violence

BRAD EVANS

This is a LARB Provocations publication
Published by The Los Angeles Review of Books
6671 Sunset Blvd., Suite 1521, Los Angeles, CA 90028
www.larbbooks.org

Brad Evans would like to thank the journals the *South Atlantic Quarterly*, *Theory & Event*, *Review of Education & Critical Pedagogy*, along with *World Financial Review* and the *Reading Lists* for granting permission to reproduce the articles and discussions here. All rights reserved. Copyright was retained by author and printed accordingly for all additional articles and discussions featured.

Cover Artwork: Chantal Meza, Genesis (40x40, Oil on Wood), Museo de Guadalupe, Zacatecas Mexico 2017.

ISBN 978-1-940660-46-2

Library of Congress Control Number: 2018965696

Contents

To Chantal Meza:
Once we were then,
Now we are now, until then.

"The media landscape of the present day is a map in search of a territory. A huge volume of sensational and often toxic imagery inundates our minds, much of it fictional in content. How do we make sense of this ceaseless flow of advertising and publicity, news and entertainment, where presidential campaigns and moon voyages are presented in terms indistinguishable from the launch of a new candy bar or deodorant? What actually happens on the level of our unconscious minds when, within minutes on the same TV screen, a prime minister is assassinated, an actress makes love, an injured child is carried from a car crash? Faced with these charged events, prepackaged emotions already in place, we can only stitch together a set of emergency scenarios, just as our sleeping minds extemporize a narrative from the unrelated memories that veer through the cortical night."

— J. G. Ballard, *The Atrocity Exhibition*

Preface

Russell Brand

I FIRST HEARD of Brad Evans while completing a degree in religion and global politics at SOAS University in London in 2016. I had come to academic study late in life mostly to arm myself with hard critical knowledge in response to an astonishing and sustained personal attack by the British media. As I had begun to publicly comment on politics, the reaction was at times unfathomable. Without rehashing the whole affair here (this is, after all about Brad Evans), the thrust of my argument — conducted through blogs, online videos, *The New Statesman*, *Newsnight*, then ultimately, oddly for a while, all media outlets — was that contemporary, centrist politics made the rituals of electoral democracy redundant. Or as *The Sun* reported it: "Russell Brand Says Don't Vote."

The whole situation got rather out of hand, the attacks increasingly personal. It was spoken about in parliament, on *Fox News*, across the pond and across the political spectrum. What I was saying was being analyzed, rebutted, condemned, and sneered at because one could assume it wasn't supported by a University "education" of a particular kind, or spoken from behind the mastery of a power-dressing suit, suitably cut into the political fabric. Eventually flattened by the deluge, I retreated from the "conversation" and a year or so later made the decision to equip myself more favorably should such a confrontation ever recur.

In SOAS's Religion in Global Politics course you encounter Professor Brad Evans's work somewhere between Michel Foucault and Edward Said. Man, you get hit up with some dense texts in that place: queer theory, orientalism, ontology, post-colonialism, post-modernism, all great icebergs of impenetrable information, with more concealed in the footnotes than visible in the text, written in tiny fonts as the language retreats into microscopic inaccessibility. Every week we'd be assaulted with another block of knowledge and I'd go home and ignore it until the next lecture. Eventually, blessedly, my teacher Sian Hawthorne gave us an essay by Brad Evans where he artfully illustrated how the 9/11 terror attacks had acted upon our shared psyche, ending the idea of a safe, outside space, elucidating how violence is framed, normalized and purposed according to the intentions of the powerful. Brad Evans's writing articulated something that I sensed but could not describe, as if the information was inside me but needed to be ignited and defined in order to become psychically activated. He explained how both the 9/11 attacks and the fall of the Berlin Wall could be understood as real time metaphors: The fall of the wall representing the end of separateness, the annihilation of the point of tension between two rival powers as one imploded; and the spectacle of 9/11 erasing the idea of bounded conflict and facilitating a state of constant terror. Brad's argument showed us that it can happen anywhere, at any time, so however scared you are, you can never be scared enough; and importantly, whatever action "we" take to counter this terror, it can never be too aggressive. In one passage he riffed on the absurdity of a 2011 headline, "9/11 Terror Threat," positing that the event now existed as a dislocated and independent icon, that could be used like a Bat Signal to summon dread and impose insipid popular order. Elsewhere in the piece I was reminded how he demonstrated the ways Tony Blair and George Bush's pre-invasion rhetoric was structurally indistinct from the doctrinaire announcements of declared religious fundamentalists. It was underwritten by an assumption that they were right — that their violence was necessary, rational, reasonable, and proper, and that this idea of "rational violence" was being used to justify actions that, without this normalizing framework, would be regarded as abominable. You could swap out the idea of rational violence for the phrase "This is Allah's will," and other than the specific vocabulary there would be no difference in the actionable words and events. Simply, the powerful use violence to achieve their goals, and then mask that violence as a necessity. And in the process, humans end up becoming what we most despise, in both our language and our actions.

For the first time during my excursion in academia I experienced the possibility that esoteric information could be smuggled from the cloud-capped towers of aloof, circuitous chin-scratchery into the public discourse. Critical thinking now meant something all too important and real: that we can create an alternative to the easy ideas with visceral appeal that spreads like ink through blank minds blotting out all nuance. This book, a series of essays and conversations, is a step toward this alternative. Dear Brad, the silver-haired, handsome and darting Clooney of philosophy, zips through topics as diverse as the 2012 Olympics, Zygmunt Bauman's "self-plagiarism," the devastatingly honest letter to murdered Mexican student Mara Fernanda Castilla, and, well, me, never failing to illuminate important and neglected facets of arguments we are used to seeing presented in specific ways that encourage particular conclusions, which are so often determined in advance. Brad is at ease with complexity and he is able to infect us with that ease. He is able to explain to us the uncertainty many feel around 9/11 and its subsequent repurposing. He fills with knowledge, reason, and passion a gap that may otherwise be filled with fear and conspiracy.

After I read more of Brad's work and felt the warmth of his lucidity, I thought 'Hang on, I have a media profile, I can probably meet him if I want' and I promptly set about tracking him down. It wasn't hard, he's forever online, harping on about violence, continually revealing its subtle presence in the quotidian. My joy at encountering this great educator through his work quickly quadrupled when I discovered he had written about me. Positively! In a glorious, serendipitous flash I came upon his writing about my appearance on *Newsnight*, my *New Statesman* issue, and the subsequent furore. It felt like finding out that Conor McGregor had my back in a pub carpark ruck. Brad's analysis of the coverage, of my commentary and activism, weeded out the confusion and shame that I had felt having been unable to be objective, since I was literally the subject, and helped me to see where I had intuitively been right, why I had been so anxiously and forensically condemned and what I could learn from the process. The essay is included in this volume and I can scarcely read it without being once more engorged with the righteousness that got me into all that bother in the first place.

When I decided to launch a new podcast in which I interviewed important and innovative thinkers, in order to colloquialize and popularize their views, Brad, in part the inspiration for the venture, was the inaugural guest. Since then Naomi Klein, Al Gore, Adam Curtis, Jordan Peterson, Brian Cox, Paul Gilroy, Yuval Harari, and many other great and illustrious guests have featured. But none have Brad's druidic ability to conjure up a complex opinion on basically anything. He must see the world in numbers and codes, the helix of our DNA must refract off the lenses of his glasses. Brad is making critical theory something more than an insular academic pursuit; he is a taut and romantic Prometheus, seizing sizzling branches of hot wisdom and laying them before us.

I've since hung out with Brad (who I now see as a good friend) a fair bit, making podcasts, discussing addiction, working on TV shows, meeting each other's children, and his excitement and sharp triangulating intellect are as powerful in person as in these pages. Within these compelling and yet accessible set of essays and conversations, I hope you will experience the brilliance, originality, warmth and vigor that first attracted me to Brad's work. A great teacher must engage in plain sorcery, this can be almost shamanic: to be able to occupy many worlds simultaneously, the world of academic expertise, rarefied and inaccessible, to be able to reach out and convey without compromise challenging ideas, viscerally, with humor and humanity. This is more than a neat trick, it is magic — power that we do not understand.

At this time, when the end of liberalism, it seems, will inevitably herald a new and dangerous populism — the full implications of which we are only starting to see emerge before our unbelieving eyes — it is important that Brad Evans's work, his compassion, his ability to tell an alternative story to the one of clamouring anthemic dread (more violence, more fear, more atrocities) is supported and spread. We need a politics that will serve the population, not further impede and incarcerate it. And Brad, with his love of popular culture, his busy inquisition into art, media, and football, has precisely the perspective that will be required to oppose the rise of hateful politics.

When we first met, Brad gave me a copy of *Alice in Wonderland*, from his daughter to mine. He said at the time it was the best book of political theory ever written (he also deals with the reasons why in these insightful pages). I hope beyond hope that our daughters will grow up in a world where nuance and complexity are investigated in order that we may experience truth, in all its beauty and sadness. I hope that Brad's mission reaches the many lost and confused people in our world that are contemplating the grim alternatives to love, openness, and trust. I hope you will, within these pages, discover the excitement and optimistic thrill that Brad's writing gave me when I discovered it. A great teacher gives us access to the dormant wisdom within us, this is what Brad Evans has done for me and I hope, through these pages, he does it for you too.

Introduction

Henry A. Giroux

WHAT BRAD EVANS CALLS "The Atrocity Exhibition" no longer hides in the shadows of power and ideological deception. Authoritarianism and the expanding architecture of violence is on the rise not only in countries such as Poland, Hungary, India, and Turkey but also in the United States — a country that, however erratic, has prided itself on its longstanding dream and embrace of democratic rights. Democratic institutions, principles, and passions are under siege not only by the vicious forces of neoliberal capitalism but also by a war culture shaped by resurgent fascism. Unbridled capitalism — with its totalizing belief in market values as a governing template for all social life — inflicts mass misery and unimaginable suffering on its populace as it shifts massive amounts of wealth and resources to the financial elite. At the same time, those in power criminalize an increasing number of social problems — turning, for instance, the war on poverty into a war on the poor, using violence as a tool to address social challenges such as homelessness, school truancy, financial debt, drug addiction, and mental health issues. *Atrocity Exhibition* underscores that politics in the age of neoliberal fascism has become an extension of war; the latter is the template for shaping all relations while state and non-state violence become the medium for enforcing such dynamics.

As its welfare function is eviscerated, the state takes on a greater role in using punishment as an organizing tool to shape all aspects of the social order. Democratic practices are now replaced by genuine horrors as the dreams of a better future turn into ever-present nightmares. The endless production of inequality, poverty, and state violence, accompanied by a growing culture of fear, precarity, and cruelty, have unleashed the mobilizing furies of fascism at a social level. Paroxysms of unchecked rage displace criticism of the genuine horrors of capitalism. Neoliberalism increasingly fuels a right-wing populism that willingly indulges the symbols, language, and logic that echoes fascist history.

As Evans makes clear throughout this book, human beings are now transformed into capital and thus subject to the dictates of privatization, deregulation, commodification, the celebration of self-interests, and a notion of freedom divorced from any sense of social bonds or moral responsibility. All relations are subject to market values and all transactions are wedded to the logic of exchange value and capital accumulation. Such a neoliberal order reduces one's fate solely to a privatized matter of individual responsibility. In return, this reduction is further diminished to questions of character, individual choice, and a faux notion of resilience. Missing from this discourse is any whiff of injustice or reference to larger structural and systemic forms of oppression. Politics now dissolves into pathology.

Older narratives tied to the social contract and welfare state are replaced by the new narratives of racial and social cleansing, which exhibit a disdain for democratic notions of solidarity, community, compassion, and empathy. Out of this disgust, if not hatred, for the basic institutions and principles of democracy, a new white nationalist narrative of disposability emerges that embraces symbolic and visceral violence aimed at those considered tainted by blood, soil, religion, race, and ethnicity. Evans understands this attack on democracy, but he also reveals the possibility of a critical and democratic community: he wants to show how the imperatives of power, war, and violence command the visions of society and produce a radically individualized, competitive, and militant subject and what it means to challenge and transform this dystopian imaginary.

Neoliberal fascism produces a new kind of devastation, particularly in the United States. It is marked by escalating poverty and misery among large sections of the public: relentless violence; an epidemic of social isolation; the opioid crisis; mass shootings; the growing presence of the police in all public spheres; and a culture of fear that strengthens the security state. These atrocities move between two modalities: spectacle and brutality. An aesthetics of depravity and an endless display of captivating spectacles turn hyper-violence into a form of sport, maximizing the pleasure of violence by giving it a fascist edge, while the real and visceral brutalities of unimaginable violence

continue — everything from the mass murder of over 2,600 people after the Twin Towers terrorist strike to the murderous attacks on the 43
college students in Iguala, Guerrero, Mexico, to the endless killing of
the innocent women and children as portrayed in the work of Mexican
artist Chantal Meza and Gottfried Helnwein.

Violence no longer shocks; it feeds the news cycles and becomes fod-
der for Hollywood blockbusters all the while numbing a wider public
to the conditions that make its existence and trivialization possible.
Atrocities have become routine, normalized in the United States —
landscapes of horror on exhibit for a social order that elevates violence
to its central organizing principle. Indeed, as Evans observes, violence
has moved from a tool of terror and punishment to an exhibition that
signals both the loss of historical memory and a flight from reason and
ethics. Is it any wonder that notions of collective responsibility have
been replaced by a collective numbing that collapses the line between
a genuine ethical crisis and the fog of political indifference? As Evans
makes clear, this is a violence that is as existential as it is visceral. There
is nothing abstract about violence, especially under the leadership of
a growing number of authoritarian leaders, with Trump at the front of
the line — leaders who both enable and legitimate it.

Fascism thrives on contradictions that serve the ruthless and powerful. For instance, Trump cages children who are separated from their
parents, stripped naked, shackled to chairs, and left in solitary con-
finement. Yet, he criticizes basketball great LeBron James who builds
a public school for at-risk youth. As Charles Blow put it in *The New York
Times*: "Hover over the irony here: the man trying to help at-risk children by opening doors for them was being attacked by the man who
has put children at risk by locking them in cages." Trump claimed he
was going to drain the swamp. Instead, he turned it into a toxic waste
site filled with corrupt and incompetent political hacks who are ethically tranquilized. His apologists, such as Ann Coulter and Alex Jones,
revel in spewing out insults about defenseless children. Right-wing
celebrity pundit Coulter shamelessly claimed that youth speaking
out against gun violence were child actors, imposters showcasing the
slaughter of innocence for fame and self-promotion. Conspiracy theorist, radio host, and ally of Donald Trump Alex Jones went further and
claimed that the Sandy Hook shooting was a hoax. This is a small and
selected snapshot of the culture of cruelty that accompanies a fascist
social order.

What these snapshots point to is a new political narrative suited to the present moment. Under current historical circumstances, the elements of fascism have reappeared most visibly in the discourse of imperial bravado, unchecked racism, anti-immigrant fervor, a hatred of Muslims, apocalyptic populism, a hyper-masculinity, an unapologetic anti-intellectualism, a contempt for weakness, and a contempt for dissent. This is the atrocity exhibition, the fragments of a dystopian present, which signals a new script for the mass, everyday violence that accompanies the rise of neoliberal fascism in the United States and the rise of illiberal democracies abroad. It demands, as Evans writes, that we "rethink historical memory, the meaning of the intolerable, the state sponsored violence," and the horror of what he calls "disposable futures."

Evans calls for a comprehensive interrogation of war and violence that is at once historical, relational, systemic, and dialectical, akin to what C. Wright Mills once referred to as the sociological imagination. Consider this book as an invitation to read against the culture of war and violence — a forum for witnessing the unsettling and unspeakable — as a critical engagement with a culture of visceral and symbolic violence. He offers a politics of ethical necessity to confront the anti-democratic forces that threaten the meaning and substance of democracy, politics, and any viable and just future.

At the center of Evans's work is a meticulous and encompassing attempt to interrogate the historical and multifaceted conditions that create a distinctive and crudely brazen politics. This is dystopian politics marked by a level of self-deceit, moral irresponsibility, and political corruption. At a time when radical and democratic horizons are closing and public spheres are disappearing, Evans highlights how real and symbolic violence turns the language and policies of those in power into weapons of hate and their victims into objects of disposability, social abandonment, and terminal exclusion. The call for walls, militarized borders, increased policing, and mass surveillance makes everyone a suspect and normalizes the culture of terror. The language of blood, purity, and belonging is now fused with expanding machineries of state repression and an attack on dissent. Terror and violence have become the DNA of everyday existence. As Evans observes, "Such violence feels its way into existence. Trusting nobody, fearing everything. That is the real meaning of terror. There is an intimate reality to its appearance." (Chapter 23, "Painting a State of Terror")

Unlike many theorists, Evans interrogates violence not only through the overt forces of the state's repressive apparatuses such as the police, military, and armed thugs, but also through the ideological apparatuses that create the visions and values that fuel right-wing populism and the ideological underpinnings of the financial state. Symbolic and pedagogical repression are crucial for forging neoliberal fascist narratives and a culture of violence. Evans highlights how language is transformed into an endless discourse of dehumanization and scapegoating, broadcast by a massive state-aligned propaganda machine. Evans is particularly insightful in examining how liberals use the language of peace and human rights to legitimate a war culture and new forms of authoritarianism.

Evans makes clear how the retreat from democracy is a betrayal and abandonment of the principles of equality, justice, and freedom. It is precisely this sense of abandonment and betrayal of the vulnerable and the working class in the United States that creates a vacuum for mobilizing the most violent energies of neoliberalism all while promoting the rise of right-wing populist movements.

The emergence of neoliberal fascism and diverse forms of illiberal democracy around the globe points to a terrifying horizon of political repression and violence. Under such circumstances, it has become all the more difficult to theorize a politics that matters, to recover a language that has real meaning, and to develop pedagogical practices that speak to concrete needs and conditions. *Atrocity Exhibition* is a clarion call to fight against the diverse registers of violence that enable emerging authoritarian regimes and to create a space for individual and collective resistance. Evans employs the language of theory, art, ethnography, and history in order to create a political tapestry; in so doing he elucidates how finance capital, militarism, state violence, and repressive ideological apparatuses work in tandem to shape repressive policies and inflict mass suffering at the level of everyday life.

Evans engages in dialogue with a number of other theorists in this book in a language that not only highlights a range of social problems but also engages in a discourse that is both rigorous and accessible. Evans and his collaborators show how education, language, and art can create radical ways of thinking about critique, dissent, resistance, and the future. *Atrocity Exhibition* works to create a new language and mode of intervention at a time when violence encourages a culture of forgetting rather than a culture that embraces civic learning and courage. *Atrocity Exhibition* recognizes that politics bears both the burden and responsibility of changing the collective consciousness so that people might understand and engage the forces that shape their everyday existence. Politics, for Evans, needs a language that allows us to remember the past, enables us not to look away, and confronts a new sense of responsibility in the face of the unspeakable. In sum, this is a call for a new language that encourages people to recognize themselves as agents rather than victims.

As I read these pages, I was reminded of Martin Luther King Jr. who believed in the "fierce urgency of now" and that "in this unfolding conundrum of life and history, there is such a thing as being too late." At the core of Evans's work is a politics of solidarity and humanity and a strong belief that one cannot escape matters of moral and social responsibility if we are to be bound to each other by something more than the narrow orbits of self-interest and crass consumerism. Evans rejects the collapse of agency into destiny. Like Tony Judt, Zygmunt Bauman, Stuart Hall, James Baldwin, and Edward Said, he believes that intellectuals have, in troubled times, a distinct responsibility to analyze power works and to construct a world that is more just and democratic. For Evans, ethics and responsibility must be placed at the center of agency, politics, and everyday existence, in the belief that current regimes of tyranny can be resisted and that human beings can be moved to imagine possible alternative futures. With these new beliefs, we will make radical change happen.

Author's Note

Brad Evans

Monday, 23 July 2018

I HAVE ALWAYS BEEN struck by the political importance of the literary imagination. Not only does literature allow for a more intimate and compelling insight into the wonder and fragility of the human condition, it also provides critical commentary about those elements of human existence the so-called "social sciences" fail to capture. What is more, it is in the literary field that the spatial and temporal markers of human existence collide in full appreciation of their complex and often blurred lines of articulation. Just as we cannot understand the problem of violence without discussing life's poetic elements — creativity, passion, and love — so it is impossible to think about the political without journeying back, like some privileged witness already armed with the plot to the final scene, into the dramas of the past, or willfully projecting ourselves into the future anterior in all its hopeful and catastrophic permutations. The person, the political subject that comes to believe in this world, has never been simply determined by reasoning and rationality. Each subject both literally and figuratively navigates the world, endlessly reconceptualizing its modes of being while thinking and feeling its way through the bittersweet vortexes of cohabitation.

This book borrows its title from J. G. Ballard's classic *The Atrocity Exhibition,* which offers such an apt description of contemporary life saturated by the onslaught of various media spectacles. Ballard understood better than many "political scientists" the importance of embodied critical thought, and his commentaries on the interplay between the social, the technological, and the all-too-human desire to break open what is inside the body provide us with some of the most sophisticated critiques of violence to date. But what might the title mean today, nearly 50 years after it appeared on the cover of this most wounding and unsettling of texts? Well, simply switch on your "smart" phone (which actively inserts what it means to be "intelligent" into the design of the user's grasp and simultaneously evacuates the need away for the user's won intelligence) and open any major news application. As you scroll through the constantly changing and replenishing news updates on the digital feed — a fragmentary world that has seemingly lost any sense of plot — from the comfort of wherever you are, so the contingent and indiscriminate "atrocities" appear, one by one, disaster upon disaster, vertically hierarchized on your screen by selected news-worthiness, yet horizontally flattened in respect to any meaningful contextualization. What is actually the exhibit on such an app? Events of human suffering are being broadcast, exhibited for our full viewing (dis)pleasure. But the gallery has also been logically inverted. We have become the exhibits, walking around in a motionless and seemingly impotent gaze, while the image has become the visitor, journeying to us with various degrees of interest and already preloaded with subjective prejudices about our worthiness.

This series of writings and discussions was written across what seems to be the longest "short decade" (2011–2019) with all its disorientating speeds and intensities. Beginning with the ongoing and calamitous wars that were predictably declared following the collapse of the Twin Towers up to the political catastrophe that is Trump (with his own presidentially gilded towers, brutally marking with their unapologetic modernist presence the same scarred New York skyline), it represents an exercise in writing from the reality of our dystopian shadows, covering a period in which terror has become normalized and war such a part of the everyday fabric of a global existence it no longer even needs to be declared. I owe it to the brilliant series editor for this *Los Angeles Review of Books* "Provocations" imprint, Tom Lutz, for capturing this moment and the various forms of violence this anthology has responded to when proposing the subtitle "Life in the Age of Total Violence." The word *total* invariably has a fraught and impassioned political history that arouses sensitivities, from the brutally oppressive ideas of totalitarianism's Total State to the devastating reality of Total War, whose physical and philosophical cuts deep into the body of earth are still all too apparent. Let's not forget here what Hannah Arendt discovered in her still-important *The Origins of*

Totalitarianism: "In an ever-changing, incomprehensible world the masses had reached the point where they would, at the same time, believe everything and nothing, think that everything was possible and that nothing was true." The "everything" Arendt wrote against was the total liberation of every prejudice and the total denial of every right to be classed merely human.

Our age and its violence are undoubtedly different than the violence of the 20th century and its willful slaughter of millions in the name of some European ideological supremacy. We can only try to imagine what World War II might have looked like, or the bombing of Hiroshima and Nagasaki, if our immediate social media platforms had been available. It would certainly have tested Judith Butler's theorizing on the powers of mourning and the aesthetics of its performance. And yet if we understand the totalizing condition to be one that suggests no alternative, then we can purposefully deploy the term "total violence" as a conceptual provocation to describe the contemporary moment — despite the sleepwalking delusions of the "enlightened" Steven Pinker. Because violence continues to shape all social relations in the world today, its ubiquitousness — as possibility and as fact — defines the age.

Violence comes in many different forms, every form of violence should be taken and critiqued on its own terms, and indeed, given its unique victims, every instance of violence demands ethical rigor and contextualization. But we also need to consider violence and its history as a whole, and it is here that representing violence as "inescapable" is unacceptable; it would mean we have already surrendered to the most totalizing of human claims: that we have accepted our species' annihilation.

The brilliance of Ballard's *The Atrocity Exhibition* lies in its fragmentary and non-teleological narrative. The very idea of sequential time now belongs to an outdated past, and chronology no longer appears to be sufficient for explaining the unfolding of the historical present, where space and time have been undone by the powers of the digital and information communications revolutions. Ours is the time of the event — the fleeting exhibition — which we can barely grasp due it to recombinant forms and unlocatable centers. And yet the fragmentary still presents to us the promise of a certain critical entry. Life in an age of total violence is life in fragments. How we pick up the pieces remains part of the task — or, as Anton Chekov once wrote, "don't tell me the moon is shining, show me the glint of light on broken glass."

Nobody understood or developed the fragmentary method more completely than Walter Benjamin. He understood that through the cracks of history, what remains are fragments of truth. This requires the assembling, juxtaposition, and conversation among things that on the surface may not appear connected. This anthology follows in a similar vein, providing commentaries and analysis on fragments of violence, not to bring out something of the universal or to naturalize a position, but to insist upon the need to critique violence in all its forms — all while looking at the ways common logics appear — whether we are talking about victims of state-sanctioned violence or the murder of a young female Mexican student who died alone.

To that end — or perhaps (as explained in the piece that appears towards the end of the essay section titled "Violence, Conflict at the Art of the Political") in a search for an alternative beginning — the hope for this set of writings is to foreground the problem of violence through a fragmentary series of responses such that the need for us to rethink the political itself in more poetic and conversational ways can become the mobilizing force against the new tide of fascism in the 21st century.

ATROCITY

EXHIBITION

Barbarians & Savages

Brad Evans & Michael Hardt

Saturday, 10 July 2010

BRAD EVANS: One of the most important aspects of your work has been to argue why Deleuze and Guattari's *Nomadology* needed to be challenged. With the onset of a global war machine that shows absolutely no respect for state boundaries, matched by the rise of many local fires of resistance that have no interest in capturing state power, the sentiment that "History is always written from the victory of States" could now be brought firmly into question. On a theoretical level alone, the need to bring the *Nomadology* treatise up to date was an important move.

But there was something clearly more at stake for you than simply attempting to correct and canonize Deleuze and Guattari. One gets the impression from your works that you were deeply troubled by what was taking place with this newfound *human*itarianism. Indeed, as you suggest, if we accept that this changing political terrain demanded a rewriting of war itself — away from geopolitical territorial struggles that once monopolized the strategic field, towards biopolitical life struggles whose unrelenting wars were now to be consciously fought for the politics of all life itself — then the political stakes could not be higher. For not only does a biopolitical ascendency force a reconceptualization of the war effort — to include those forces which are less militaristic and more developmental (one can see this best reflected today in the now familiar security mantra: "war by other means") — but also, through this process, a new paradigm appears that makes it possible to envisage, for the first time in human history, a global state of war or a civil war on a planetary scale.

While it was rather easy to find support for this non-State paradigm during the 1990s — especially when the indigenous started writing of the onset of a fourth world war that was enveloping the planet and consuming everybody within — some have argued that the picture became more clouded with the invasion of Iraq, which was simply geo-politics as usual. The familiar language that has been routinely deployed here would be of US exceptionalism. My concern is not really to attend to this revival of an outdated theoretical persuasion. I agree with your sentiments in *Multitude* that this account can be convincingly challenged with relative ease. Foucault has done enough himself to show that liberal war does not demand a strategic trade-off between geopolitical and biopolitical aspirations. They can be mutually re-enforcing, even, or perhaps more to the point, *especially* within a global liberal imaginary. And what is more, we should not lose sight of the fact that it was when major combat operations were effectively declared over, that is when the borderlands truly ignited. My concerns today are more attuned to the post-Bush era, which, going back to the original War on Terror's life-centric remit, is once again calling for the need to step up the humanitarian war effort in order to secure the global peace. Indeed, perhaps more worrying still, given that the return of the Kantian-inspired humanitarian sensibility can now be presented in an altogether more globally enlightened fashion, offering a marked and much needed departure from the destructive but ultimately powerless (in the positive sense of the word) self-serving neo-con. What do you feel have been the most important changes in the paradigm since you first proposed the idea? Is it possible to detect a more intellectually vociferous shift taking place, which is rendering all forms of political difference to be truly dangerous on a planetary scale? Would you argue that war is still the permanent social relation of global rule?

MICHAEL HARDT: The notion of a global civil war starts from the question of sovereignty. Traditionally, war is conceived (in the field of international relations, for instance, or in international law) as armed conflict between two sovereign powers, whereas civil war designates conflict within a single territory in which one or both of the parties is not sovereign. War designates, in other words, a conflict in some sense *external* to the structures of sovereignty and civil war a conflict *internal* to them. It is clear that few, if any, of the instances of armed conflict around the world today fit the classic model of war between sovereign states. And perhaps even the great conflicts of the cold war, from Korea and Vietnam to countries throughout Latin America, already undermined the distinction, draping the conflict between sovereign states in the guise of local civil wars. Toni Negri and I thus claimed that, in our era, there is no more war but only civil wars, or, really, a global civil war. It is probably more precise to say, instead, that the distinction between war and civil war has been undermined in the same way that one might say, in more metaphorical terms, not that there is no more outside but, rather, that the division between inside and outside has been eroded.

This claim is also widely recognized, it seems to me, among military and security theorists. The change from the framework of war to that of civil war, for instance, corresponds closely to thinking of armed conflicts as not military campaigns but police actions, and thus a shift from the external to the internal use of force. The general rhetorical move from war to security marks in more general terms a similar shift. The security mantra that you cite — "war by other means" — also indicates how the confusion between inside and outside implies the mixture of a series of fields that are traditionally separate: war and politics, for example, but also killing and generating forms of social life. This opens a complicated question about the ways in which contemporary military actions have become biopolitical and what that conception helps us understand about them.

Rather than pursuing that biopolitical question directly, though, I want first to understand better how the shift in the relationship between war and sovereignty that Toni and I propose relates to your notion of liberal and humanitarian war. In a war conventionally conceived, it is sufficient for the two sovereign powers to justify their actions primarily on the basis of national interest as long as they remain within the confines of international law. Whereas those *inside* are, at least in principle, privilege to the liberal framework of rights and representation, those *outside* are not. When the relationship of sovereignty shifts, however, and the distinction between inside and outside erodes, then there are no such limits of the liberal ideological and political structures. This might be a way of understanding why contemporary military actions have to be justified in terms of discourses of human rights and liberal values. In turn, this same relationship relates to what many political theorists, like Wendy Brown, for instance, analyze as the decline of liberal values in the US political sphere at the hands of neoliberal and neoconservative logics. In other words, perhaps when the division declines between the inside and outside of sovereignty, liberal logic must be deployed (however inadequately) to justify the use of violence over what was formerly the outside on the one hand, while on the other, liberal logics are increasingly diluted or suppressed in what was formerly the inside.

BRAD EVANS: What I am proposing with "The Liberal War Thesis" borrows from some pioneering works, which have already started to cover the main theoretical ground (Mark Duffield, Michael Dillon, Julian Reid). Central to this approach is an attempt to critically evaluate global liberal governance (which includes both productive and non-productive elements) by questioning its will to rule. Liberal peace is thus challenged, not on the basis of its abstract claims to universality — juridical or otherwise — but precisely because its global imaginary shows a remarkable capacity to wage war (by whatever means) in order to govern all species of life. This behavior is not to be confused with some militaristic appropriation of the democratic body politic — a situation in which liberal value systems have been completely undermined by the onslaught of the military mind. Rather, this undermining exposes the intricate workings of a liberal rationality whose ultimate pursuit is global political dominance. Traces of such an account can be found in Michael Ignatieff's book *Empire Lite*, which notes how the gradual confluence between the humanitarian and the military has resulted in the onset of an ostensibly humanitarian empire that is less concerned with territory (although the State no doubt still figures) than it is with governing life itself for its own protection and betterment. Liberalism as such is considered here (*à la* Foucault) to be a technology of government to strategize power, which necessarily takes life as its object. As a technological implement, it is compelled to wager the destiny of humanity against its own political strategy. Liberalism can therefore be said to betray a particularly novel strategic field, in which the writing of threat assumes both planetary (macro-specific) and human (micro-specific) ascriptions. Although it should be noted that it is only through giving the utmost priority to life itself — working to secure life from each and every threat posed to an otherwise progressive existence — that its global imaginary could ever hold sway. It is no coincidence, then, that the dominant strategic paradigm for liberals is *global human security*. What could therefore be termed the liberal problematic of security naturally registers as a liberal biopolitics of security, which, in the process of promoting certain forms of life, equally demands a reconceptualization of war. Ultimately, not every life lives up to productive expectations let alone shows its compliance.

In a number of crucial ways, this approach offers both a theoretical and empirical challenge to the familiar international relations scripts, which have tended to either valorize liberalism's visionary potential or simply castigate its misguided idealism. Perhaps the most important of these is to insist upon a rewriting of the history of liberalism from the perspective of war. Admittedly, there is much work to be done here. Not least, there is a need to show with greater historical depth, critical purpose, and intellectual rigor how liberal war (both externally and internally) has subsequently informed its juridical commitments and not vice versa. Here I am invariably provoking the well-rehearsed "Laws of War" sermon, which I believe more accurately should be re-phrased as the "Wars of Law." Nevertheless, despite this pressing need to rewrite the liberal encounter in language whose familiarity would be capable of penetrating the rather conservative but equally eso-teric specialist field of International Relations, sufficient contempo-rary grounds already exist which enable us to provide a challenging account of global civil war from the perspective of liberal biopolitical rule. Michael Dillon and Julian Reid's *The Liberal Way of War* encap-sulates these sentiments, with the following abridged passage worth quoting:

> A biopolitical discourse of species existence is also a biopo-litical discourse of species endangerment. As a form of rule whose referent object is that of species existence, the liberal way of rule is simultaneously also a problematization of fear and danger involving threats to the peace and prosperity of the species. Hence its allied need, in pursuing the peace and prosperity of the species, to make war on whatever threatens it. That is the reason why liberal peacemaking is lethal. Its violence is a necessary corollary of the aporetic character of its mission to foster the peace and prosperity of the species ... There is, then, a martial face to liberal peace. The liberal way of rule is contoured by the liberal way of war ... Liber-alism is therefore obliged to exercise a strategic calculus of necessary killing, in the course of which calculus ought to be able to say how much killing is enough ... [However] it has no better way of saying how much killing is enough, once it starts killing to make life live, than does the geopolitical stra-tegic calculus of necessary killing.

This brings me to the problem of inside/outside. It is possible to account for the conflation of the two by acknowledging the onset of a global political imaginary that no longer permits any relationship with the outside. One could then support the kind of hypothesis you mention, which, rather than affirming the best of the enlightened liberal tradition, actually correlates the hollowing out of liberal values to the inability to carve out any meaningful distinctions between inside/outside, peace/war, friend/enemy, good/evil, truth/falsehood, and so forth. But this approach would no doubt either re-enforce the militaristic paradigm or raise further critical doubts about the postmodern/post-structural turn in political thought, and it is misleading. The collapse of these meaningful distinctions is not inimical to liberal rationality. To the contrary, the erosion of these great dialectical interplays now actually provides liberalism with its very generative principles of formation. I felt that you began to explore this in *Empire* by noting how Foucault's idea of biopolitics was inadequate to our complex, adaptive, and emergent times. To rectify this, Deleuze's notion of "societies of control" was introduced, which is more in line with contemporary systems of rule. My interest in this, however, is what actually lies behind: namely, the realization that societies of control are informed by a fundamental change in the biopolitical account of life, which, although affording life great potentiality, presents it in an altogether more dangerous light. This is what I would term the "liberal paradox of potentiality" — revealing contemporary liberalism's irresolvable biopolitical aporia. On the one hand, the body liberated from the former disciplinary regimes is a body whose capacity to be free is assumed to increase exponentially — not implying that every situation presents a certain degree of freedom, or, for that matter, that one can simply "be free," but that freedom is something which needs to be continually *produced*. And yet it is precisely because a body is now endowed with adaptive and emergent qualities — capable of *becoming* other than what was once epistemologically certain — that a life sets off more alarms. After all, who knows what a body is now capable of doing? Deleuze's reading of Spinoza thus seems rather prophetic. For what a body is capable of becoming is the war cry heeded by contemporary security practitioners, which is reflected in recent developments in counter-terrorism. A marked shift is now clearly taking place in this field, which is moving us away from the traditional actions-based (punish after the event) or intentions-based (punish if intentions can be established) approaches, tending instead towards a more pervasive *capabilities assessment* (punish if one can establish the capability to strike).

MICHAEL HARDT: I find it interesting how the decline of the division between inside and outside does not undermine liberal rationality, as you say, from the perspectives or in the fields of international relations and security studies, although it does undermine the logic of a variety of liberal and radical democratic projects in the field of political theory. It seems to me that the collapse of a meaningful distinction between inside and outside *is* inimical to liberal democracy — or radical democracy — for these authors. For the critique and/or redemption of liberal democracy in political theorists such as William Connolly and Wendy Brown, a discrete and bounded space is required for the effectiveness of liberal rights, formal equality, freedoms, and representation. Ernesto Laclau's notion of the people, Chantal Mouffe's concept of hegemony, and Etienne Balibar's idea of citizenship (even in a supranational context such as Europe) all similarly require a delimited sovereign space and a specific population. The focus in all these cases, it seems to me, is not on the outside or the conflict across the inside/outside border, but rather on the circumscribed nature of the inside. The people to whom these notions of liberal or radical democracy apply must be determinate and limited. That is not to say, I should repeat, that the projects of these political theorists require the definition of an enemy or focus on mechanisms of exclusion, but rather that they rely on a definite conception of the "inside," that is, a coherent social body (such as a people) and a delimited sovereign space (whether national or not).

Perhaps this disjunction regarding the status of liberalism between International Relations and Political Theory is due, in part, to disciplinary differences that make it difficult to communicate between those fields. Perhaps it is due also to the ambiguous topological metaphor of inside and outside, which might be doing too much work here and thus leading to confusion. In addition, some difficulty certainly arises from the different meanings attributed to the term "liberalism." We already have the problem of a primarily economic conception of liberalism (more prevalent in Europe) that refers to the freedoms of trade and markets, and a primarily political conception (more prevalent in North America) that emphasizes rights, the rule of law, constitutional freedom, and so forth. In your work, however, as well as that of Dillon and Reid, and perhaps more generally in the field of International Relations, there seems to me a somewhat distinct idea of liberalism, which is certainly based on juridical notions of the international rule of law but also highlights humanitarianism and the preservation of life as grounding principles. This is perhaps why the discourse of liberalism in International Relations moves so easily into questions of biopower — and also why the division between inside and outside is not necessary as a ground here. Tracing the meaning of liberalism across these disciplinary fields to separate the terminological differences from the differences in argument can certainly help clarify the question.

More interesting, though, is the possibility that the disjunction I'm highlighting is not merely explained by metaphorical ambiguities and terminological differences but really points to a conceptual and political conflict, which is revealed by looking at the issue and phenomena from different disciplinary perspectives. In other words, perhaps if political theorists were to adopt the disciplinary framework of International Relations scholars in this case, they would be forced to question their grounding in a coherent "inside," that is, a determinate population and a circumscribed space of sovereignty, for liberal or radical democratic projects. In turn, such an exchange might force International Relations scholars to think more critically about what kind of democratic projects are possible in a context in which the division between inside and outside has declined.

BRAD EVANS: Agreed. There is a need for much greater cross-fertilization of ideas across the disciplines not only to permit more sophisticated meaningful critiques but also to have a more fruitful search for common political alternatives. To begin this process (with the intention of outliving it), I would suggest that we need to be more definitive about "What is liberalism?". While it could be argued that the "many liberalisms" we can speak of show the richness of the tradition, one can speak the language of freedom and give juridical pronouncements without ever acknowledging the liberal recourse to war and violence. To my mind, the only way these various disciplines can be brought together is to insist upon an inclusive understanding of liberalism that factors in both its political and economic dimensions. How else could we assess whether the ideal matches reality? Such a "political economy" perspective will be resisted in many quarters, especially since it implies a need to show how the tremendous political power and moral suasion (that liberalism wields on a planetary scale) rests upon the power of economy. What is more, if we take a political economy perspective, liberal rationality is revealed as primarily driven by biopolitical imperatives, which, in turn, force us to acknowledge that notions of sovereignty/law are merely one generative principle of liberal formation. We can simultaneously appreciate that the juridical/emancipation story, with its definitive sense of grounding, assumes secondary importance behind the biopolitical task of making life live in productively compliant ways.

Looking at this from a global perspective, it could then be argued that the "*nomos* as camp" hypothesis, with its impending "states of exception," makes no conceptual sense, especially given the collapse of those neat demarcations that once permitted the Schmittean decision. Foregrounding instead the internal problem of emergence — with emergence here associated with the propagation of all types of circulations — liberalism replaces the state of exception paradigm with an internal state of unending emergency, capable of leaving life "bare" within the remit of law. Not, then, the camp as *nomos*, which even some liberals have been glad to announce, but a *nomos* of circulation.

If we accept this new biopolitical security architecture, then it inevitably follows that the sovereignty over life becomes purely contingent. For not only are territorial integrities irrelevant when the political destinies of life are at stake, but, given the highly complex and adaptive strategic situation, there can be no universal value systems or grand blueprints to follow. This is especially acute in zones of instability, when not only is life subject to the forces of biopolitical experimentation, but the liberal commitment to democratic regimes and political rights becomes subject to contingent factors as well. There have been, for example, many occasions when the most sacred of rights (that to life) has been cast aside for the most speculative utilitarian calculations. What once was the surest litmus test of one's democratic credentials — election victories — has in recent times had liberals scrambling for new methods of de-legitimation. My personal favorite here is the story of the "democratic coup."

A logical corollary of this is the mixture of the strategic fields you mention. It is no coincidence today to find renewed priority being afforded to the insurgent. The RAND Corporation, for instance, has, for some time now, been calling for a more comprehensive and nuanced strategic paradigm that incorporates counterinsurgency into the wider remit of the Global War on Terror. I am reminded of a wonderful observation Foucault makes in a few incisive pages of *Society Must Be Defended* in which he identifies the three key figures that make up the modern condition: barbarians, savages, and the civilized. Barbarians, he argues, are a function of sovereign power. Existing beyond the constitutional pale, although sometimes penetrating with purely destructive intent, they represent those lives that show no respect for the constitutional order and, hence, have and should be afforded no moral or political value. Savages, on the other hand, are a function of biopolitical power; open to remedy and demanding engagement, they represent those lives which are capable of being redeemed. No great conceptual leap of imagination is required here to draw out meaningful connections between barbarians/terrorists and savages/insurgents. Indeed, in the theaters of war today, one can write of that all-too-familiar historical tendency of waging war by getting savages to fight barbarians in order to prove their civilizing credentials. Even here, however, the lines in the sand have been blurred. Terrorists no longer occupy a place of exteriority to the political realm; they are fully included within the biopolitical order. What is more, the ability to set out clear parameters between the terrorist and the insurgent has proved rather elusive. This is compounded even further by a realization that terrorists are no longer simply intent upon wanton destruction but have shown a willingness to actually cross over to become insurgents, posing a much wider social problem. This approach is clearly evidenced in the recent United Kingdom CONTEST II National Security Strategy (2009). What is particularly striking about this document is the style in which these threats are presented. Terrorists are now presented in a manner which is biopolitically fitting: like some cancerous cell, not only are they seen to be capable of damaging a vital organ within the body politic, but they also now hold the potential to infect the wider bodily terrain. The significance of this sovereign/biopolitical merger can be read in two ways. First, through this coming together, it is possible to detect a certain reprioritization of affairs in which the once familiar problem of the sovereign encounter can now be dealt with biopolitically. And second, given that the biopolitical is now tainted by the specter of terror, then the biopolitical becomes truly moralized in that the war to redeem savages is equally a war to expel evil.

MICHAEL HARDT: I find intriguing and very productive your translation of barbarian to terrorist and savage to insurgent, along with the correlate that, from the standpoint of the sovereign, the latter couple has the potential to be civilized or redeemed whereas the formal couple does not. It strikes me that what is at play here, in part, are two relations to the body. In the first years of the new millennium, at the inception of the "War on Terror," I recognized in much of US military theorizing a fascinating doubling and inversion regarding the body of the terrorist and the body of the US soldier. On the one side stood the horrifying, barbaric figure of the terrorist, defined by not only its power to destroy others but also its acceptance of corporeal self-destruction, characterized paradigmatically by the absolute negation of the body in the act of suicide bombing. On the other side stood the body of the US soldier that, it was thought, could be kept at a safe distance from all danger by technological innovations and new military strategies associated with the so-called Revolution in Military Affairs (RMA). Precise missiles, drone airplanes, and other devices could aid a military strategy aimed at no soldiers lost — at least, no US soldiers. So, I was interested in the way that these two figures — the barbaric body guaranteed destruction and the civilized body guaranteed preservation — arose at roughly the same time and seemed to be bound together in dialectical negation.

You are right that the insurgent body occupies an entirely different position. It does not threaten self-destruction or corporeal annihilation. The insurgent must be transformed through the mechanisms of biopower just as the savage must be redeemed and civilized. It is interesting, in fact, that at the same time (in the military and security discourses) there has been a shift from the barbaric terrorist to the savage insurgent, as you say, there has been a parallel move away from the dreams of bodiless military actions and the strategic principles of the RMA. Anti-insurgency biopower is aimed at the transformable body. This gives us another level, I suppose, to the relation between war, biopower, and liberalism that you were insisting on earlier.

BRAD EVANS: Exploring the relations you identify between war, biopower, and the transformable body is one of the most important critical tasks we face today, especially since these relations force us to directly confront the legitimacy of liberal interventionism. Military interventions can, of course, be rather easily assigned imperial ascriptions. The scene becomes more complicated, though, when we encounter humanitarian interventions, which tend to be presented in an altogether more benevolent light. And yet, if the history of civilizing missions teaches us anything, then surely war is taking place there, too,

albeit on different terms. We can see this reflected today in the way violence is understood. Barbarian violence is always subject to the neat
them/us, outside/inside, evil/good, unreasonable/reasonable marks
of absolute differentiation. Theirs is a violence that by its very nature
is always unjust. Savage violence, in contrast, is seen to be an internal
problem that is subject to a progressive/regressive imaginary. It is the
product of local conditions of *underdevelopment*. Hence, unlike barbarian violence, which offers no possibility to remedy the cause (aside
from outright elimination), savage violence is marked out by modes
of relative differentiation, in which the source of the problem can be
identified and, with enough resource allocation, the causes of conflict
alleviated. Clearly, each of these different problematizations has its
own unique relationship to power. For instance, given that resistance/
insurgent violence is the surest indicator of a local population's capacities for their own (un)making, then it necessarily follows that more
liberal engagement is required. What is needed is the ability to turn regressive violent economies into more productive and profitable local
conditions of possibility. That people may be resisting liberal forms of
biopower and its "wars by other means" (the "other" having a figurative as well as strategic use) is never entertained.

As you mentioned, something different is taking place here than with
the RMA's terms of engagement. Displacing the full *spectrum* spatial
doctrine, which sought to dominate land, sea, air, and space, primacy
now tends towards a life-centric full *spectral* doctrine which aims to
capture the more complex terrain of hearts, minds, bodies, and souls
(the latter referring not only to what a body is, but what a body is capable of becoming). Invariably, in order for such a war to be successful, it
is necessary, as Colonel Rupert Smith argues in his book *The Utility of
Force*, to wage "war among the people." The concept of zero casualties
thus becomes a misnomer, since warfare can no longer be fought at
a distance; instead, military leadership relies upon the most intimate
micro-specific knowledge — what the anthro-military establishments
now term "mapping the human terrain." Ironically, then, this more humane liberal approach does not translate into a lessening of the war
effort in order to secure the global peace, pacifying all non-liberal elements; instead, war becomes a normalized biopolitical condition in
which the attempted closure of geopolitical space merely proves to be
an initial experiment at setting out the all-embracing political terrain.
Importantly, within such terrains, not only does the inside/outside lose
its strategic primacy, but the meaningful distinctions which once set

out the citizen from the soldier also enter into a zone of indistinction. Everybody becomes part of the liberal war effort. I, therefore, agree with the claims you made in *Multitude* that "war has become a *regime of biopower*," which is intimately aligned with the task of "producing and reproducing all aspects of social life." Indeed, with global liberal rule shown to be shaped by a commitment to war (globally and locally), unending or permanent war become a very real condition.

So, as you suggest, the relations between war and the body provide us with another (perhaps the most incisive) opportunity to challenge that formidable school of liberal thought. Indeed, once we begin to recognize that the ultimate object for liberal war is the productive/transformable body, it then becomes possible to begin questioning the transcendental or divine principle which allows liberalism to draw out such an unreserved global will to rule.

I want to turn to a crucial aspect of your work in *Empire*. You single out Kant and Hegel for particular critical attention. While I share your anti-Hegelian sentiments (especially regarding the dialectical method's suffocation of political difference), it is the intellectual heritage set by Kant that really troubles me. Zygmunt Bauman is correct to observe, in *Society under Siege*, that "These days, it is a hard task to find a learned study of our most recent history that would not quote Kant's Universal History as a supreme authority and source of inspiration for all debate of world citizenship." One could even go further to argue that if there is a modern "image of thought" (to invoke Deleuzian conceptual vocabulary), then it is a Kantian image of thought, which, as you have indicated, not only demands that one *needs* metaphysics in order to think, but also, given that the world is reduced to ideal forms of representation, it exorcises any possibility of immanent political and ethical relations.

Despite these problems, Kant's notion of "perpetual peace" has become a sort of manifesto for liberal internationalists and cosmopolitan theorists who advocate a shift towards a bounded/inclusive humanity. Whilst this notion of a bounded humanity is itself enough cause for political concern — not least since certain politicians have now made it their task to begin speaking on behalf of an endangered humanity, a formidable power which serves to provide humanity with an authentic voice — what worries me here is the strategy of deception that is taking place. For even though Kantian-inspired liberals continue to use transcendental humanitarian notions of universality in order to justify their global ambitions, a more critical eye would note how humanity has always been misplaced in this script. Humanity has never been the unifying transcendental principle for liberal theorists and practitioners since humanity is always assumed to be flawed. Why else would you require the continuous juridical watch if not to keep an omnipresent eye on the pious subject? Indeed, as Kant himself taught, given that the negative lacuna of juridical power alone is insufficient to ensure that life does not side with the unreasonable, then something beyond juridical power is also required.

Kant takes up this challenge in his essay on perpetual peace. In a part of the essay that contemporary liberals tend to ignore, Kant notes how ending conflict depends upon setting in place the right economic system. Thus, invoking what he termed "the spirit of commerce" (a phrase which Agamben recently notes has obvious theological connotations), for Kant, the task of settling conflict by reaching the highest stage of political development also rests upon the productive power of economy — something which clearly represents more than mere economic transaction and exchange. What Kant implied with his positive cosmopolitan ethic can be said to appear today in its full theological and economizing glory. Existing above and beyond the law, the unifying driver for liberal practitioners is not the humanitarian principle but the pure regulatory principle governing this flawed humanity. What then constitutes the divine principle for liberal practitioners is not the divine endowment of a universal freedom of rights or individual reason but the regulative and productive economy of life itself. When Tony Blair therefore remarked, in a very Kantian way, that the wars of the 21st century are global wars for the very politics of life itself, he was revealing more about the contemporary nature of liberal power than is readily accepted. For today, not only is the nature of threat being extended to give priority to the wider political problem of globally insurgent populations, but since this is also matched by a broadening of the security agenda (which is increasingly drawing into the same strategic framework non-political accidents), the productive economy of liberalism now begins to appear in all its divine earthly light.

MICHAEL HARDT: It might be interesting to set the liberal paradigm you are challenging back in relation to Carl Schmitt since, in a way, the movement we are tracing in the nature of warfare in the last few years might be understood in terms of a shift from Schmitt to Kant or, really, from transcendent forms of power and domination to transcendental ones. For Schmitt, the political has the same form as warfare since both are defined by the friend-enemy distinction. That is why, he insists, there is no relation between the economic and the political: in the economic realm (or at least in the capitalist market), one has no enemies, only competitors. Similarly, for Schmitt, the sovereign decision stands outside the constitution and the legal realm. In the liberal paradigm you articulate and identify with Kant, however, these terms are all scrambled. Liberal war is no longer separated from but rather identified with both economic life and the legal sphere. This is where I find useful the Kantian distinction between the transcendent and the transcendental — used a bit against the grain. The ground for politics and war is not located in the transcendent position of the sovereign but rather in the transcendental position of capital and the law. These are the dominant forces today that primarily determine the conditions of possibility of social life. And, as you point out, this liberal configuration of politics and war is perhaps just as theological as the sovereign, transcendent one, focusing now on the constant action required to limit the negative effects of and govern a humanity characterized by its imperfections. This theological-political difference might even be understood as separating Schmitt's Catholicism from Kant Protestantism.

Aside from the pleasures of mapping out such correspondences, what are the political and theoretical consequences of this analysis of the liberal war paradigm along with the claim that it has become dominant today? One important consequence, from my perspective, is that it poses a limit to the utility of understanding politics today in terms of sovereignty. For the last decade, the concept of sovereignty has played an important and expanding role in political theory and focused attention on transcendent forms of power that stand outside the social and legal constitution, ruling over states of exception. The sovereignty paradigm has even led many theorists to decry new forms of fascism. The George W. Bush administration and its "War on Terror" certainly did provide numerous "exceptional" instances — such as the functioning of Guantánamo and Abu Ghraib prisons, the officially sanctioned use of torture, the establishment of extraordinary rendition programs, the widespread violation of international law, the passage of the Patriot Act, and so forth — that were read, under the rubric of sovereignty, as essential to the current political scene. The liberal war paradigm suggests instead that, although such exceptional acts of a sovereign power should be challenged and defeated, they are not the essence of the current political situation. (And, in my view, this has not altered fundamentally with the change of US administrations but has only become more obvious in the wake of the failures of the Bush regime.) One problem for political theory is that focus on such dramatic instances has generally diverted attention from the primary, transcendental pillars of domination and war today: law and capital, which function through "normal" rather than exceptional means. The continuous juridical watch to police humanity and guard against the effects of its imperfections that you mention is matched by the naturalized social divisions and hierarchies constantly reproduced by capital. And the argument goes one step further to claim that, at times, war is necessary to maintain this liberal order, but the form, rationale, and ideology of such war rests on the values of the transcendental realms of economy and law.

Another consequence of this shift from a sovereignty paradigm to a liberal war paradigm has to do with the nature of resistance and alternative that each implies. Whereas critiques of and resistance to transcendent, sovereign forms of power do not generally nurture alternative powers, critiques of and resistance to the liberal paradigm do uncover powerful alternative subjectivities. The critique of capitalist political economy can reveal not only the exploitation but also the power of social labor. Capital, as Marx and Engels say, creates its own gravediggers as well as the subjectivities capable of creating an alternative social order. The critique of the liberal legal order, too, can bring forth powerful subjects of rights. The resistance to and critique of sovereignty, in contrast, offers nothing to affirm. In Giorgio Agamben's biopolitical framework, for example, what stands opposed to sovereign power is bare life. And the numerous recent analyses of various states of exception and new fascisms have generally merely combined moral outrage with political resignation. Perhaps equally important, then, to the ability of the liberal war paradigm to identify how power and domination primarily function today is the kind of subjectivity generated by the critique of and resistance to it. Recognizing liberal war as our primary antagonist can be an extraordinarily generative position.

Originally published in somewhat different form in Theory & Event.

The Liberal War Thesis

Brad Evans

Thursday, 1 September 2011

WHEN THE HISTORIAN Sir Michael Howard delivered the prestigious Trevelyan lectures at Cambridge University in 1987, he posed one of the most pertinent questions of our times: What is the relationship between liberalism and war? For many, the fact that this question was posed at all represented a remarkable political departure. In international politics, liberalism has conventionally been associated with the Kant-inspired virtues of perpetual peace, along with the commitment to uphold human rights and justice. Preaching peaceful cohabitation among the world of peoples, liberal advocates have therefore made claim to the superiority of their enlightened praxis on the basis that they enjoy a monopoly on the terms "global security," "peace," and "prosperity." While liberals take this for granted, for Howard therein lay the dilemma: despite being shrouded in universalist and pacifist discourse, liberal practice has actually been marked historically by war and violence. Howard's concern, not unlike criticisms of Carl Schmitt's, was clear. Michael Dillon and Julian Reid summarize:

> [Howard's] target was the way in which the liberal universalization of war in pursuit of perpetual peace impacted on the heterogeneous and adversarial character of international politics, translating war into crusades with only one of two outcomes: endless war or the transformation of other societies and cultures into liberal societies and cultures.

Despite the importance of Howard's initial provocation, he nevertheless failed to come to terms with the exact nature of liberal war-making efforts. He merely chided liberals for their naive faith in the human spirit, which, although admirable, was at best idealistic and at worst dangerous. Liberalism is not simply a set of ideals; neither is it some conscience of the political spirit. Liberalism is a regime of power that wages the destiny of the species on the success of its own political strategies. Before we map the implications of this for our understanding of war, an important point of clarification should be made. Unlike reified attempts in international relations thinking to offer definitive truths about war, what I present here as the liberal war thesis does not pretend to explain every single conflict. It does not deny the existence of geostrategic battles, and neither does it deny the fact that any single war can reveal a number of competing motivations. Like security, war can be written and strategically waged in many different ways depending on the key strategic referent. Wars can be multiple.

So, what then makes a war liberal? Here I offer ten fundamental tenets that set liberal war apart from conventional political struggles:

1. *Liberal wars are fought over the modalities of life itself.* Liberalism is undoubtedly a complex historical phenomenon, but if there is one defining singularity to its war-making efforts, then it is the underlying biopolitical imperative, which justifies its actions in relation to the protection and advancement of modes of existence. Liberals continuously draw reference to life to justify military force (cf. Ignatieff). War, if there is to be one, must be for the protection and improvement of the species. This humanitarian caveat is by no means out of favor. More recently, for instance, it has underwritten the strategic rethink in contemporary zones of occupation that is seen, by David Kilcullen and Rupert Smith, for instance, to offer a more humane and locally sensitive response. If liberal peace can therefore be said to imply something more than the mere absence of war, so it is the case that liberal war is immeasurably more complex than the simple presence of military hostilities. With war appearing integral to the logic of peace insofar as it conditions the very possibility of liberal rule, humanity's most meaningful expression actually appears through the battles fought in its name. It would be incorrect, however, to think that this logic represents a recent departure. Life has always been the principal object for liberal political strategies. Hence, while the liberal way of rule is by definition biopolitical, as it revolves around the problems posed by species life, so it is the case that liberal ways of war are inherently biopolitical, as they, too, are waged over the same productive properties that life is said to possess.

The reason contemporary forms of conflict are therefore seen to be emergent, complex, nonlinear, and adaptive is not incidental. Mirroring the new social morphology of life, the changing nature of conflict is preceded by the changing ontological account of species being that appears exponentially more powerful precisely because it is said to display post-Newtonian qualities.

2. *Liberal wars operate within a global imaginary of threat.* Ever since Immanuel Kant imagined the autonomous individual at peace with the wider political surroundings, the liberal subject has always been inserted into a more expansive terrain of productive cohabitation that is potentially free of conflict. While this logic has been manifest through local systems of liberal power throughout its history, during the 1990s a global imaginary of threat appeared that directly correlated liberal forms of governance with less planetary endangerment. This ability to collapse the local into the global resulted in an unrivalled moment of liberal expansionism (see *The Human Security Report 2005*). Such expansion did not, however, result from some self-professed planetary commitment to embrace liberal ideals. Liberal interventionism proceeded instead on the basis that localized emergency and crises demanded response. Modes of incorporation were therefore justified on the grounds that although populations still exist beyond the liberal pale, for their own betterment they should be included. This brings us to the martial face of liberal power. While liberalism is directly fuelled by the universal belief in the righteousness of its mission, since there is no universally self-evident allegiance to the project, war is necessarily universalized in its pursuit of peace: As Dillon and Reid put it:

> However much liberalism abjures war, indeed finds the instrumental use of war, especially, a scandal, war has always been as instrumental to liberal as to geopolitical thinkers. In that very attempt to instrumentalize, indeed universalize, war in pursuit of its own global project of emancipation, the practice of liberal rule itself becomes profoundly shaped by war. However much it may proclaim liberal peace and freedom, its own allied commitment to war subverts the very peace and freedoms it proclaims.

3. *Liberal wars take place by "other" means.* Liberalism declares otherness to be the problem to be solved. The theory of race dates back to canonical figures like Kant, John Locke, and Jean-Jacques Rousseau,

whose progressive account of life originally conceived of noble savagery. While this desire to subjugate "the other" is a permanent feature of liberal biopolitics, the idea of human security that emerged in
the early 1990s instilled it directly into policies that sought to pacify
the global borderland, as Duffield demonstrates. Directly challenging
the conventional notion of state-based security, human security discourses found a remedial solution to the problem of maladjustment
in sustainable development. This led to the effective "capitalization
of peace," since conflict and instability became fully aligned with the
dangers of underdevelopment. Inverting Carl von Clausewitz's for-
mula that war represents a continuation of politics by other means,
war-making efforts were increasingly tasked with providing lasting
capacities for social cohesion and peace. Liberal ways of war and
development thus became part of the same global strategic continuum. While it could be argued that, in the immediate aftermath of
9/11, concern with sovereign recovery unsettled this narrative, giving
sure primacy to military force, the contemporary post-interventionary phase of liberal occupation signals its effective reawakening. The
veritable displacement of the figuration of the terrorist by the body
of the insurgent fully reveals this strategic reprioritization. Unlike the
problem of terrorism — that is, a problem of (dis)order — insurgents
are a problem of population whose violence is the product of causal
resentment. Their resistance pertains from unfortunate locally regressive conditions that can be manipulated to resuscitate the vitality of
local life systems. Since insurgencies, then, are open to remedy and
demand engagement, like the savages of the colonial encounter, they
are otherwise redeemable.

4. *Liberal wars take place at a distance.* The Clausewitzian inversion
above does not simply incorporate every aspect of civic governance
into the global war effort. Since the unity of life incorporates every
political strategy into a planet-wide battle, the destiny of the species
as a whole is wagered on the success (or failure) of its own political
strategies. As recent liberal incursions make clear, however, global war
cannot be sustained by relying on interventionary forces. Not only do
such interventions lead to localized resistance, but the relationships
to violence they expose are politically unsustainable. Waging war at
a distance is the favored policy choice. This policy of getting savages
to fight barbarians in the global borderlands involves a broad range
of interconnected strategies. These include the abandonment of political neutralities; arming and training of local militias; instilling the

correct political architecture to prevent credible political opposition; funding development projects that have a distinct liberal agenda; and marginalizing any community that has the temerity to support political alternatives. This distancing does not simply reveal the microphysics of liberal biopolitical rule. Creating conditions wherein the active production of all compliant life-sustaining flows (biopoliticized circulations) does not jeopardize the veritable containment of others, liberal war makes possible the global partitioning of life. This is not simply about security understood in the conventional sovereign sense of upholding territorial integrities. It is about deciding what must be made to live and what must be allowed to perish in the global space of flows.

5. *Liberal wars have a distinct relationship to territory insomuch as spatiality is firmly bound to active living space.* Liberal power triangulates security, populations, and territory in a way that binds geostrategic concerns to the active production of ways of life. Through the capitalization of peace, this triangulation has gone global as the management of local resources has become a planetary security concern. The development-security nexus tied the dramatic materialization of life to conditions of social cohesion. More recently, it has widened its security ambit to include protection of the environment and climate adaptation strategies. Leading to the generalization of liberal biopolitical rule, the development-environment-security nexus (DESNEX) is now part of a mobilization for war on all fronts — from human to biospheric (see Evans and Duffield). As the security apparatus of a new liberal environmentalism, DESNEX is no longer satisfied with policing and maintaining the life chances between the globally enriched and the globally denied. This is a highly politicized maneuver predicated on the geographical containment of the poor and dispossessed. It is forging a new global settlement around the control and management of the biosphere. A new speciation of global life is therefore taking place according to its ability to properly manage and care for the environment and, at the same time, maintain capitalist accumulation. For DESNEX, containment is now not enough — a locked-in global poor must be made fit for such stewardship.

6. *Liberal wars are wars of law.* One of liberal power's foundational myths is its commitment to law. Constitutional law is presented as being the natural foundation for any civilized society. Without this arrangement, the concept of "a people" — understood to be a legally

binding community of political beings — appears to hold no meaning. A people, however, is never made by laws. Neither are laws politically neutral. Whatever the jurisdiction, laws are enacted in a highly tactical way largely in response to crises that are never value free. This brings us to the problem of the norm. Advocates of liberal war reconcile their commitment to law by relating juridical safeguards to agreed normative standards. Norms as such appear to be the logical outcome of reasoned political settlement. Our discourse of battle, however, appreciates that power defines the norm such that those who deviate from it pose a threat to the biological heritage of life. The norm is another way of suppressing political differences. There are then no universal, all-embracing, value-neutral, timeless, or eternal a priori norms that inhibit some purified and objective existential space where they await access by the learned justices of the peace. There is no absolute convergence point to human reason. Every norm is simply the outcome of a particular power struggle. Its inscription always follows the contingency of the crisis event. That is why no universalizing system of law can ever account for or suppress the particular calls for justice that directly challenge moral authority. When Philip Bobbitt advocates for a more tactical and strategic approach to law, he is not calling for some neorealist revival. He is simply asking for liberal market states to be more efficient and effective in response to those problems than they now are.

7. *Liberal wars move beyond states of exception to take place within a condition of unending emergency.* Walter Benjamin warned that while exceptional moments of crisis were politically dangerous, the effective normalization of rule could be far more sinister. With order finally restored, what previously shattered the boundaries of acceptability now begins to reside in the undetected fabric of the everyday. Ours is no longer a time of exception. What marks the contemporary period is terrifyingly normal. While there is no law without enforcement, no enforceability exists without intimate relation to crisis, as Derrida points out. Every law and every decision respond to an exceptional moment. It brings force to bear on what breaks from the norm to rework the basis of normality anew. There is therefore no pure theory of the exception, no absolute break from law. Law reserves the right to transgress its own foundations, where it encounters continuously emerging crises — untimely moments that require varying degrees of intensity in the subsequent deployment of force. It is no surprise, then, to find that states of exception are all too frequent once the broad sweep of

liberal history is considered. Not only do crises permit the reworking of the boundaries of existence, but the fluctuating shift from (dis)ordered sovereign recovery (external modes of capture) to progressive security governance (internal modes of interventionism) defines the liberal encounter.

8. *Liberal wars depoliticize within the remit of humanitarian discourses and practices.* Even when some epiphenomenal tension exists, the inclusive image of thought invoked by liberals immediately internalizes the order of battle. This is no mere sovereign affair. Liberal war has always been immeasurably greater than the juridical problem of order. It has always pertained to the life and death of the species. Since what is at stake in contemporary theaters of war is the "West's ability to contain and manage international poverty while maintaining the ability of mass society to live and consume beyond its means," as Duffield writes, each crisis of global circulation marks out a terrain of "global civil war, or rather a tableau of wars, which is fought on and between the modalities of life itself." With depoliticization therefore occurring when life is primed for its own betterment — that is, within humanitarian discourses and practices — it is possible to offer an alternative reflection on Giorgio Agamben's "bare life." Agamben's notion of bare life draws on sovereign terms of engagement. Life becomes exposed on account of its abandonment from law. The biopolitical encounter, in contrast, denies political quality as the "bare essentials" for species survival take precedence. No longer reduced bare in a juridical sense of the term, life is stripped bare since its maladjusted qualities impede productive salvation. Hence, while this life is equally assumed to be without meaningful political quality — though in this instance because of some dangerous lack of fulfilment — allowing the body's restitution displaces exceptional politics by the no less imperial and no less politically charged bare activity of species survival.

9. *Liberal wars are intimately bound to the active production of political subjectivities.* Security discourses have always had a particular affinity with political authenticity, which sets out who we are as people and defines what we are to become. It places limits around what it means to think and act politically. The liberal approach to security implies that political authenticity is not simply tied to those identity formations defined by epiphenomenal tension. It breaks free of such static demarcations. The liberal subject instead is constructed by living freely through contingent threats to insecurities around its existence.

Within a broader and more positive continuum of endangerment, liberal subjectivity has never been in crises if we understand those to be the disruptions to fixed modes of being. Born of the paradoxically anxious conditions of its ongoing emergence, the liberal subject is the subject of crises. It lives and breathes through the continual disruption to its own static modes of recovery. While this subject has gone through many key changes, the disrupted subject is made real today on account of its need to be resilient. Again, this does not infer a static state of ontological affairs. Resilient life must uphold the principles of adaptation and change held true by our radically interconnected age. Since what is dangerous today is seen as integral to the very life processes that sustain liberal life, danger is directly related to the radically contingent outcomes on which the vitality of existence is said to depend. With liberal societies having to endure what Dillon has termed the "permanent emergency of its own emergence," our predisposition to the unknowable contingency of every new encounter — the event of contemporary life itself — appears at the same time to be the source of our potential richness and the beginning of all our despairs.

10. *Liberal wars are profoundly ontotheological.* When Barack Obama reconciled the problem of "evil" with the "imperfections of man" in his Nobel laureate speech, he reaffirmed the Kantian belief that evil is very much part of this world — not that people are born of evil but that unnecessary suffering results from bad or dangerous political judgment. Offering then a humanistic reworking of the story of the fall — one in which life, always assumed to be perpetually guilty of its own (un) making, must continually seek its own recovery from the ashes of its own potential demise — we uncover why sovereignty is not the transcendental frame of reference for liberal power. Kant-inspired liberalism preaches universality but accepts that the universal is beyond the realms of lived experience. It preaches the international virtues of law but accepts that one's encounter with moral law has to be contingent. It insists on life's autonomy even though it offers an account of freedom in which humankind has fallen to the guilt of its own unmaking. It promotes human progress yet puts forward the thesis of infinite regress to highlight humankind's imperfections. And it claims that all life has an original predisposition to good and a simultaneous propensity to evil. Liberal life is forced to endure a self-imposed temporal purgatory — life is always guilty of the moral deficiencies of the past yet incapable of exorcising them in the future. These imperfections are actually demanded so that the antiproductive body can prove its moral and

political worth. While this morally deficient default setting invariably moves us beyond any metaphysical attachment to the humanitarian principle (humanity is, after all, too flawed to become the unifying principle) and while the power of law alone is insufficient to overcome the imperfections of modern people, faith is restored by something in the order of the divine economy of life itself.

One could argue here that contemporary liberalism is, in itself, facing terminal crises. Whatever one's opinions of the wars in Iraq and Afghanistan, it is clear that Western populations have no taste for new forms of military interventionism and lasting engagement in the global borderlands. And whether one considers a resurgent socialism in Latin America, the emergence of new forms of capitalization by alternative geopolitical powers, the changing nature of religious movements that have used democratic procedures to their own political advantage, or the continuation of indigenous struggles that challenge any hold over the terms "rights," "freedom," "democracy," and "justice," liberalism appears to be operating within a declining zone of political influence. As recent events in Libya illustrate, however, we must be wary of signaling its lasting demise. Throughout modern history, liberalism has proved to be resilient when faced with its own crises of legitimacy and authority. Its claims to violence in particular seem to enjoy a remarkable ability to regenerate as the memory of indigenous subjugation and depoliticization fades with time. One could be more cynical and suggest that given the only things that liberal regimes in Western zones of affluence can materially export today are war and violence, rather than write of its demise, the liberal war thesis is only beginning to enter a new retrenching chapter, which will resonate for a considerable time.

Originally published in somewhat different form as "The Liberal War Thesis: Introducing the Ten Key Principles of 21st Century Biopolitical Warfare" in The South Atlantic Quarterly.

New Thinking is Needed About September 11

Brad Evans & Simon Critchley

Thursday, 31 August 2011

THE TEN-YEAR DISTANCE from the attacks of September 11, 2001, gives us an opportunity to reflect on the significance of that day's violence. Common sense asserts that our world is changed forever because of 9/11. But if true, shouldn't we have spent more time considering the stakes of the event? The attacks were abhorrent and criminal, but our response so far represents a profound failure of the political imagination.

The many human faces to the tragedy provided a passing glimpse into a genuine ethical response mobilized by grief. But all too quickly the mourning ended as matters turned to the usual militarism. The invasion of Afghanistan, the illegal bombardment of Iraq, the establishment of torture camps and, most recently, the execution of Osama bin Laden.

Perhaps this shouldn't surprise. Despite paying lip-service to global security, peace, and justice, the West's history is marked by violence against those who refuse to capitulate to it. After 9/11, Giorgio Agamben wrote that security was fast becoming the main criterion of political legitimacy. Elections would be won on claims to protect domestic populations from rogue elements. This means taking the fight to enemies who, it seems, hate our existence. But when this happens, the state can itself become a terrorist entity.

Our political response has been pitiful. The left accuses the right of suffocating politics by taking advantage of so-called "exceptional" conditions. The right accuses the left of blindness to the ideological dangers of Islamofascism. The left condemns the unmediated abuse of power but supports or remains silent on NATO-led violence. The right draws connections between Islam and one of the most shameful episodes in modern history to justify violence.

Without trying to critically understand why people support the willful oppression and slaughter of "others" — especially within the shallow remit of international "norms" — our justification to control through violence is rarely questioned.

Modern politics is infected by a utilitarian mindset that bets the future against the present. "Our present actions are justified because they will make the world a better place" is a hypothesis that cannot be disproved. But these supposedly reasoned deliberations have underwritten the collateral slaughter of millions. Nor can they answer these questions: when is too much killing enough, and how many deaths must there be before a well-intentioned action loses its moral credibility?

We require new ethical ways of thinking about living in a radically interconnected world.

Originally published in somewhat different form in The Guardian.

9/11 – A Duty to Remember, but What?

Brad Evans & Simon Critchley

Thursday, 31 August 2011

THE VIOLENCE WITNESSED TEN years ago was spectacularly horrifying. Mass death quite literally broadcast "live." Many images of that fateful day linger. We still recoil at the moment the second plane impacted, the point at which we knew this was no accident. Our memories can still recall that frozen transience, the same experienced shared by President George W. Bush, who, in a room full of children, cut a powerless figure. And still, we are traumatized by the thought that any one of us may have faced that terrifying predicament, whether to jump or not as the searing heat became too intense to bear. Such an impossible decision thankfully most of us will never have to face.

Let us be clear from the outset. 9/11 was both unjustifiable and abhorrent. Not only did it defy logical reasoning, completely blurring beyond all intelligible meaning the enemy and the innocent, the target and collateral damage. As an event, it offered no promise that the future could be opened to better ethical relations amongst peoples of this world. Indeed, if being terrified is the defining political criterion for what happens in devastating times, for those of us who live in advanced liberal societies, the term "terror" is indeed a more than satisfactory explanation.

One of the most remarkable results of that memorialized day was the way the shared sense of grief translated into something like a genuinely felt shared sense of human sensibility. Operating on an emotional level, our sympathies extended the hand of friendship to victims who we would most likely never meet. If the humanitarian principle has any real meaning, it must be in times like these it finds its most affective power. This responsiveness wasn't about universal legal proclamations. Neither was it about retributive calls for justice. Less grandiose, yet certainly charged with more potent realism, human togetherness showed itself through the willingness to affirm life in the face of the most indescribable suffering.

Yet all too quickly, this time of civic grief would be seized upon to inflict violence upon those deemed complicit. Tragically Orwellian, the dream of global peace would be transformed into a planetary war. In Afghanistan and Iraq, our retributive justice would soon adopt its own limitless utilitarian logic. "To save us at home, the war must be taken to them," politicians reasoned. Hunting down perpetrators in this way inevitably produced its own collateral damages — blurring, once again, perceived enemies from those caught within the violent crossfires of ideological rage.

While the numbers of dead in those countries seem countless, and we imagine their terror, being terrified resonated here with the same petrifying force. Well intentioned bombs don't do less damage. A wound inflicted by a stray humanitarian bullet has the same impact no matter the righteousness of the cause. A just cause cannot sanction an innocent death unless we subscribe to the belief that some lives are more disposable than others.

So, what could we have done differently? Surely not taking the fight to them (whatever the cost) shows weakness in the face of danger? Proposing here a more liberalized war effort is certainly not the intention. Students of colonialism will quickly appreciate that "war by other means" smacks of the worst cases of deeming others savage. Just imagine if we had not rushed into the all-too-predictable counter recourse to war and violence. What if the claim that the day our "world changed forever" demanded more considered philosophical reflection? More radical still, what if our response was to say to the Muslim world: We will do nothing, then wait for you to clear your own political name? That is was up to Islam to show its genuine ethical persuasion by dealing with the al-Qaeda problem on its own terms?

This is no more hypothetical than what we have now. We cannot know for sure whether the world is safer or not because of our actions.

We have been travelling on a pre-emptive rollercoaster which can only deal with the future by attempting to create it through the rule of force. One thing is, however, clear. As Obama speaks at the site of the tragically fallen, the sentimentality of liberal humanism still reigns supreme. But one source of our problems is that liberalism preaches tolerance but only shows it to those who show it first. Its moral sentiments are predicted on peace yet, in practice, only amplify the reasons for war. While liberalism talks of humanity, its only method for realizing it is to wage war endlessly, so while we have a duty to remember the suffering of 9/11, political ignorance still remains our afflicted curse.

All this may sound remarkably emphatic. Maybe that is the point. For too long, our politics have been depleted of emotional considerations. Yet as we all know, life is full of emotional experiences which affect the way we see and relate to the world. Let's not blind ourselves here. The politics of emotion is fraught with dangers. The history of fascism taught us that much. Attempting to remove our emotions as a frame of reference, however, not only clouds our political judgements, it also prevents us from making meaningful political distinctions between those emotions that positively affirm human togetherness and those that, in the face of dangerous uncertainty, call for the suffocating forces of militarism at any given opportunity.

Originally published in somewhat different form in Social Europe.

Militarization of London Olympics Shows One More Host Country's Fetish for Displays of Force

Brad Evans

Thursday, 26 July 2012

SO, THE OLYMPIC GAMES are finally upon us. Whether we perceive this global extravaganza to be a triumphant social gathering which reveals all that is remarkable about the human spirit or yet another corporate feast of plenty, it nevertheless provides us with a pertinent moment to evaluate the operations of power in contemporary liberal societies. Not only does it illustrate how our postindustrial lifestyles are increasingly defined by "event-based" experiences, it also shows how terror has become normalized in the current historical conjuncture. As securitization policies become more visible, the corporate militarization of public space appears routine. It is even to be applauded as a reasoned and rational choice.

For the past few weeks, the British public has been caught in an emotional crossfire that has become the hallmark of liberal societies. From one direction, we have been encouraged to positively embrace the "spirit of the Games," with its promise to transcend the daily miseries affecting people the world over; the official sales pitch is that this is more than a sports event, that it holds the seed of global togetherness and peaceful cohabitation. From another direction, however, we have been made acutely aware of the dangers forever lurking in our midst; that we need to "secure the Games" is not in any doubt — from what, exactly, only speculative reason or a catastrophic passage of time may begin to reveal.

The security operation for the games is itself an Olympian effort. More than 18,000 military personnel are deployed on the streets. This includes some 1,000 combat support troops, a number that is greater than British forces on the ground in Afghanistan. They are accompanied by state police and private security personnel, who by conservative estimates add another 30,000 staff. Drones hover over the London skies. HMS Ocean (the Royal Navy's biggest warship) is moored in the Thames; RAF Typhoon jets remain on permanent standby with the directive to use "lethal force," while surface to air missiles are deployed on housing estates in East London, leaving us in no doubt about the lethality of the freedom our liberal societies gratefully receive.

None of this appears out of the ordinary for us despite its schizophrenic (dis)orientation. We have learned to fear what we actually produce. One only has to track the various terrorist elevation systems still in background use to discern this paradox. The more significant the public occasion — the more spectacular celebration — the more the risk of something catastrophic happening is heightened. Color-coded systems of anxiety management have become the fear heartbeat of nations. Compulsive securitization invariably becomes the allied response.

While many in the post-9/11 moment questioned the abandonment of democratic principles and the violent excesses of the Global War on Terror, the privately-driven securitization of all aspects of life has continued unabated. Indeed, as Walter Benjamin understood all too well, what previously appeared "exceptional" (especially the abuse of power) quickly comes to reside in the normalized fabric of the everyday. Although the "War on Terror," for instance, is perhaps notable by its sudden absence from the discursive arena of political polemics, its militarized logic has been sophisticatedly incorporated within an expansive strategic framework that connects all things endangering.

Stephen Graham has pointed out how this security terrain is embodied in the Olympic Mascot, "Wenlock." As Graham wrote,

> For £10.25 you, too, can own the ultimate symbol of the Games: a member of by far the biggest and most expensive security operation in recent British history packaged as tourist commodity. Eerily, his single panoptic-style eye, peering out from beneath the police helmet, is reminiscent of the

all-seeing eye of God so commonly depicted at the top of Enlightenment paintings.

For Graham, this represents the onset of a new type of surveillance society, one which openly declares its strategic priorities:

> The Olympics are society on steroids. They exaggerate wider trends. Far removed from their notional or founding ideals, these events dramatically embody changes in the wider world: fast-increasing inequality, growing corporate power, the rise of the homeland security complex and the shift toward much more authoritarian styles of governance utterly obsessed by the global gaze and prestige of media spectacles.

Underwriting this security effort is the catastrophic imaginary that defines contemporary liberal governance. The Games have produced their own novel and fitting headline — "Olympic-geddon" — to account for all potential disasters that could erupt and force the capital's vital networks to break down. This shift toward an all-hazard continuum of threat is the real legacy of the militaristic vision of full-spectrum domination. Threats have become indistinguishable from the general environment. Every petty anxiety can become the source of our deepest fears. And all potential racial prejudices are waiting to be resurrected as the nature of the threat offers no clear profile in advance.

But what actually is "security"? Our problem here lies in the question. Ever since Thomas Hobbes wrote his landmark text *The Leviathan*, security has become the foundation stone of modern politics. Security is not, however, a "what" – it is a "how." While Hobbes wrote of the anarchical war of all against all to prevent the masses from resisting the injustices of feudal exploitation, beneath the veil of his sovereign deceit was the arrangement of society into hierarchies. Liberal security uses this same inner logic, which is less about showing some allegiance to the principal object needing security (i.e., the State, the People, the Games), than it is with guaranteeing access to resources deemed essential to contested ways of living.

Like Sauron, the all-seeing eye in J.R.R. Tolkien's wonderful trilogy, the controlling gaze nevertheless has its weak points — it is insecure by design. This, however, is not a source for lament or dismay. It is a further condition of possibility. That the system cannot be made totally secure only serves to ratchet up securitization all the more. Resilience thus becomes a new term of art for a security-conscious society that has all but abandoned the dream of final security in exchange for a profitable existence. Those attuned to global risk-taking are, after all, the real moneymakers.

Any informed critical theorist knows that the political depends upon the ability to bring into question what is not seen as problematic. This drives us to question why something is not on the public agenda. How does power operate to prevent us from critiquing its most visible traces? Questioning the unquestionable requires making the implicit explicit. When we do so, it allows us to really open up the functioning of power as it impacts everyday lives. This is not about abstract eso-tericism but about the desire to question power — especially liberal power — on the basis of its effects.

So, what still remains largely unquestioned? Many of us will now be fa-miliar with the G4S security debacle that led its director, Nick Buckles, to apologize for the "humiliating shambles." But who are G4S? And, more importantly still, what are the political implications of this shift toward private security? The company is the world's largest private security provider with marquee statistics: some 657,000 employees and a "unique global footprint" that covers 125 countries. It provides a range of global security details, including safe passage for the global financial elite and for high-end leisure tourism, airport and embassy security, and managing asylum centers, prisons, and other detention facilities.

While politicians have taken G4S to task over its contractual failures, any critique of private security provision is absent from the debate. It is left to us to raise the questions of public accountability and political legitimacy. Private contractors invariably work for the private interest. They service particular constituencies. They are allegiant to the flag of currency exchange and profit making. While such organizations claim to be professional and socially responsible, it is a mistake to see them as apolitical. Embodying the (neo)liberal pursuit of power and its will to planetary rule, they represent a profound change in liberal security governance — the political sphere and the very nature of sovereignty itself are replaced by a technocratic ensemble of private/public, mil-itary/policing, local/global contractors. As G4S's social responsibility statement proclaims: "Our size and scale mean we touch the lives of millions of people across the globe and we have a duty and desire to ensure the influence we have makes a positive impact on the people and communities in which we work."

The distinction between private security contractors and the military has become a false dichotomy (the lines between the private and the public long since abandoned), but the British soldier has nevertheless returned as the reliable face of civic protection. The British soldier embodies the freedom that society is said to enjoy, freedom that is understood as a result of soldiers' sacrifice and commitment: making the streets safe from Kabul to Islington so we are left in no doubt that our protection cannot be otherwise.

But what does it mean politically to have trained killers on the capital's streets? Should this have happened in North Korea or Iran, politicians would have undoubtedly lambasted the despotic state of military affairs. We, however, reason it to be an efficient use of resources to maintain the democratic peace. In the process, we fail to question what it means to live in a time when the distinctions between war and peace, global and local, private and public, soldier and citizen, once again blur.

We are invariably left to ponder here the perceived source of threat. One hundred thousand soldiers on the streets of Manhattan would not have prevented 9/11. The horrifying violence of that day illustrated the futility of conventional force. And yet, conventional force is the only illusion of power that liberal societies can hope to maintain now that the ability to wage war has become one of its most profitable and dependable exports. On the social aside, the psychological brinkmanship of full militarization, the brazen show of potential force, echoes Susan Sontag's famous paraphrase "shocking and awful." Whether the intended audience for such a performance is external or internal, it is clear that militaristic posturing — as both a symptom and defense of the emerging carceral state — demands a more serious discussion than is currently being entertained.

It is well documented that President George W. Bush tried to instill a military spirit into the civilian bodies of American citizens. As he once famously declared, "Every American is a soldier and every citizen is in this fight." While some may explain this in terms of the logic of "ex-

ceptional times," it does not account for the more normalized practices of militarism we witness in our liberal societies today. George
Chesterton observed some time before the Olympics buildup: "The
only place you could be sure of seeing a British soldier used to be outside a pub in a garrison town at chucking-out time. Now there are soldiers on talent shows, parading in sports stadiums and singing on day-
time television." Soldiers are rewarded with on-television spots and
garrison towns with royal patronage. We are left with the militarization
of the public realm that we witness on the streets of London today:
"We have turned the reality of war into an emotionally nourishing theater ... [that] serves an ideological and financial function."

Some will invariably counter here that the militarization of the public
realm simply reflects the dangerous world in which we now live. After
all, none of us would wish to be blown up by a suicide bomber. Where
is the freedom in that?

While the high-profile nature and location of the Games undoubtedly
makes it a target, what is required is a more somber and considered
response. It was common after 9/11 and 7/7 to question why these
people hated us. Many politicians and embedded academics insisted
that we were endangered simply because of who we were and have
been — the simple laws of physics tell us that we need to account for
our actions and our histories of violence. Only then can we deal with
the problem at the level of power and, hence, political contestation.

Michel Foucault put forward the idea of the biopolitical in order to
critically assess the racial-, gender- and class-based dimensions of securitization practices.[1] Foucault was acutely aware that making life secure was not about setting limits, as if everything stemmed from legal
declaration, but about creating conditions that benefited particular
constituencies. The regime of determining what needed protection by
means of risk assessment, conceals the disposability of others behind
an objective mask of scientific verification. This brings us to one of the
most sinister dimensions to Olympiad security.

------

1 Between 1971 and 1984 Michel Foucault gave a series of lectures dealing
with his research at the Collège de France. Those relevant to this study are the
following (the last of which his seminal notion of biopolitics emerges): "Society
Must be Defended" (1976-1976), "Security, Territory and Population" (1977-
1978), and "The Birth of Bio-Politics" (1978-1979).

The placing of rapier missiles on the Fred Wiggs Tower block in Leytonstone, along with five additional sites across the city, brings into critical question the very meaning of the term "Terror." Not only have the tenants living in marginal social conditions expressed their concerns that the missiles actually make them more of a target, they have identified the somewhat obvious point that sleeping with a high-velocity missile system on your rooftop is truly terrifying. While the residents have famously protested with banners proclaiming, "THIS IS NOT A WAR ZONE," their opposition was overruled by High Court Judge Charles Haddon-Cave, who stated that missile deployment was lawful and proportionate to the level of threat faced. He did, however, note that the residents' concerns demonstrated "something of a misapprehension" about the equipment.

This is not a critique of the tremendous effort and dedication of the athletes, of course. Neither is it a challenge to major sporting events and their genuine ability to have a marked impact upon the emotional well-being of people. It is to question who benefits financially and politically from Olympiad security in the longer run. While it is too early to tell the lasting effects, if the previous experience of the Games in Athens is anything to go by (when private contractors feasted on a security bill of some $1.5 billion), the weight of austerity to follow will be similarly selective in its target audience.

Major sporting events will always be deeply political. For too long, we have placed politics in a neatly defined box, owned by a distinct political class, which has benefited only a select few. This, despite the fact that some of the most significant political moments in the history of human struggles asked a blessing neither of politicians nor universal moral theorists. Nor do we wish to banish from memory the victory of Jessie Owens from the 1936 Olympics or the dignity showed by Tommie Smith and John Carlos as the idea of global revolt entered the political lexicon during the troubled year of 1968. And just as Diego Maradona claimed some divine intervention against the forces of British colonial oppression in 1986, so the terrain seems ripe for a further act of Argentinean political defiance as the Falklands question refuses to go away. We should not, however, be blinded to the wider political project at work here. As Will Self critically explains:

> The modern Olympics is a fatuous exercise in internationalism through limbering up and then running down to entropy.

The modern Olympics have always been a political football — nothing more and nothing less — endlessly traduced and manipulated by the regimes that "host" them. This one is no different, presenting a fine opportunity for the British security state apparatus and its private security firm hangers-on to deploy the mass-suppression and urban paranoiac technologies in the service of export-earning. Some Peace. Some Freedom.

Olympiad security provides us with a glimpse into a possible future. It is a bit like the airport experience where the idea of perfect regulation of life is played out — albeit with lifestyle benefits more seductive than the latest perfumes. Overtly militarized enclaves deploy the most advanced security technologies to ensure the frictionless (i.e., resistance-free) circulation of all things commodifiable, so that, as with airports, once you enter "the zone," you begin to realize that you have no political rights. Our choice is straightforward. Either we accept this manufactured simulacrum of experience or we demand the return of the political into social discussion. This requires us to start questioning that which is concealed within the vacuous politics of normative deliberation. It is not to accept the privileged boundaries of the debate. It is to question the framing of the question such that we expose the power and violence of its discursive framing.

Originally published in somewhat different form in TruthOut.

Public Intellectuals Resisting Global Violence

Grace Pollock & Brad Evans

Sunday, 27 January 2013

GRACE POLLOCK: The *Histories of Violence Project* began, I believe, as a cultural and intellectual intervention to address the escalation of global violence in the aftermath of the terrorist attacks on September 11, 2001. In your work, you've stated that our collective response to 9/11 represented nothing short of "a profound failure of the political and philosophical imagination." I'm wondering if you could elaborate on what you meant by that, and what kind of trends emerged from 9/11 which led you to that conclusion?

BRAD EVANS: One of the impetuses for doing the film *10 Years of Terror* was to make sense of what was taking place in the post-9/11 moment, particularly in the UK, around the July 7, 2005, bombings in London. At the time, I was living in the city of Leeds, and I was also living in the Hyde Park area, which was where a number of the suicide bombers had a particular association, so it was quite literally the War on Terror coming home. And what you found in the UK, which was similar to the whole discourse around 9/11, was very much a sort of "we have no complicity in this whatsoever, these people just simply hate us" and "this is an exceptional moment which demands an exceptional response." There was no understanding that there was a history prior to 9/11. Of course, now we're in a moment a decade on from 9/11 — which allows for much broader political and philosophical reflection.

A number of academics, sometimes with the best intentions, were caught by this politics of the exception — and this happened on the

41

right and on the left. The discourse on the right was "this is profoundly exceptional, let's have an exceptional response" such that "shock
and awe" became the natural outcome. The left equally — particularly
those familiar with the work of Giorgio Agamben — followed this idea
of "we are living in a state of exception, there's the abandonment of
morals," and so forth.

If we just simply take the date of 9/11, however, and look 10 years prior
and 10 years afterwards, you can see that, actually, 9/11 is more of a
continuum in a much wider historical process. And a lot of the dynamics that had taken place which led up to the violence of 9/11 had been
slowly maturing for considerable time. It's there in the ideas of Carl
Schmitt, from whom Agamben borrows his terms. Carl Schmitt says
what comes after a state of exception is a state of emergency. And the
emergency is the return to the norm, and equally — of course Walter
Benjamin writes about this, too — there's this move from exception to
emergency, exception to emergency — so, actually, states of exception
are not that exceptional in the broad sweep of history.

That was one of the main issues I really wanted to start bringing out:
this idea that actually clinging to this politics of exceptionalism represented a failure of the political imaginary, a failure in our ways of
thinking about 9/11 historically. And also, tied to that is the question,
how did this discourse of exceptionalism — "the world begins with
9/11," "Ground Zero is Year Zero," "all history projects forward from this
moment" — how did that particular memorialization of the event lend
itself to the discourse of war?

If we see the response to 9/11 as actually something that's not exceptional but altogether normalized, we begin to enter into a new political
discussion. And this discussion centers on the realization that none of
us was actually surprised by the intervention in Iraq or Afghanistan —
there was nothing exceptional to it. The way that Western Liberal societies — and that's Liberal with a big L — the way we deal with violence
is through violence and retribution. Such is the altogether normal way
of dealing with problems which exceed our limits of expectation. So,
in other words, our response to 9/11 wasn't in any way exceptional. It
was, actually, from the perspective of our political history, "business
as usual."

There was a wonderful piece written in *The New York Times* on the 10th anniversary of 9/11 by Simon Critchley called "The Cycle of Revenge." Simon posed the simple question: "What would have happened if we had done nothing after 9/11?" What if there had been no intervention in Iraq, no intervention in Afghanistan, if there had been, instead, a politics of forgiveness? It might seem absurd for us to say this now. It would certainly have seemed absurd in the immediate 9/11 moment. But I think Simon is onto something significant here in that a nonviolent response to 9/11 would most certainly have been an exceptional politics. Not violence as usual. So, in that sense, all we have done, as Simon suggests, is perpetuate the cycle of violence. And this is what I meant by a profound failure of the political and ethical imagination.

GRACE POLLOCK: So, approaching the 10th anniversary of 9/11, you saw an opportunity to make an intervention. The *Histories of Violence Project* compiled a series of video interviews with eminent public intellectuals talking about how we can rethink violence in ethical ways. I'm wondering what informed your choice to have critical, publicly engaged scholars at the forefront of this kind of intervention?

BRAD EVANS: Well, it was painfully obvious to anybody within and outside of the academy when you were looking ahead to the 10th anniversary that it was always going to be a very sentimental affair. It also evidences a certain sacrament — by this I mean there were a lot of political-theological discourses circulating around that time. The sentimentality you could understand from the victim's perspective — I'm not in any way critiquing that. There is a need to memorialize violence such as 9/11. But, as an academic, you do have an ethical obligation to say, "What is the politics of this memorialization? How do we understand the events of 9/11 historically so we can think better about the future?" And I think that is the move which is incumbent on the public intellectual.

I'm very hesitant, and I'm immediately turned off when you read an academic book, or any book, which basically tries to prescribe the future. Whilst we all have ideas about what better democracy and better justice look like, those academics who speak the universal truth for everybody I find completely totalitarian. But I do think the one way we can think about the political better, to echo Judith Butler here, is in terms of framing the problem. So, for me, it is: How do we frame the problem of 9/11 at the 10th anniversary in a way which brings the political back into the discussion?

There was also another question: What did it mean to arrive at that 10th anniversary? In many senses, you could take the in-between period of "ten years of terror" as a point of temporal departure that would allow us to bring into question whether we were actually talking about a much broader sweep of history. It seems there were a number of critical scholars who were writing about this in a very fragmented way, and there were a number of key questions which needed to be addressed about 9/11 which weren't being addressed in the mainstream media. So, *Ten Years of Terror* was my attempt was to bring those questions to the fore — even just posing the questions seemed to me an important intervention.

GRACE POLLOCK: So, there were individual academics addressing these types of questions, and one goal of the *Histories of Violence Project* was to bring them together as a group of critical voices. But they are by no means homogenous in their perspectives — there is quite a diversity of voices being represented.

BRAD EVANS: I think that has to be central to the way we need think about critical pedagogy and the way we try to deal with such a colossal event as 9/11. There is this narrative which comes out — that 9/11 is the day the world changes forever — but if that's the case, then shouldn't we spend a bit more time reflecting on the philosophical significance of this horrifying moment rather than in 20 days we declare war?

One of the major problems we've had in terms of the buildup to the militarization — and this is not unique to 9/11 — is that you have a catastrophic event and then you have a single truth which appears. And that singular truth is "these people hate us, this was an unprovoked attack, 9/11 happens," and so forth. This is not in any way to justify the violence of 9/11, which was quite clearly abhorrent. But it is to understand that even in terms of the discourses and narratives of people's experiences with 9/11, and also certainly within the academic world, there are many different problematics. A number of the academics who were filmed for the project I profoundly disagree with. But you have an obligation to critical thinking to acknowledge that, actually, this is a contested space of politics. Otherwise, I would just be offering another universal truth of 9/11, which is just as bad, for it follows what led to the mobilization of war in the first place.

GRACE POLLOCK: The project was largely about posing the questions?

BRAD EVANS: Absolutely, and to understand that the legacy of 9/11 is contested as much as it is a contested history, as it is a contested experience of the meaning of the event, and so forth.

GRACE POLLOCK: You work within the university and also with cultural organizations outside the university. The university at the present moment — is there potential there for resisting violence? I'm thinking in terms of pedagogy and in terms of collaborative work with other scholars, in terms of looking to models of public intellectuals — where would you draw your inspiration from for the future prospect of a collective nonviolent world?

BRAD EVANS: My inspirations are very widespread, and they stem from within academia and beyond academia, but it's generally from those academics who put their necks on the line and are precisely willing to ask the questions which don't get asked. There's nothing conspiratorial about this — it's about revealing what is painfully obvious to many people. So, it's not about unearthing some magical secrets behind the operation of power, it's actually to question what is altogether normalized. I have a deep fear of normalization. The norms. For they often conceal the more formidable forms of intellectual violence.

If only the world was all about the "state of exception," that would be easy for us. We could say, "yes, we're going to condemn Guantánamo Bay." And we should condemn Guantánamo Bay, but that would be easy for us. It's those academics I find inspiration from who are willing to question the norm, question the everyday violence, question the everyday abuses of power which happen right throughout society. There are obviously a number of pioneering figures, particularly people like Zygmunt Bauman, Henry Giroux — certainly Simon Critchley, Michael Shapiro are also great examples as well — academics who are willing to go that extra step and just basically say, "okay, how can we think a new angle of vision on this problem, which everybody doesn't see as a problem?" So, it's to question what is not being questioned — that is my first source of my inspiration.

I don't necessarily subscribe to the logic that politics is a science. I'm deeply skeptical of political science as it is conventionally understood — as if it's some objective, literal, perceptive study or inquiry as to the way people behave. Not that there's no room for some of that type of investigation, but I prefer to side with the poetic elements of the political. As much as philosophical poetry, politics has to have an affective relationship with you, it has to have performance with you. Why can't we try to make political language beautiful and poetic? Why does it have to follow structures, or "this is the right way you write things"?

So, certainly the academics and the scholars whom I find most compelling write in a wonderfully poetic way that appeals to, resonates with you. Not just in terms of the problems you're dealing with, but also in a very affirmative, creative way which also highlights deeply troubling, necessary problems — a way which gestures towards "actually, things can be thought otherwise."

GRACE POLLOCK: I would like to go back to the idea that, before the *Histories of Violence Project*, there was no medium through which these critical voices who were presenting different ways of thinking could be brought together and be placed in conversation for the public to hear. I'm wondering if you could talk a little bit about the choice to use a website, to use digital media — but also how they present an alternative to what might be called the dominant media and the perspectives represented there?

BRAD EVANS: Coming from my teaching experiences in the university, I quickly learned that students are much more new media savvy than my peers. And that's just one generation. You know, as an academic, I strongly believe that we have an ethical obligation to use new media. But when we do, we must address more detailed questions of what new media can enable while being alert to the potential closure of political space. New media are ambivalent, they can be enabling or disabling. There's a wonderful essay written by Gilles Deleuze on the idea of control societies, and this should inform our critique of new media technologies.

But, also, to say that we won't engage with new media at all is preposterous. There's one thing I find completely compelling about new media in terms of the political. If we say that 9/11 is a global event, then it has global political significance and the aftermath has global political consequences. Surely the way we theorize about this has to be de-bounded from any sense of sovereign territoriality, and new media provide us with that opportunity. They not only allow us to transcend — that is, take on different critical questions beyond any sense of territorial confine — but also allow us to intellectually break down the borders as well.

Again, the video *Ten Years of Terror* quickly jumps from a philosopher to a sociologist to a social scientist to a linguist to a world-respected literary scholar, so there is this whole shift or breaking down of institutional boundaries, national boundaries, intellectual boundaries, which new media allow us to do. The lesson for me was therefore straightforward. The way you have to do this, making it meaningful, is to connect it to a problematic, and my problematic is violence. That is the way I found it meaningful to address global violence. And judging by the number of visitors to the site, we arguably really touched upon something.

GRACE POLLOCK: So, in terms of your motivation and ongoing work with the *Histories of Violence Project*, is it possible (without speculating too much on the future) that the present itself is something that can be transformed so as to lead to a better, more hopeful future?

BRAD EVANS: Well, absolutely. Social transformation always happens. We can't speculate on the future — who knows, the future might be worse than the contemporary — but we can always say abuses of power, and fascist abuses of power, always eventually get overturned in one way or another because there's always resistance. Now, where that resistance comes from sometimes resides in the most unexpected places. Who would have thought in 1994 when the North American Free Trade Agreement was declared that the poorest people of Southern Mexico would ignite a global resistance movement?

Now, where the spaces for intervention in the future come from, we've got no idea. And how that's going to look, we have no idea. But we can be sure in some senses that it will arrive. Not even the horrors of Nazism were so total that it could destroy the affirmative politics of people's demands for freedom, justice, and right — and effective resistance will not be conceived in a universal "this is the one truth" because, you know, all those terms of "freedoms, rights, and justice" are very contested across different cultures and different spaces, and we have to be open to that idea as well.

But, certainly, we can remain 100% confident that there will be sites for new interventions and new ways of thinking about the political, which will erupt in the most unexpected places, and that is, I guess, the wonder of politics — that we have no idea where this is going to erupt, but we can be certain that it will erupt somewhere. And so, that always gives you affirmative hope: people — the poorest of the poor sometimes — find ways to exercise their political subjectivity in the most creative and wonderful ways, and it doesn't necessarily lead to a cult of violence.

Originally published in somewhat different form in TruthOut.

London's Violent Spectacle: What is to Be Gained by Calling it Terror?

Brad Evans

Thursday, 23 May 2013

POLITICIANS KNOW BETTER than most that words function politically. More than offering some definitive truth to a situation, the use of language conditions what is further possible. The decision therefore to label the horrifying spectacle of violence witnessed on the streets of Woolwich in South London Wednesday as a "Terror Attack" will have consequences. But what is actually to be gained from labeling it in such a way instead of as a criminal act, politically motivated violence, or just pathological derangement?

Let's be clear from the outset, the murder of Lee Rigby, a British soldier, was appalling and should be condemned. Whatever the political grievance, there is no justification whatsoever for the attempt to severe the head of a person in broad daylight. Such violence is undoubtedly beyond the comprehension to many of us around the world. Unfortunately, that cannot be said for some places where our military continues to have a lasting presence and where horrific violence is a daily occurrence.

Before all the facts were established, politicians and media alike were quick to declare that the violence "looked like Terror." This justification was made on two counts. Firstly, it was presumed that the target for the violence was military personnel. The second, more compelling at the time, was the footage of an assailant who stated without remorse for the action: "We swear by almighty Allah we will never stop fighting you. The only reasons we have done this is because Muslims are dying every day. This British soldier is an eye for an eye, a tooth for a tooth. We must fight them."

He further added, as if to claim that the burden of history left him with no option: "I apologize that women had to witness this today, but in our land our women have to see the same. You people will never be safe. Remove your government. They don't care about you."

British Home Secretary Theresa May immediately responded by declaring that the vicious assault on the soldier was more than an individual crime but an "attack against all of us." This, however, raises a number of serious questions. Assuming that the violence was politically motivated, does that necessarily imply that the attack was on the entire fabric of our society? And what does it mean to collapse the military with the civic so that no distinction can be established?

Not only has the role and function of our militaries been radically transformed beyond "defense," since they have been given the oxymoronic task of *fighting for peace* under the auspices of the War on Terror, many of us have been deeply uncomfortable and openly critical with their continued use of force, which has produced a veritable small country of casualties for political change. Violence, it must be added, is widely believed, even in the policy world, to be the source of today's fundamentalism. Moreover, if we are to use the words of the assailant as justification for our response, should we not take these more seriously and open them up to rigorous scrutiny?

Like the violence witnessed at the Boston Marathon last month, it is evident that this violent spectacle was markedly different from the horrors of 9/11 and 7/7 (the 2005 London bombings that killed 52 and injured 700 plus). No longer purposefully aiming for "mass casualty" shock appeal, the numbers of victims are fewer in number. That does not demean the nature of the tragedy. It does, however, raise the question as to why these localized acts of violence can still be presented as part of a continuum of threat that endangers global security?

Michael Clarke, the director of United Kingdom's less-than-impartial think tank the Royal United Services Institute (RUSI), speaking on the BBC, called the perpetrators of the attack "homicidal exhibitionists." They represented a handful of individuals — possibly lone — who crave the media spotlight and shock through the celebratory nature of violence as a public spectacle. This may well be true, but the question remains: Why do these particular acts resonate while comparable events in other parts of the world are barely considered? Indeed, why are we so fixated in the contemporary period on these types of "media events" instead of the continual violence many suffer on a daily basis, which just so happen to occur outside of the spotlight?

Deadly events continue to be presented to us as random. This is not incidental. Random events strike without warning. They offer, in other words, no credible foresight. Some even reason that we need to accept their inevitability. Surely, however, if we accept that the violence is political, then there is nothing random whatsoever about its occurrence? Political violence is always a process. It always has a history, and thus its spectacle cannot be divorced from the violence that precedes it. Neither can a solution be found unless we face up to an altogether more difficult political task.

Perhaps one of the more disturbing aspects of the violence was the manner in which the video of the assailant went viral. This should not escape our attention. Neither can it simply be explained in terms of digital and technological capabilities. Our culture is fascinated by spectacles of violence. From Hollywood movies, video games, to nightly dramas, violence seems to grab our attention more than any other performance. Maybe this alone demands more in-depth scrutiny and more ethical consideration?

We must remember that "Terror" by definition is morally and politically loaded. Far from offering to us an objective assessment, it immediately invokes ideas of barbarity and evil, even though the act of violence is deemed to be premeditated, rationally calculated, and politically motivated. What is more, neatly setting apart bad guys from good guys, it rightly delegitimizes some forms of violence yet morally authors others as necessary for the protection of the core values of societies.

Terror's peculiarity, however, is that while it is a political term, once applied, it fulfills its design to prevent serious politically discussion. Terror offers no compromise. There is nothing to be negotiated. There is no credible politics to be spoken of. More than failing to even entertain that the term may be brought into critical doubt, what remains is a framing of the violence in such a way that militarism reigns supreme.

Terror, in other words, sanctions the need to meet violence with a violent response.

It is no doubt disturbing to see this type of violence come to our city streets. It is also deeply unsettling to witness the assailants remaining at the scene and continuing to calmly walk about justifying their actions as if the violence was totally normal to them. This exposes the fundamental duality to the logic of violent spectacles. For violence to have any shock value on its intended audience, it must appear somehow exceptional. And yet, to understand it fully, we need to take seriously the claim that its exceptional qualities are wholly dependent upon highly contingent factors, not least: on which side of the political divide we just so happen to have been born.

We may remain shocked, angry, and outraged by the violence witnessed on our screens. This is an understandable human response, and too often we forget that emotions matter. There is nothing, however, to be gained by labeling it a "Terror Attack" other than to perpetuate a climate of fear that fuels hatred and extremist positions on all sides. Dealing, instead, with it either as a localized form of criminality that should not be dignified with a political response or as a politically motivated attack outside of the Terror frame might just allow us to break this tragic cycle of violence.

Originally published in somewhat different form in TruthOut.

Branding the Revolution

Brad Evans & Julian Reid

Monday, 25 November 2013

BRITISH COMEDIAN AND ARCH-PROVOCATEUR Russell Brand has been causing quite a storm of late. Having mocked the corporatization of global media networks on MSNBC in the United States, he proceeded to upset organizers of the GQ Awards with a historical quip about one of their more illustrious sponsor's sordid fascist affinities. He then had the audacity to make a public call for a "revolution" in his guest editorial contribution to *New Statesman*. This latest provocation subsequently went viral (in excess of one million views) following an interview with Jeremy Paxman on BBC's *Newsnight* program.

While Brand's call to revolution has been met with the usual derision by the ruling political classes and wealthy elites with whom he has long had an uneasy relationship, what has been particularly notable about the backlash is the vitriolic nature of the attacks from leftist intelligentsia. This is to be expected. As Brand, like many would-be radicals, quickly learns, there are few things quite as venomous as the offended liberal.

But what is it about Brand's revolutionary calling that so offends? Or to put it in more explicit terms, what gives this flamboyant, sexually extroverted, self-confessed ex-junkie, comedian, and public celebrity, who is not a recognized expert in politics nor established member of "the left," the right to speak about politics and revolt? Could it be that Brand perturbs simply because he doesn't know his place, speaks out of turn, and commands attention on subjects in which he has no recognized expertise or historical record of engagement? Could it be that the Russell Brand "brand" offends the sensibilities of leftist liberals because he challenges their own intellectual monopoly on questions concerning the stakes of political struggle, social transformation, and indeed, the very future of "the left" itself? And is it not the case that in having the temerity to speak on these issues, he effectively exposes the poverty of the prevailing branded visions of politics to be found available on the liberal left?

Let's begin by focusing on three of the most frequently made charges against Brand in the backlash.

> 1) Russell Brand lacks a developed political awareness, resulting in petulant and immature posturing and encouraging a militancy that could be dangerous in its results.

> 2) Russell Brand is biographically "flawed" in ways that disqualify him from being able to claim any right to speak in the name of emancipation.

> 3) Russell Brand is himself a wealthy member of the celebrity elite, a fact that denies him any right to speak against a system that makes him wealthy and services his narcissistic craving for public attention.

Under Brand's editorship and intellectual leadership, *New Statesman* posed the question of the meaning of revolution to a number of public figures and artists including Noam Chomsky, Naomi Klein, and Ai Weiwei. This collective hardly constitutes the politically ill-informed! Brand's own contribution titled, "We no longer have the luxury of tradition," is an honest and self-reflective 4,500-word personal journey that begins with the assertion, "before we change the world, we need to change the way we think." Following which, he goes on to write:

> Like most people I am utterly disenchanted by politics. Like most people I regard politicians as frauds and liars and the current political system as nothing more than a bureaucratic means for furthering the augmentation and advantages of economic elites. . . . I don't vote because to me it seems like a tacit act of compliance; I know, I know my grandparents fought in two world wars (and one World Cup) so that I'd have the right to vote. Well, they were conned. As far as I'm

concerned there is nothing to vote for. I feel it is a far more potent political act to completely renounce the current paradigm than to participate in even the most trivial and tokenistic manner, by obediently X-ing a little box.

One of the most high-profile criticisms of Brand's intervention has come from Deputy Prime Minister Nick Clegg. Clegg took aim more directly at Paxman for his sympathy with Brand's political disillusionment and refusal to vote. The fact that Clegg leveled his criticism primarily at Paxman instead of Brand reveals who he regards as possessing more credibility to speak on politics. Paxman is, after all, Clegg might reason, one of them, as he remains a product of the same Oxbridge schooling that continues to produce the political class in the UK. But let's focus on the substance of Clegg's criticism. As he goes on to explain:

> We know that politics is not perfect, but at the end of the day it is the way that we decide how you pay your taxes, how we support our hospitals, our schools, whether we are going to war or not, how we deal with climate change. . . . Of course it is sometimes unedifying, but this idea that you can just sort of sneer at the whole thing, dismiss everyone as being rogues and charlatans and therefore "I am going to wash my hands of the whole thing" — I think it is a total abdication of responsibility.

Really? Not only does Clegg engage here in the crudest form of intellectual blackmail, saying we cannot imagine or pursue an alternative to existing political systems without committing "a total abdication of responsibility," so does he engage in a fraudulent public deception that relies upon the delusions of his own historical amnesia. Paxman has already taken him to task for the fact that his Liberal Democrats party engaged in one of the more shameless political deceits of recent times by reneging on their campaign commitment not to increase student fees. Hence, serious questions have already been raised about the worth of the entire process he claims is the only responsible choice. But what about Clegg's further claim that we get to "decide" on issues of import? What about going to war in Iraq? We must have been out of the country when that occurred. Whether we'd be happy to accept crippling austerity measures? What about whether we should put the likes of Bush, Cheney, and Blair on trial for war crimes, or profiteering bankers for crimes against the future of hope now viciously denied to youth across the world?

Democracy should not be reduced to the act of voting for the same selection of petit bourgeois actors who are identifiable solely by wearing different color suits and neckties. Neither can it be found in a system that by its very definition is "representative." Democracy means people having the ability to influence those decisions that fundamentally shape their own lives. So, like Brand, we too have a "confession" to make. We don't vote and never have done so. Not because we have no commitment to politics or the possibility of improving societies. It is because we believe the entire charade to be a stage-managed performance that continues to express the sheer poverty of contemporary political imaginations. People don't refuse to vote because they are apathetic or because they have abdicated any sense of political responsibility. Indeed, not voting is more than some passive or negative act. It is *preceded* by the belief that politics can be otherwise.

A more brutal attack on Brand's political awareness and strategic choices has come from fellow comedian Robert Webb. According to Webb, Brand is effectively an appeaser of the worst kind since he makes light of something truly "important," and as a result, has not thought through properly the real consequences of his ideas. Immaturity, then, writ large! As he writes:

> I understand your ache for the luminous, for a connection beyond yourself. Russell, we all feel like that. Some find it in music or literature, some in the wonders of science and others in religion. But it isn't available any more in revolution. We tried that again and again, and we know that it ends in death camps, gulags, repression and murder. In brief, and I say this with the greatest respect, please read some fucking Orwell.

Webb's typically reductionist argument suffers from a self-righteous and narrow reading of history. He embodies the "reasoned liberal" who remains deluded in the belief that music, literature, science, religion, and politics can be neatly separated into distinct spheres of action and engagement. Even though, of course, there is "fucking Orwell." God forbid that we find poetry in the political, beauty in styles of living and affirmative joy at the wonder of philosophical enquiry to take us beyond the stripped-down reasoning of his sense of political agency. While Webb accuses Brand of being unaware of the consequences of history — especially the history of mass violence — he effectively forces Brand into a modernist paradigm wherein politics becomes a matter of deciding between different State models. If Webb had the slightest understanding of less Eurocentric approaches to history, he would appreciate how (a) it has been precisely the modern State (which Brand is effectively bringing into question) that has been responsible for the atrocities he mentions (and for which liberal states are some of the worst offenders); and (b) alternative political actors the world over have long since appreciated the limits of liberal democracy just as they are fully appreciative that its notions of freedom, democracy, and justice are illusionary. Indeed, in the contemporary period, the impetus for a radical rethink doesn't emanate from privileged students with a revolutionary urge but from places like Chiapas in Mexico, where the capillary ends of neoliberal power and violence are most clearly felt.

Perhaps it is Webb who should read some "fucking Orwell"; not as a historical document grounded in time but as a way to interrogate the contemporary period. Then he might appreciate that reason alone can easily become a sickness that reasons thousands to slaughter for the moral good.

The second criticism leveled at Brand concentrates on his biographical history, effectively disqualifying him from speaking on issues of emancipation in the present. While his admission of drug taking has been periodically raised to question his soundness of mind, it is really his sex life that is the major "flaw." Brand, it seems, stands guilty as charged for "objectifying" women. Laurie Penny, responding in *New Statesman*, has exemplified this position. While Penny doesn't disagree with anything Brand says in terms of his critique of liberal democracy, she nevertheless feels compelled to point out that he (like many other celebrity men) "boasts a track record of objectification and of playing cheap misogyny for laughs." This, apparently, is "just what a rock star does." For Penny, this sexism is not to be dismissed as incidental to the cause. It reveals the wider "rape apologism on the left" that deems women to be a hindrance to the "real struggle":

> But what is this "real struggle," if it requires women and girls
> to suffer structural oppression in silence? What is this "real
> struggle" that hands the microphone over and over again

to powerful, charismatic white men? Can we actually have a revolution that relegates women to the back of the room, that turns vicious when the discussion turns to sexual violence and social equality? What kind of fucking freedom are we fighting for? And whither that elusive, sporadically useful figure, the brocialist?

Is Penny, however, not equally guilty here of disqualifying Brand's intervention by offering a more authentic concept of the "real struggle?" Indeed, outside of Brand's widely reported sexual adventures, where is the evidence that he is fundamentally a sexist? Does the quantity of Brand's encounters, or indeed the way these female partners look, necessarily translate into objectification?

Some will no doubt recount here the radio incident that resulted in the comedian Andrew Sachs of *Fawlty Towers* fame being mortally offended by comments about his granddaughter in the name of comedy. The media outrage was evident and somewhat inevitable given that during the same show, Brand also chastised the *Daily Mail* newspaper for its support of Nazism and Hitler. Even here, the debate tends to stop at the fact that Brand is a sexist because he talked about sexual relations in public. Having an active sex life that is widely reported is not the same as being a sexist. We are equally curious how many actually bothered to interview Sachs following his outrage and concerns with stereotyping about his own stereotyping in the name of comedy. Nobody asked him how many Spanish waiters he thought had suffered the derogatory chant of "Manuel" after *Fawlty Towers* was aired.

One of the real tragedies of a particular strand of leftist thought, contributed to by puritanical trends within feminism and elsewhere, has been to forget that sexuality and desire are affirmative political categories, not in a way that sees them simply as enslaving and responsible for all the world's problems but integral to the creation of emancipated subjects liberated from normalizing repressions. We are all desiring subjects, and to forget this is the gravest of political deceits, one that is complicit in the operations of power. This is not in any way to apologize for gender inequalities. They are inexcusable. Nor is it to make light of the feminist struggle. It remains integral to the fight against fascism in all its forms. But to argue that Brand has no right to speak in the name of emancipation because of his sexual activity is to engage in puritanism of the most suffocating kind. It is tantamount to reverse sexism that uses its claim of more authentic victimhood to refuse to see itself.

Brand's celebrity status invariably raises many questions. Why is it that only celebrities manage to get their voices heard? Would the same criticism be levelled at a different kind of celebrity, say Stephen Fry? Is this a problem with the individual or the system that produces this logic? While it might be right to question the fact that Brand profits from the very system he now has the luxury to critique, could we not say the same of some of the current darlings of the intellectual left such as Judith Butler and Slavoj Žižek, who also have a mass populist following that is wholly compatible with a celebrity culture? After all, as people have long noted, it requires the luxury of time to study Marx's critique of capitalism.

Let's take, for example, *Salon* writer Natasha Lennard, who raises directly this question of Brand's celebrity status. Although she acknowledged him to be a "well-intentioned, wildly famous performer with a 'fuck-this' attitude and some really nice thoughts," she nevertheless is compelled to question:

> We have to be willing to obliterate our own elevated platforms, our own spaces of celebrity; this grotesque politico-socio-economic situation that elevates a few voices and silences many millions is what Brand is posturing against. Would he be willing to destroy himself — as celebrity, as leader, as 'Russell Brand?' I think he'd struggle, but I don't really know the guy.

Suey Park and Isabelle Nastasia argue that Brand's "so-called revolution" is "particularly ridiculous" as it is the corporate media that is holding him up as this revolutionary icon, while "young people of color, and women, queer kids, working class and poor youth are leading organizations that are building a robust movement across issues, strategies, and identities; a movement that is not looking to celebrities or elites for direction but is informed from below."

So how is one authenticated as being from below? What qualities do you need to possess in order to qualify as a valid member of this inverted vanguard? What does one need to renounce about oneself before being able to speak with an authentic voice? Are there degrees,

for instance, of "belowness" that create levels of subaltern verification? Does this invalidate the voices of all white men, especially those
who garner a public profile? Does this preclude we who, although
from working-class backgrounds, now find ourselves part of well-established academic institutions? Indeed, does having a presence in
the corporate media world necessarily disqualify the quality of the
criticism and the political intervention? We wonder whether Park and
Nastasia would apply the same logic to Pussy Riot, whose plight and
message is equally reported on account of their stardom and corporate agenda?

Surely what matters is that a person appreciates the conditions in
which they are located and chooses to resist on such terms. Otherwise
we risk becoming revolutionary vanguards in the most exclusionary of
senses. We might recall here Brand's justification for his outburst at the
GQ ceremony, which is worth quoting at length:

> In case you don't know, these parties aren't like real parties.
> It's fabricated fun, imposed from the outside. A vision of what
> squares imagine cool people might do set on a spaceship. Or
> in Moloko. As we come out of the lift, there's a bloody great
> long corridor flanked by gorgeous birds in black dresses,
> paid to be there, motionless, left hand on hip, teeth tacked to
> lips with scarlet glue. The intention, I suppose, is to contrive
> some Ian Fleming super-uterus of well-fit mannequins to
> midwife you into the shindig . . . I could see the room dividing
> as I spoke. I could hear the laughter of some and louder still
> silence of others. I realized that for some people this was re-
> garded as an event with import. The magazine, the sponsors
> and some of those in attendance saw it as a kind of ceremo-
> ny that warranted respect. In effect, it is a corporate ritual,
> an alliance between a media organization, GQ, and a com-
> mercial entity, Hugo Boss. What dawned on me as the night
> went on is that even in apparently frivolous conditions, the
> establishment asserts control and won't tolerate having that
> assertion challenged, even flippantly, by that most beautiful-
> ly adept tool: comedy.

> I do have some good principles picked up that night that
> are generally applicable: The glamour and the glitz isn't real,
> the party isn't real, you have a much better time mucking

around trying to make your mates laugh. I suppose that's obvious. We all know it; we already know all the important stuff, like: don't trust politicians, don't trust big business and don't trust the media. Trust your own heart and each other. When you take a breath and look away from the spectacle it's amazing how absurd it seems when you look back.

What Brand terms absurd, we call tragic. Our current predicament is most certainly a tragedy. As utopian ideas and the belief that we may transform the world for the better are displaced by an open horizon of inevitable insecurity, more tightening of the belt and future catastrophe, politicians tell us that there is no way out of this already fated existence. This is where Brand's "comedy" represents something far more than frivolous entertainment. It crosses firmly over into the political, for comedy can be the most potent and disruptive of political weapons when tragedy prevails, as Simon Critchley discusses in *Infinitely Demanding: Ethics of Commitment, Politics of Resistance*.

For too long have we been sold the idea that politics is a "science" through which humans can be studied like lab rats and prodded into action through the simplest of participatory mechanisms. Anything else simply confuses the docile masses! But we prefer to see the political as a poetic art that is defined by the creation of new modes of living and new ways of thinking. Revolution in such terms is not about storming the palace or even returning to outdated political categories such as communism. It is, as Brand argued quite rightly, about changing the way we think about the political. Such a task demands embracing the impossible and transgressing the limits of what is simply the "natural" order of things. This is why we find Brand so compelling. He has become a lightning rod to expose all that is outdated with the left's political imaginary. The liberal left obviously cannot abide Brand; because his discordant, unlicensed, and, for many, unwelcome "entry" into politics actually demonstrates in its temerity the existence of a political imagination worthy of the name. The rules of the game must be changed, and another way of deciding on how we all live together must be fought for.

Originally published in somewhat different form in TruthOut.

The Promise of Violence
in the Age of Catastrophe

Brad Evans & Julian Reid

Sunday, 5 January 2014

OURS IS AN AGE of catastrophe. New Yorkers understand this better than most. To live there is to be forever in danger. From "terror" to weather and everything in between, its pasts and futures collide as the city is haunted by the spectral promise of violence. Such a reality is at odds with the narrative through which the city has attempted to re-brand itself. Manhattan is said to be a safer, more inviting, cleaner, and less seedy environment. Sections have been renamed: West Harlem is now Manhattanville, as if to indicate a clean break from the past in terms of the neighborhood's identity. Much of the change has been attributed to zero-tolerance policing implemented during the Giuliani and Bloomberg years which resulted in a notable decline in recorded violence and homicides. Indeed, the possibility of a return to the grittier New York so often dramatized during the 1970s and 1980s continues to frame contemporary political debates, as shown in the police policy of stop-and-frisk.

If its streets are no longer mean, they are nevertheless spaces of vulnerability. New York is a paradigm that suggests spaces of all kinds are fundamentally insecure by design.

Something dramatic occurred in the decade after September 11, 2001. It was common to write about the events of that day as something exceptional. It was "the day the world changed forever," as Tony Blair told us, the global broadcasting of mass violence that brought us all together for the first time in a shared sense of planetary grief and outrage. This notion of the exceptional moment became a rallying cry on the right and the left, evidenced most clearly in the revival of the work of Carl Schmitt. Some insisted that the old rules of war needed to be scrapped because the nature of the threat was like nothing we had witnessed before. Others bought into the idea of exceptionalism and extended it to the abuse of sovereign power, most evident at Guantánamo Bay. This was expected. Such a retreat at least offered some sense of security and certainty.

True to form, as Schmitt would have appreciated, representations of the violence of 9/11 in the mass media were notably uniform. They reprinted, to the point of monotony, images of the exploding towers, leaving no doubt that a state of war was in effect. Such analysis, however, gradually unraveled as the decade went on. Not only was it increasingly clear that power and danger needed to be understood in planetary terms, the politics of exceptionalism led to the disastrous war in Iraq.

Let us turn to a more unsettling image of that day: Richard Drew's infamous sequence of the Falling Man. Only a handful of media outlets initially published these difficult yet serene compositions. Critics argued that publication disrespected the victims as the final moments of their lives were presented in horrifying detail. Why did these images meet such a backlash while the images of the towers' destruction became accepted? There is undeniably a personal dimension at work here that these images force us to confront. Had any of us happened to visit Manhattan that day, a trip to the World Trade Center could have been on the itinerary. How would we have reacted in such a terrifying predicament? Perhaps these images were more contentious because, unlike exploding towers, which function in a militaristic way, depicting a state of spectacular warlike devastation, the Falling Man shifts the analysis from material destruction to the more personal, human aspect of the tragedy, which is complex and indiscernible.

Fast-forward to a few months after the 10th anniversary of 9/11. Here, we witness a remarkable shift in attitudes. The fifth season of *Mad Men* was launched with a series of images that depicted silhouettes of a suited businessman falling from a building. The comparisons with 9/11 were all too evident. But what did these images reveal about the political moment? We arguably were in a different period that revealed the limits of time and the simplicities of exceptionalism. The image of a falling person, it seemed, was no longer sacrosanct; it was, as the producers insisted, simply advertising. It wasn't that "the terror" had been defeated. The enemy is, after all, unbeatable by definition. The discourse simply had become part of the everyday lexicon. Such a condition is better described as "terrifyingly normal," in which the normalization of violence overwrites the need for critical examination. In the terms of the falling businessman, as Matt Weiner, the creative director for *Mad Men* pointed out, there was a need to have a more nuanced understanding of the history of catastrophe and the human response: "I hate to say it, but a businessman falling out of a window is a symbol that far precedes that event."

The falling subject embodies the contemporary liberal subject. It is a life form that is assumed to be vulnerable because the complex order of things produces systems that are what hackers call "insecure by design." It is a life that must accept the inevitability of another disaster. The dream of lasting security belongs to a bygone era. To be politically astute and socially responsible requires an acceptance of the age of catastrophe and its assumptions about the fleeting order of things. As Juliette Kayyem, policy adviser on homeland security to the Obama administration and Harvard academic, puts it:

> One day it will be acceptable, politically and publicly, to argue that while homeland security is about ensuring that fewer bad things happen, the real test is that when they inevitably do, they aren't as bad as they would have been absent the effort. Only our public and political response to another major terrorist attack will test whether there is room for both ideologies to thrive in a nation that was, any way you look at it, built to be vulnerable.

This brings us directly to the problem of resilience, which is the new dominant trope for thinking about life and its environment. It is worth dwelling here on the events of the 10th anniversary of 9/11. A few days before the commemoration, media outlets started reporting on the possibility that New York may be targeted — the nature of the event always raised this prospect. By September 8, Mayor Bloomberg announced "credible" but "unconfirmed" details of the impending attack. While newspapers such as the *Daily News* headlined in the most tragically Orwellian way, "9/11 Terror Threat," CNN encouraged New Yorkers to be "vigilant." Vigilant against what? How can one be vigilant when the threat was unknowable in nature? What remains is to be suspicious of everything. No sooner had the threat shifted from white vans to the water supply that it was then the subway's turn to be the site of possible danger. This prompted then-Mayor Michael Bloomberg to publicly ride the subway that day. Showing what he proclaimed to be the spirit of New Yorkers, he embodied the hardened resilient subject who wasn't afraid to face the enemy on its terms. While, in the end, no attack materialized, this episode also made clear that the nature of the threat was, in fact, ubiquitous. It was integral and hence indeterminable from the lived environment.

Like threat, the doctrine of resilience was ubiquitous. *Newsweek* set the tone with a cover feature of a passenger jet against cloudless blue sky, headlining with an increasing font size, "Ten Years of Fear: Grief: Revenge: Resilience." The image used was painfully reflective in its normality. Time magazine was equally reflective as its "Beyond 9/11" cover, designed by Julian LaVerdiere and Paul Myoda, co-creators of the original "Tribute in Light" memorial. The rationale being, as *Time*'s managing editor, Richard Stengel, noted, to represent "something that literally and figuratively moved beyond 9/11." *People* magazine's emotional tribute was the "Legacy of Love — The Children of 9/11 — Portraits of Hope," which showed photographs of those who lost fathers that day. It read: "Their fathers died on that terrible day, before they were born. Today, these 10 kids and their moms have triumphed over tragedy." The spirit of the nation was defined by its ability to bounce back from the catastrophe.

Battery Park in Lower Manhattan offered another scene of survivability. Surrounding Fritz Koenig's partially disfigured "The Sphere," which was formerly at the Austin H. Tobin Plaza (between the Twin Towers), 3,000 whitened flags that featured the names of the deceased symbolically memorialized the past while celebrating that it is possible for certain things to emerge, if slightly transformed, in design, meaning, and political resonance. "The Sphere" became a living symbol of resilience because it literally provided an optimistic center for reflection in a sea of tragic memory. Perhaps, however, it was Marco Grob's "Beyond 9/11: Portraits of Resilience" exhibition in the Milk Gallery and various additional public spaces across Manhattan that proves most revealing. Featuring stark black-and-white photographs of the 40 faces said to encapsulate the spirit of recovery, such resilience is ubiquitously framed by politicians, the major, the admiral, the general, the military hero, the CIA covert operative, along with the CEO, New York firefighters, artists, and everyday survivors. The messages here were poignant. Resilient life is fully inclusive. It made no distinction. Catastrophe had strengthened the resolve. We learned more about ourselves by living through the terror. Shared experience of trauma brought a people together. Despite vast differences in lifestyles, not to mention wealth, the resilient subject was universal.

What remains of interest to us are the political stakes. A visit to the National September 11 Memorial at Ground Zero proves most instructive. Michael Arad's design is poignant in its symbolism. By footprinting the Twin Towers, the past is drawn into the present as the names of the victims are etched into the granite. This is accompanied by a cascading symmetrical flow of water in keeping with what Zygmunt Bauman calls the "liquidity" of our modern times. Descending some 30 feet into a darkened void, it also can be seen as representative of the black hole phenomena so often associated with theories of catastrophe. Everything is drawn into this void. Nothing escapes. Such memorialization thus emphasizes trauma by making visible what is no longer there. And it draws into sharp relief the central void, which reminds visitors that the unknowable horrors of the experience lie inaccessibly beneath the surface of the memorial's fixed frames.

Beyond the symbolism of the memorial, visitors are left in no doubt as to the closure of the political. Upon entering the site, all are immediately reminded that the memorial is "a place of remembrance and quiet reflection." This is accompanied by another sign warning against political or religious discussions of any kind. But if the world truly changed on that day, surely more time should have been spent debating the significance of the event and the consequences of any actions that followed. Reflection is a substitute here for the incontestable demands of quiet acceptance. The truth of the event is not open to public discussion. Neither should we confuse the reflective moment with any notion of political sensibility. Why it mattered is inconsequential. The undeniable message is that a catastrophe occurred and that there remain dangers still lurking on the horizon of future possibility.

The militaristic dimensions to this are evident. We have noted how resilience offers a new social morphology that transforms everything from the nature of neoliberal governance to the way the military is rethinking the entire practice of engaging with the problems war brings.

Indeed, while it is tempting to focus on the doctrine of resilience as originating within ecological circles, the humanities and social sciences reveal something more about the implicit political stakes. One of the more perverse cases of this doctrine's symbolism is found in the recently "christened" USS New York. "Forged from the steel of the World Trade Center," this latest warship evidences the most potent expression of "bounce-backability." As New York Governor George E. Pataki explains,

> We're very proud that the twisted steel from the World Trade Center towers will soon be used to forge an even stronger national defense... The USS New York will soon be defending freedom and combating terrorism around the globe, while also ensuring that the world never forgets the evil attacks of September 11, 2001 and the courage and strength New Yorkers showed in response to terror.

While resilience for many appears to be common sense, our argument is that it actually leaves people "dangerously exposed." More than simply accepting the inevitability of future catastrophe, it preaches the folly of even thinking we might resist danger and, instead, accept the necessity of living a life of permanent exposure to endemic dangers. Indeed, not only does it expose us to the possibility of the violent encounter before it happens such that we may be more responsive should it arrive, it promotes our adaptability so that we are also less of a threat politically. Accepting the imperative to become resilient means sacrificing any political vision of a world in which we might be able to live free from dangers, looking instead at the future as an endemic terrain of catastrophe that is dangerous and insecure by design. Resilient lives are forced to embrace an art of living dangerously that can imagine the future only as occupied by the ruins of the present. It is fully compatible with the neoliberal model of economy, its promotion of risk, and its emphasis on care for the self to the evacuation of the social state. Without the confidence that the world may be transformed for the better, what remains are vulnerable subjects forced to partake in a world that is catastrophically fated unto the end. How we might break from this demands a new political imaginary and poetic sense of spatial belonging.

Originally published in somewhat different form in TruthOut.

As We Remember the Atrocities of the 20th Century, We must Change the Way We Think about Violence

Brad Evans

Tuesday, 4 February 2014

MASS VIOLENCE IS POORLY understood if it simply refers to casualties on battlefields or continues to be framed through conventional notions of warfare. We need to interrogate the multiple ways in which entire populations are rendered disposable on a daily basis if we are to take seriously the meaning of global citizenship in the 21st century.

The next few years provide us with a timely opportunity for serious reflection. As we begin memorializing the "Century of Violence" — including the 20th anniversary of the Rwandan genocide, the centenary of World War I, the 70th anniversaries of the bombings of Hiroshima and Nagasaki, and the 40th anniversary of the "killing fields" in Cambodia — confronting the suffering of the past will become part of contemporary debate.

While there is no doubt a need to collectively memorialize these traumatic and horrifying world events, it is not sufficient to simply use them as an opportunity to claim that we now live in more secure and peaceful times.

A number of authors, including Steven Pinker, have us believe that mass violence is on the decline due to the expansion of liberal zones of influence and pacification. This all rests on points of definition.

While it might be possible to offer an account of more peaceful times by reducing our analysis to questions of violence between nations or ideologies, such accounts fly in the face of the lived realities of many of the world's citizens.

What we need is a sober and honest reflection on the memory of violence so that we are better equipped to understand its subtler and more sinister qualities.

Although our understanding of war and violence has been altered over the past few decades, rightly accounting for the daily insecurities people face in zones of instability and crises, our analysis still remains largely tied to rather tired 20th century political categories that oscillate between authoritarian and failing states, ethnic tensions, or the problem of insurgencies. We need a new vocabulary and a different angle of vision if we are to interrogate its novel and contemporary forms.

Defining rape, for example, as a weapon of war has allowed us to relate what appears to be personal incidents to widespread systematic abuse. And yet such methods are selectively applied in ways that appear all too convenient to the political fortunes of liberal societies.

Even in terms of conventional warfare, we seem incapable of connecting individual deaths with broader questions of mass violence and policies of systematic abuse. In the five years of the Obama drone policy, for instance, comparable numbers of people have been killed as were in the horrors of September 11, 2001. Even if we accept that a significant number of these are suspected militants, the policy of assassination denies us any recourse to verifiable modes of justice. And how many innocents are to die before this violence is explained in comparative terms?

This says nothing to the broader questions of endemic gun crime or the mass incarceration of people of color in the United States that is numerically comparable to forced imprisonment witnessed during the global slave trade. Neither does it talk to the socially engineered conditions of extreme poverty and inescapable despair so commonplace throughout the world.

As we therefore set about the process of memorialization, it is also imperative that we start to question whether aspects of our contemporary societies make it possible to think and act in ways that render specific people disposable. How can we use these historical moments and the legacies of atrocity to begin meaningful debate on the state of the world today?

This requires open dialogue between public figures, academics, artists and creative visionaries, NGOs, activists, along with religious and community leaders regardless of political affiliation. Only then might we start to think seriously about the meaning of global citizenship, peaceful cohabitation, our shared responsibilities, and what it means to live a dignified existence.

Originally published in somewhat different form in The Independent.

Are Some Lives Disposable?

Brad Evans & Adrian Parr

Friday, 14 February 2014

WHAT TYPICALLY SPRINGS to mind when one speaks of "violence"? Would it be the systematic murder of civilians during the Holocaust or the massacre of Tutsis by Hutus in the Rwandan genocide? Perhaps we are prompted to reflect upon all those killed during the two world wars of the 20th century or the more recent wars in Afghanistan and Iraq? Is it the suicide bombers who blow themselves up in a public place or the lone gunmen taking fire on groups of school children and their teachers?

If the horrors on the nightly news or government warnings on the limits of nonviolence are the benchmark we use to think about violence, then maybe it is all of the above. Such narratives certainly dominate most of our contemporary discussions and demands for remembrance.

But can we reduce violence simply to a matter of state or non-state actors entering into conflict? Indeed, does violence necessarily have to be related to some form of physical violation?

What about all the species that have gone extinct as the climate changes and habitats disappear, while greenhouse gas emissions persistently rise? What might we say about the malnourished and starving living with crippling hunger pains and thirst on a daily basis while millions of tons of food waste enter landfills each year? Or for that matter, the victim of psychological abuse who learns to live with the torment such that the eventual physical blow becomes a relief from what is imagined?

And then there are those who find themselves homeless and without a livelihood as a result of the global financial crisis, all the while the corporate architects of this very real and systemic tragedy continue to profit in these crippling times of crises and austerity. Surely we might argue that all these are equally worthy of being described as instances of everyday violence, where political strategies and economic systems render some lives invisible and inaudible while affirming and legitimating others?

There is a fundamental problem of representation here. Many of our assumptions on violence are linked to forms of political authenticity and the right to claim monopoly over the terms "peace," "security," and "prosperity." And beneath the veneer of these discourses is the ability to strip lives of the ability to precisely identify the source of oppression and suffering.

What remains is a narrative that focuses on individual failure without any attempt to address the wider conditions of disempowerment, let alone change them for some alternative.

In January, 2014, the United Nations announced it would suspend updating the death toll from Syria's civil war, explaining that the organization could not confirm casualty figures. But do the numbers adequately encompass the systematic nature of violence as it plays out in the contemporary world? The numbers used to summarize, measure, monitor, know, and evaluate life cannot possibly translate the exhaustion that must arise when living in a conflict zone that apparently has no end in sight or the physical and emotional pain of losing a limb and the frustration of navigating rubble-filled streets on crutches.

While the attempt to rethink violence may unsettle the belief that the liberal variant of democracy faithfully represents its constituency, we cannot simply rely upon diagnosing conflict with matters of both national and human security as if only "bad actors" inflict violence, as if liberal societies do not produce their own novel and deeply embedded structural forms of violence.

To reason otherwise is to reduce many of the world's citizens to being statistics devoid of system, thereby failing to raise critical questions of agency and responsibility so often relied upon by the most oppressive and tyrannical systems of rule. To account for widespread suffering without diagnosing the conditions that continue to render lives disposable is to engage in a seriously remiss intellectualism of the most banal and ethically compromised form.

This lands us straight back where we began, with violence deciding what is seen and heard and what life is disposable. What needs to be interrogated is less the exceptional nature of different acts of violence, less the actions of violent individuals, than the chilling normality of violent circumstances intrinsic to our contemporary societies.

It is somewhat easy to condemn violence when it appears in those moments of spectacular and terrifying rage. We are less comfortable looking directly at the daily forms of violence each of us might gaze upon as we simply walk down the streets of any major city.

We need new and more imaginative ways for interrogating violence if we are to take seriously the meaning of global citizenship in the 21st century. This demands that we reframe the memory of violence and challenge the politicization of remembrance, which attempts to absolve us of the violence we have committed in the name of better futures.

We can all accept that what happens in the past has a profound bearing on the historical conjuncture in which we currently live and from which we currently benefit. Instead of getting caught up in emotional or humanistic sentimentality, we should begin by asking what the past says to us about the world we inhabit today. We need to encourage our fellow citizens to consider the relations between violence of the past and the structure and logics of modern life in ways that don't simply write off these atrocities as illiberal aberrations of our otherwise peaceful and civilized times. Violence is not simply a series of unrelated moments of extraordinary violence. We do ourselves a great disservice by continuing to reason violence by applying outdated 20th century paradigms.

Originally published in Al Jazeera.

Turning a Blind Eye to the Political Promise of the Financial Crisis

Adrian Parr & Brad Evans

Friday, 21 March 2014

ON SEPTEMBER 15, 2008, the financial services company Lehman Brothers filed for bankruptcy. The week beginning Monday October 6, the Dow Jones Industrial Average fell at least one percent a day for six consecutive days as the S&P 500 fell 22 percent in six trading sessions. By Friday October 10, 2008, the London stock market had "suffered its third largest fall ever" with the FTSE 100 falling by over 10 percent in early trading, "wiping about £89.5 billion off the value of Britain's biggest companies." The global economy went into free fall as the world's leaders and business figures scrambled to stop it. A domino effect of bankruptcy, foreclosures, and rising unemployment set in.

Five years on, and not much has changed since the world catapulted into one of the worst financial upheavals since the Great Depression of the 1930s. A vibrant people's movement had briefly bubbled to the surface, demanding change and a redistribution of power and wealth. Yet the opportunities to test-run brave new economic alternatives and equitable forms of social organization are rapidly frittering away.

For a moment there, all eyes and hopes were on the Occupy Movement as it reclaimed public space in New York City, London, Madrid, Rome, Sydney, and Taipei, just to name a few. The slogan, "We are the 99 percent," struck a chord loud and deep in the hearts of people in all walks of life. People from around the world joined forces to demonstrate en masse against the financial corruption and greed that had triggered the 2008 global financial meltdown, demanding an end to the gross inequities and skewed power relations a capitalist economy produces.

In October 2011, hunger strikers in Mexico City protested outside the Mexican Stock Exchange. Occupy movement student protesters were pepper sprayed by police in the campus quad of UC Davis on November 28, 2011. The incident went viral, sparking a lively public debate over the tensions between democracy, militarism, and public space. Meanwhile, in January 2012, over 40 people were arrested as they attempted to occupy Rondebosch Common, one of the wealthiest suburbs in the most unequal city of South Africa: Cape Town. Lives once treated as a means to an end — that end being the accumulation of capital and the centralization of power in the hands of few — had come together to collectively demand politics be placed in the service of the 99 percent.

The unseen, unheard majority had transformed into a loud visible minoritarian force, peacefully rallying around shared aspirations, outrage, anxieties, and optimism for a new world order. That is, a world not organized around catering to the excesses of capitalism or around irresponsible financial markets and the interests of a few reckless bankers or around investors maximizing the short-term financial interests of shareholders. How would such a world work? For one, it would have a renewed sense of public governance: a political condition premised upon intolerance toward the artificiality of democratic consensus and compromise, which in practice amounts to private interests persistently undermining the public good through campaign contributions and lobbying activities; a new world order that would respond to the growing number of poor and unemployed by improving social safety nets, healthcare, and education opportunities; a society that promotes and nurtures long-term value; a political system committed to the redistribution of wealth; and a society unafraid to work toward ideals.

With the financial crisis, the neoliberal notion that social and environmental problems can be left up to the free market to solve came into question. UK Prime Minister Gordon Brown blamed the crash on the systemic failures of capitalism. European Central Bank President Jean-Claude Trichet criticized the neoliberal turn toward deregulation, urging the Bretton Woods agreement be reinstated. During his speech at New York's Economic Club, Trichet announced: "It's absolutely clear that financial markets need discipline: macroeconomic discipline, monetary discipline, market discipline."

Even socialism appeared to have lost its controversial taste. The February 6, 2009, issue of *Newsweek* featured an article by Jon Meacham titled "We Are All Socialists Now." Americans needed to recognize, he wrote, that the age of Reagan had come to a close and a new age of big government had ironically been ushered in under the US Republican Presidency of George W. Bush. Bush had bailed out the financial sector to the tune of US$700 billion. Picking up on the growing sympathy for socialist approaches, Meacham nevertheless argued the European welfare state was the cause of high unemployment in Europe. He forewarned readers against following in the footsteps of their European comrades, contending government intervention in the economy would restrict economic growth at a time when it was needed most.

Three main criticisms shaped the explanations for why the situation occurred. Firstly, it was bad people, such as the bankers and "rogue traders" selling mortgages to the poor, who couldn't afford their repayments, and the unrestrained avarice of the private sector. Secondly, it was bad government with policies that favored the rich and loosened regulation. Thirdly, it was bad ideas: the illusion that prosperity would be endless, for example, or people comfortable with unsustainable levels of debt.

The dominant narrative describing the impact of the financial crisis was economic. The housing bubble had burst, putting a serious dent in that market. The global financial market was completely destabilized. This spooked investors, and, in turn, sent further shock waves throughout the economy. Banks and corporations were either going bankrupt or teetering on the verge of bankruptcy, and layoffs ensued. Governments the world over were on the brink of falling; indeed, a large chunk of the US presidential campaign of 2008 was fought over whether or not markets needed to be more or less regulated.

The upshot is that a series of economic solutions were put on the table: lower interest rates, promote consumption, encourage more personal debt, and, most of all, use public money to save the private sector. The question of a fair response to the vulnerabilities and disadvantage the financial crisis has exacerbated, however, continues to be sidestepped. Disadvantage and vulnerability are multifaceted problems, and, within the landscape of poverty, it is women, immigrants, children, the sick, and elderly, of course, who continue to experience deeper hardships and whose situation largely falls below the radar.

Such populations constitute an invisible majority; lives that are abstracted by the technical language so often favored by macro-economists and political scientists.

In the Eurozone, drop-in construction jobs directly impact low-skilled immigrant migrant workers, otherwise difficult to reintegrate into the economy, and, as informal workers, they run the risk of losing their visa status. Immigrant workers are caught in a terrible double bind — unable to return home where there is no work and stuck in a country where there is little work, all the while servicing whatever debt incurred in migrating. Worse still, they become the obvious targets for adherents to new forms of nationalism and fundamentalism that purposefully emerge in times of crises.

From 2000 to 2009, the number of US children living below the national poverty rate of $22,050 a year for a family of four grew 33 percent. The majority of poor children are African American, with 36 percent of black children living in poor families. In some states, such as Ohio and Michigan, this figure increases to 46 percent. That says nothing to the levels of mass incarceration that overwhelmingly victimizes poor people of color and migrants. What does it say of a society that it favors the mass imprisonment of a racially distinct underclass at a yearly financial cost comparable to full board graduate study at an Ivy League university?

Nancy Birdsall of the Center for Global Development came out in February 2009 urging the world's wealthiest countries to develop a coordinated fiscal stimulus to deal with the situation. The International Labor Organization predicted the developing world would lose 50 million jobs; the World Bank projected Africa would have zero growth in per capita income. In response, Birdsall explained:

> Five billion people living in developing countries are innocent victims of the global economic crisis. Most live in countries with limited resources for stimulus packages, let alone for food stamps and unemployment insurance. This is true even in the many developing countries that have had re-

sponsible government and economic management for some
two decades.

The focus on resuscitating the global market and national economies
has meant that the most vulnerable continue to suffer the consequences of reckless and irresponsible behavior and policies that they
have had little or no say in creating. What is more, as a recent study
by Oxfam suggests, the levels of measurable inequalities have grown
to such levels that it now seems impossible to argue that neoliberal
policies benefit all the world's citizens. As the paper finds, one percent
of the world elite have now amassed nearly half the planet's wealth in
their personal fortunes. This control over some $110 trillion equals the
total wealth of the poorest 3.5 billion people.

The paper also finds that a mere 85 of the world's richest people have
as much income as the poorest 50 percent; while nearly 70 percent
of world citizens have seen a marked increase in relative poverty. The
implications, they argue, could not be more pronounced and stark:

> This massive concentration of economic resources in the
> hands of fewer people presents a significant threat to in-
> clusive political and economic systems. Instead of moving
> forward together, people are increasingly separated by eco-
> nomic and political power, inevitably heightening social ten-
> sions and increasing the risk of societal breakdown.

What we therefore confront is the possibility of widespread resentment and social unrest. Indeed, while we don't simply buy into the
reductionist economic arguments that poverty itself is the principle
cause of violence — it becomes all too easy to blame the global poor
for conditions of instability and crisis — it is nevertheless clear that
such contrasts in fortunes, economically or politically, are not sustainable.

So, what might it mean to bring the political back into the discussion
of the ongoing financial crises? For a start, we can point to a number
of basic historical lessons we might draw from this and political principles that could be followed.

First, we need to be clearer that policies of austerity don't simply represent a universal tightening of the belt. Austerity is not an ideological

position — it is the expression of the logic of capitalism whereby production is placed in the service of capital accumulation, and an ethos of privatization, commodification, and competition holds sway. Eerily reminiscent of the socially disastrous structural adjustment policies imposed upon many in Latin America, Sub-Saharan Africa, and South East Asia during the 1980s and 1990s, the policy of austerity is tantamount to a redistributive tax that benefits the rich while the pain it causes is felt more acutely by the global poor.

Second, we need a new vocabulary for describing the conditions of hardship and daily suffering endured by many of the world's citizens. This requires a more sober and honest reflection on the connections between policies of enrichment and policies of despair. As the eminent sociologist Zygmunt Bauman has written, there is a need to deploy more compelling terms that truly impress the political and social stakes:

> Casualties are dubbed "collateral" in so far as they are dismissed as not important enough to justify the costs of their prevention, or simply "unexpected" because the planner did not consider them worthy of inclusion… Thinking in terms of collateral damage tacitly assumes an *already existing inequality* of rights and chances, while accepting a priori the unequal distribution of the costs of undertaking action.

Third, we need to ask more uncomfortable questions about the ways in which entire populations are continually rendered disposable as a matter of systemic design. That is to say, we need to question more critically the real violence of poverty in ways that force us to confront both the daily tragedies of lives on the margins of existence and the intellectual neglect that creates such conditions in the first instance.

Fourth, we need to move beyond the analytical reductionism in policy discourse that strips human life of any political agency. The global poor are not simply a problem to be solved. Neither is the human subject some undifferentiated mass that can be governed as if all that mattered was aggregated levels of growth. Such assessments too often conceal the concentration of power and mask the true scale of human suffering.

Fifth, we need to move beyond outdated ways of thinking about politics, as if the only way to conceive of engagement is through the framework of the State. Power has long since been elevated into what Manuel Castells has called the "global space of flows." This is not a call to simply replicate a deeply flawed "representative" model on a global level, with a new cadre of political professionals. It is to take heed of the voices from below in ways that empower them to influence those forces that profoundly shape their lives, forces that, at present, they have no viable say in whatsoever.

And finally, we need to start a new conversation at a systemic level about the real political consequences of financial irresponsibility. For if we accept that economic activity is always political, this requires us to move beyond simply calling out unscrupulous banking practices as criminal or individualizing cases of rogue activity. The catastrophe brought upon many by the systematic abuse of power should raise more serious questions about what actually constitutes a crime against humanity.

Originally published in somewhat different form in World Financial Review.

Zygmunt Bauman's Warning from History

Brad Evans

Monday, 31 March 2014

WE ARE ABOUT to enter into a sobering period reminding us of the human capacity for destruction and devastation. As we begin to commemorate a number of key historic moments marking out the "century of violence," there will be a need to honor the dead and remember the failures of our political imaginations and our failure to prevent the widespread slaughter of tens of millions.

But we cannot simply memorialize without asking difficult and searching questions about the contemporary moment, about the way contemporary global society makes it possible to think and act in ways that render specific populations disposable.

The memory of violence is always deeply embedded in "regimes of truth" that are the outcome of power struggles. History is never value neutral or self-evident. What Michel Foucault often termed the "history of our present" is the outcome of many fraught intellectual battles, often perpetrated by the victors, who try to hide continued oppression and the most systematic of abuses in plain sight.

Zygmunt Bauman remains one of the most important intellectuals connecting the violence of the 20th century to the disposability of populations in the contemporary period. The author on some 50 books, Bauman is undoubtedly one of the most important critical voices of our generation. His eloquent and incisive writings are not the product of ivory tower privilege. Bauman talks to the present, having personally seen, intimately known, and lived through the worst excesses of

20th century totalitarianism. His warnings for contemporary generations carry weight precisely because he understands all too well the
ability for mass violence to regenerate in novel forms, whatever their
historical traces.

Bauman has continually shown remarkable sensitivity and courage when dealing with the question of violence. In *Modernity and
Ambivalence,* he offered an account of the different approaches modern society adopts toward the stranger. He argued that, on the one
hand, in a consumer-oriented economy, the strange and the unfamiliar is always enticing; in different styles of food, different fashions, and
in tourism, it is possible to experience the allure of what is unfamiliar.
Yet this strangeness also has a more negative side. The stranger, because he cannot be controlled and ordered, is always the object of
fear; he is the potential mugger, the person outside of society's borders
who is constantly threatening.

In Bauman's most famous book, *Modernity and the Holocaust*, he
gives a fuller account of the dangers of these kinds of fears. Drawing
upon Hannah Arendt and Theodor Adorno's books on totalitarianism and the Enlightenment, Bauman developed the argument that
the Holocaust should not simply be considered to be an event in
Jewish history, nor a regression to some form of premodern barba-
rism. Rather, he argued, the Holocaust should be seen as deeply connected to modernity and its order-making efforts. The metaphor of
the "Gardening State" was invoked here in particular to address the
violence of modernist regimes that can rationalize the most abhorrent
acts for the most progressive ends and calculated reasons. This has
come to define a particular novelty of the modern period.

Such warnings permeate Bauman's extensive intellectual corpus. As
he noted in *Modernity and the Holocaust*:

> The unspoken terror permeating our collective memory of
> the Holocaust (and more than contingently related to the
> overwhelming desire not to look the memory in its face) is
> the gnawing suspicion that the Holocaust could be more
> than an aberration, more than a deviation from an otherwise
> straight path of progress, more than a cancerous growth on
> the otherwise healthy body of the civilized society; that, in

short, the Holocaust was not an antithesis of modern civilization and everything (or so we like to think) it stands for.

As a historic event, it was "fully in keeping with everything we know about civilization, its guiding spirit, its priorities, its immanent vision of the world — and of the proper way to pursue human happiness together with a perfect society."

Hence, the violence was:

revealing of the characteristically modern zeal for order-making, the kind of posture which casts the extant human reality as a perpetually unfinished project, in need of critical scrutiny, constant revision and improvement. When confronted with that stance, nothing has the right to exist because of the fact that it happens to be around.

Such reasoning has been carried through in remarkable texts, such as *Wasted Lives*, that highlighted with real purchase the modern compulsion to render things disposable — life included; while his more recent works on liquid modernity, such as *Society Under Siege* and *Liquid Fear*, dealt more specifically with new forms of violence, which societies witness as they lose their traditional sovereign moorings. With considerable foresight, in fact, Bauman understood all too well what it meant to live in a "planetary frontierland" wherein all sense of space and time have been radically transformed, from the death of the so-called Westphalia Peace to conventional ideas on security and cohabitation. Bauman explains this as the fundamental separation of power and politics.

Bauman's work continually forces us to consider how the production of "disposable lives" at a systematic level is entirely fitting for contemporary societies. Liberal modernity, in fact, is yet another chapter in the story of the production of "disposable humans," or what he terms elsewhere "collateral casualties," retaining the two defining and notably modern preoccupations: order building and economic progress. Order building creates lives which simply don't belong as a result of their fixed identities; the incessant drive to progress continually casts aside those deemed to have no productive value and no qualities worth extracting.

Significantly, for Bauman, it is precisely the continued production of disposable lives that defines all modern projects, regardless of their ideological emblem, and in a world where ideas of technological progress continue to shape ideas of human progress, the ability to cast aside entire populations is easier than ever.

Bauman warns us that being disposable today means being systematically excluded from the increasingly concentrated benefits and riches of globalization. Not only do current conditions force us to rethink the meaning of mass violence in the 21st century; they demand new ethical responses and political imaginaries to increasingly distanced others — others in a world that is paradoxically understood as "full" even as the planet in now taken as completely accessible.

Originally published in somewhat different form in Social Europe.

Education, the Politics of Resilience & the War on Youth

Tyler J. Pollard & Brad Evans (excerpts)

Monday, 30 June 2014

TYLER J. POLLARD: Given the corporatization and privatization of nearly all forms of education over the past several decades, how do you think the university and its faculties of researchers, teachers, and students should be communicating their work — in particular, work that engages the problematic of youth and education? How can academic laborers speak to or counteract the neoliberal forces that are working to render education into little more than worker training and begin to reconceive of education as a public good fundamental to democracy?

BRAD EVANS: I think a good place to begin — when talking about the role of academics and what we can do to respond to the corporatization of education — is with the question of what we actually mean by "education." When we do so, it becomes quite evident that education *subjects* students — that, quite literally, education is a subjective matter. Education is framed through a hierarchy of subjects, creating spheres of knowledge and power, producing political subjectivities, authenticating knowledge, and disqualifying forms of knowledge and power through what is not taught. Once you start with this premise — that the subject matter of education is integral to the production of political subjectivity —you open up an entire field of analysis: education is necessarily a form of political intervention and has always been a form of political intervention. You can then start to meaningfully interrogate the organization, the roles, the meanings, the functions, and the modalities of education right across the board, from primary school right up to the university, and indeed, beyond into other educational spaces.

Knowing that education is always political allows us to make sense of the fact that recent changes — ideas around efficiency, equality of opportunity, and opening up the educational sector to market forces — cannot be divorced from the production of neoliberal subjects. The conflict that is taking place in the university sector and beyond is precisely a conflict over this question of education as a form of political intervention. This makes it incumbent upon academics and teachers to, first of all, be aware of the starting point — that you are always involved in a relationship between power and politics. This, of course, requires a lot of critical self-reflection. How do you function as an academic? What shameful concessions are you forced into on a daily basis if you disagree with the very type of subjectivities that are being produced? How can you operate within that system such that you don't comply with the prevailing logic that the only purpose of education is to manufacture a productive work force, reducing it to methods and labor skills quantified only in terms of the jobs available at the end of the process? I think if you can only see education in such a limited way, you lose sight of the fundamental value of learning itself.

Where we can take this a stage further as academics and intellectuals is to reinscribe more forcefully the value of critical pedagogy. We find less and less importance being put on the value of critical thinking, and to conceive of the political stakes and the power relationships in which we are all increasingly embedded, the first site for intellectual struggle must be to fight once again for reinscribing the value of critical pedagogy, encouraging students to challenge their role in an academic system that is becoming increasingly neoliberalized.

TYLER J. POLLARD: Adequately responding to the war on youth requires an interdisciplinary engagement with the variety of different conditions that impact what it means to be young, to grow up, and to learn to mediate an assortment of challenges, institutions, systems, and technologies. How does your own work and research contribute in a direct or indirect way to these interdisciplinary discussions about youth? In your view, what manner of intellectual work is necessary in order to create a space in which dissimilar disciplines are able to enter into a dialogue with one another?

BRAD EVANS: I intellectually grew out of a discipline that is commonly termed the *continental political and philosophical tradition*. An integral element of the tradition, which is why it received so much hostility, particularly during the 1960s, 1970s, and 1980s, was precisely its insistence on the need for transdisciplinarity. If you wanted to study politics, you could read Thomas Hobbes, but you could equally read Franz Kafka and gain just as much purchase on political concepts, political ideas, and, indeed, ideas around what it means to be a political subject. Growing out of this tradition, it has seemed to me to be self-evident that you need a transdisciplinary pedagogy. And yet, in the academy today, for all the talk of the value of transdisciplinarity, particularly in the field of politics, it is still regimented into disciplinary silos, or what we might call "academic sovereignties." Neoliberal educators talk about the need to break down borders and barriers between disciplinary paradigms, but the pressures placed on academics continue to force hyperspecialization, making true interaction among disciplines seem almost impossible, schizophrenic, or both.

Much of the hostility that critical scholars in the field of politics and international relations have experienced is because they abandoned the sovereign privilege particular to the discipline. Too many academics still assume they have some privileged access to the world because they are rooted in a theoretical paradigm in which theory comes first, even as that theory becomes self-referential and self-validating. If we are going take the question of transdiscipinarity seriously, it has to come together around shared, specific problematics. This, in itself, can then become a form of political intervention. How do we frame the shared question such that different disciplines can bring their own logics to bear on it? The obvious ethical starting point involves abandoning the idea that we have any privileged access to the world and appreciating that every single discipline will come at the problematic differently.

I have tried to do this in my research with the shared problematic of violence. Violence is such a complex phenomenon that there is no one dominant narrative or disciplinary matrix that has all the answers. So, whether we would deal with violence from a political perspective, a psychological perspective, a sociological perspective, a geographical perspective, or any other perspective, violence has to be interrogated across multiple terrains to gain a better understanding of it. If we are going to see a fundamental change in the meaning and function of education in the university as we go through the 21st century, perhaps it will be precisely around the emergence of different schools of thought or ideas which are less disciplinary and more problematically driven. So, violence, the Anthropocene, the war on youth: where this becomes fraught, or where you can at least see the power relations embedded within the university sector and the funding that makes research possible in the first place, will be very much around what kinds of problematics will be allowed to be interrogated. No one is saying that transdisciplinarity in itself is going to lead to the interrogation of the types of questions which are deemed to be socially imperative.

TYLER J. POLLARD: You mean what sorts of questions are allowed to be asked in the neoliberal university?

BRAD EVANS: Absolutely, for sure. The critical academic's function here is precisely to bring into question what is *not* being questioned and to keep pressure against those who are setting the research agenda to allow such questions. And let's not be under any illusions: research agendas are largely set today by those organizations that can allocate resources. So, we have the financialization of a research agenda, which necessarily plays into a particular politics and a political ideology.

Great research never starts from a theory. It always starts from an urgent shared problematic. And every new problematic demands new thinking. This approach does away with the idea of the sovereign expert academic who thinks they have the ultimate truth in the world. It also places academics in a more precarious intellectual position — you have to accept that sometimes your discipline doesn't have the answers, doesn't have the solutions to these problematics. Not that intellectuals are not equipped with the intellectual resources to work things out — we just can't rest on our pre-existing theoretical laurels or retreat into a sovereign conceit.

TYLER J. POLLARD: I wonder, then, if we might turn briefly to the problematic of the future. The assault on young people has been intensified by a failure on the part of multiple parties to imagine the future otherwise, to challenge common sense, and to resist and respond productively to the commodification, privatization, and criminalization of the spaces young people occupy. What would you say is essential that we take away from the concerns raised here at the Summer Institute? And how might these interventions give us a language with which to speak differently about, on the one hand, the future of young people and, on the other hand, the role of education and the university moving into the future? To what extent might we say that education is always about a struggle for the future?

BRAD EVANS: Education has always been about a struggle for the future. The production of particular political subjectivities is always premised on the basis of what subjects are to come. What kind of subjects are we going to invest in to create the future? One of the ironies here is that education policy is always set in the present, and hence, like every regime of political power, it always believes itself to be in the right, and it will invest in the present largely in such a way that political subjectivities will emerge, which will reaffirm what are deemed to be acceptable political standards, political values, and political meanings. But the one thing the future always does is outlive the present very quickly. This, in itself, is one of the tensions that educators, and certainly political leaders, invariably feel, which is perhaps why they often fear youth as much as they see them as a source of political optimism — because the future will always be different than the present.

The question of the future is, I think, profoundly significant in terms of understanding education as a form of political intervention. If we form a prevailing mantra of this idea that education is all about equality of opportunity, we start to see the future as an open terrain, or an open horizon of possibility, where nothing in the future is set, nothing is established. In other words, the future is disembodied: no one occupies it, and as such, there are no power relations at play. When you're young, whether you go to an overtly militarized inner city school or you go to the best private school in the country, it doesn't matter — the future is still open to you. Of course, we know that that's preposterous. The future is already embodied. Education is always a fight for the future.

In fact, such battles are already being waged *in* the future. Gilles Deleuze invokes "the virtual" as a term for the realm of possibilities. Education expands the capacities or the possibilities for certain youths and diminishes the capacities for certain others (as Henry Giroux writes). This expansion and diminishment are not so debilitating or disempowering that people don't break through the system. But the future itself is already inscribed in the imagination of the present, and people do very much act in the present as if the future is at stake, and evaluating the power politics invested in the education system demands we ask: How is the future analyzed today? And how does the way we understand the future today impact upon the present pedagogical imperatives of the education system and, in particular, how we look at the question of youth?

One thing that I've written about in my work is the slow shift towards what I call the catastrophic topography of endangerment, the way the future seems to us a terrain of unending catastrophes. Only a small minority of the Earth's citizens are able to secure themselves from those catastrophes, but the larger tragedy is that catastrophe is now repackaged back to us as a condition of possibility, a learning process; indeed, something we can become more empowered from by accepting the *crisis of crisis*.

TYLER J. POLLARD: Perhaps I'll ask you about this then: You argue that governance, or more specifically, neoliberal self-governance, operates increasingly according to a logic of what you call *the resilient subject* — a logic which naturalizes and renders common sense an ontological state of vulnerability and precariousness. Such a state is ordered around the production of populations with the capacity to withstand ecological, political, social, historical, and psychic crisis. One of the impacts of this governance has been a collapse of imaginative and political forms of *resistance* into a default mode of *resilience*. I wonder if you could talk a little bit about how a critique of resilience works, and in what ways does this resilient mode of subjectivity mark a novel historical development?

BRAD EVANS: It's really quite remarkable in terms of the pace of change with which resilience has become the lingua franca of the age. Resilience now appears in any and every discipline, and it's presented as purely positive, purely benevolent. The first thing to do if you want to analyze the explosion of discourses around resilience is to simply type the term into Amazon and see the plethora of self-help books, from cradle to grave. All put forward the proposition that life is now forever in crisis and you need to accept the inevitability that you're in a full life crisis. Psychological interventions around resilience are all about the ability of the individual to bounce back from some traumatic experience. I know this sounds wonderfully benevolent. Why wouldn't you train someone to recover from trauma or crisis? The other place where resilience has been dominant is in the field of ecology and the idea that ecological systems are actually resilient, so they will themselves recover and bounce back from catastrophes. I'm not in any way in my work, or the work I've been doing with Julian Reid, arguing that resilience does not exist in ecological systems. However, there is something profoundly different in saying that plants are resilient and saying that the fundamental basis for political subjectivity is resilience. Indeed, one of the dangers that we try to interrogate in our work is the reduction of life into basically a system of weeds: the debasement of the political subject.

When you come at the problem of resilience politically, the first question you need to ask yourself is: What's being masked and precluded from the analysis? What are the gendered, racial, and classed aspects being omitted by saying that the basis of subjectivity is the resilient subject? What does this discourse already take for granted?

Resilience assumes the inevitability of the catastrophic — another attack is going to happen, in one way or another. As Nietzsche once said, to live is to forever be in danger. Resilience takes that mantra and runs with it. Thus, it encourages an art of living dangerously. Resilience accepts insecurity by design and thus abandons thinking about security, accepting insecurity as the new normal for human cohabitation. I think in this you find a collapse between different discourses on what it means to be resilient. To be resilient now is not to be resistant. And what that means of course, largely, is that the political has been settled.

Resilience is big business; it doesn't refer to some natural aptitudes that people innately possess; it's not a naturally existing state of resourcefulness. Resilience has to be a learned behavior, and resilience is therefore both an educational commodity and a form of political intervention — people have to be *taught* to be resilient. What this, of course, requires is, first of all, a fundamental assessment of those populations that are currently deemed to be non-resilient such that power can intervene to make them more resilient. These tend to be the most vulnerable populations in society and in order to teach youth the meaning of being a resilient subject, the first thing you need to do is get them to accept and highlight their vulnerabilities. Then, they have the starting point for thinking about how they might, to use the term, "bounce back."

TYLER J. POLLARD: And this, of course, naturalizes vulnerability.

BRAD EVANS: It naturalizes vulnerability, but it also *ontologizes* vulnerability. Vulnerability becomes the starting point for thinking about empowerment and emancipation. We're not saying that vulnerability does not exist. Of course it does. But, what does a pedagogy of vulnerability do as opposed to a pedagogy of oppression? And what does it mean to say that everybody is ontologically vulnerable as opposed to saying vulnerability is produced out of conditions of oppression? Here we get into an entirely different political discussion. What are the pedagogic implications if you start from a pedagogy of vulnerability? Then, educational policy and practice go into accepting that everything changes such that everything can politically remain the same. You bounce back so you don't fundamentally challenge those structures of power that create those conditions of vulnerability in the first place. A pedagogy of oppression is fundamentally different because, instead of focusing on vulnerabilities, you would rather instill confidence in subjects to say "no" to abuses of power. An ontology of vulnerability and an ontology of political confidence take you into two entirely different political avenues for rethinking the meaning of political subjectivities in the 21st century.

TYLER J. POLLARD: I wonder if you could talk a bit about some of the recent work on the left that has attempted to do just that, to ontologize the category of vulnerability and precariousness. How might a more critical approach to resilience add something to those theories?

BRAD EVANS: One thing necessary to understand regarding the way power operates is that it appropriates concepts and refashions them for the conditions of the present. What we are calling "resilience" is in many ways the neoliberalization of what Michel Foucault called "care for the self"; resilience evidences many of the hallmarks of what some people have called Deleuzian ontology (the embrace of emergence, the acceptance of the politics of events, accepting that everything is in crisis); ontologies of vulnerability play into the ways that power wants subjects to operate and to function, as in the work of Judith Butler and Alan Badiou, whose book *In Praise of Love* discusses love as a vulnerable condition; and Žižek reads love as violence, and thus a politics of love requires resilience, it requires you to bounce back at every given opportunity.

The question is: does power fear vulnerable subjects or subjects who have the confidence to say, "No, we're going to transform the world differently"? This is one of the profound political questions of our time and the answer, I think, is that power does *not* fear vulnerable subjects. Actually, power *produces* vulnerable subjects. If we are going to make a fundamental rupture or break with the power of the present, then we need to start to think the political differently and not simply conform to the subjectivities that dominant forms of power and oppression demand from people. Rethinking the political requires a new vocabulary and language that is no longer simply grounded in the emancipatory politics that emerged in the 1990s.

TYLER J. POLLARD: Your work with the *Histories of Violence Project*, which I believe you began as a kind of response to the escalation of violence across the world after 9/11, has gone to great lengths to provide a public forum for outlining the ways in which violence is understood or not understood today. Perhaps you could speak generally about the ways in which forms of structural violence are affecting young people in particularly troubling ways? To what extent is a certain experience of violence or violation constitutive of what it means to be a young person today?

BRAD EVANS: It became vogue very quickly to talk about the violence of 9/11 as an exceptional moment in history — and an exceptional act of violence, of course, requires an exceptional response. Tony Blair, for instance, came out and said, "This is the day the world changes forever." So, there's a futurity instantly embedded in this narrative. Everything has changed, and the future will never be the same as the past. This narrative also played into the critical mediations around so-called ideas of the state of exception. The response was exceptional, transgressing ideas of international law and international norms, and the justification was precisely that we're in a new political terrain. This was reactionary, very short-term, and it failed to look at the broader trajectory of neoliberal empowerment and the way war had been a condition of possibility for liberal power since the collapse of the Cold War. It was as if the state of exception discourse enabled certain liberal and neoliberal scholars to reduce everything to American hegemony and, thus, remove the broader framework from the analysis.

What we have increasingly seen in the decade that followed 9/11 has been the shift from a sense of exceptionality to what I call *terror normality* — terror has become terrifyingly normal and an accepted part of the everyday political vocabulary. We thus require a much more rigorous assessment of the ways in which violence and power operate within the remit of everyday life, within the remit of law, within the remit of civilization. And it requires a much more critical self-reflection about our society and about what kinds of regimes of power we exist and operate in.

This normalization of terror and crisis has impacted youth in profound ways. They live in a world of ubiquitous threat and endangerment, with those closest to potential modes of radicality the most dangerous. Hence, the veritable collapse between fundamentalism and radicalism — to be radical now is to be a fundamentalist, and vice versa. This results in a conscious and direct targeting of youthful populations since their youthfulness lends itself to more radicality and more radicality is more dangerous.

One of the best ways of interrogating and diagnosing the logics of violence at any time is to look at the scapegoats; to look at what populations are being scapegoated for the way the system doesn't function. The crisis we are now in owes itself largely to my generation and the political leaders that came through my generation and before, but overwhelmingly the burden of failure is placed on youth. They are the ones that are not able to get jobs, and so they are the ones who are looking for illicit means for survivability. They are disenfranchised, and so they are potentially dangerous. Young people between 17 and 24 are presented in the media today as rising up and taking to the streets. They are recruited by radical groups to become bombers, fighters. They are, in other words, being scapegoated for the instabilities that the system has already created.

Regimes of power always fear those who see the future differently. Why? Because it's a fundamental challenge to their regime of power. Youth have hope, youth have confidence, and youth have an innate desire to live differently than those generations that have come before. They don't buy into the conceit that this is as good as life is going to get or that you need to accept the inevitability of the catastrophic or that you need to simply play the game. In fact, part of the purpose of education is to domesticate radicality such that youth learn to live to play the game. Indeed, if education ever manages to do that completely, then the battle will be lost.

But the great thing, what history teaches us more than anything, is that no system of power can ever be total, can ever be complete. Indeed, the ability to refuse the operations of power appears in the most unlikely of places. The one thing that regimes of power really do fear today is the large population of unemployed youth with a view of a catastrophic future. That in itself has become the basis for really rethinking what it means to be political, and it's wonderfully imaginative. It doesn't conform to any of the political registers that the political class has been taught to accept as gospel and which are deeply troubling for those in power. They try to dismiss this emerging political imagination as doomed to fail, but it's already been wonderfully successful, already created a new political vocabulary. We have to learn from them, and this is deeply unsettling for those in power.

TYLER J. POLLARD: If young people are figured as a threat to neoliberal security, which I agree they have, how might this help us to better understand the reasons for the rise of a militarized punishing state, which is increasingly a defining feature of life for poor and minority youth? To what extent is liberalism co-extensive with — if not outright constituted by — a logic of discipline, punishment, and abandonment?

BRAD EVANS: To start with, I think there are two questions here. First, you're right, the category of life has become essential to theorizations of power. The explosion of interest in Foucault's work on biopolitics has not been incidental but rather has been a response, in particular throughout the 1990s, to emergent discourses around human security into the 21st century and an attempt to think about what happens when life becomes the object of power and the forefront of thinking about political analysis and political discussion. Previously, life appeared as an emancipatory political category, and this was part of the early impetus around theorizations of human security. We've never been so saturated by mediations on life as we are today. However, life is not a sufficient basis for rethinking the political because power is already caught up in this discourse on life: power talks to life consistently. Nietzsche misunderstood this in *Human All Too Human*. What he was actually gesturing towards was that there's something to the human condition that is more than human, which has to be the starting point for the meaning of the political.

Biopolitics is all about promoting good and bad forms of circulation, which is a much more enriching way of analyzing power in the post-9/11 moment. What global forms of circulation are allowed to flow and function? What are the dangerous threatening forms of global circulation? Circulation is not abstract — the circulation of money, numbers on a computer screen, etc. Circulation is also worth dealing with as an embodied form — that is, what people and ideas are allowed to circulate the planet without any form of sovereign intervention, without any hindrance? The next question, of course, is what is not allowed to flow and function, which constitutes the majority of the world. Migration itself is biopolitical, and the body that's not allowed to cross demonstrates the logic, politics, racism, class, and gendered distinctions around what are deemed bad or unnecessary or unwanted forms of circulation. But what we're increasingly finding is the crisis of liberalism globally and almost the declining zone of influence of liberalism globally. Liberalism and neoliberalism are in crisis; they're quite precarious, actually, and so their regime of managed circulation is in crisis.

Which helps explain the increased incarceration of populations. There is an explosion of enclosure of the global poor in terms of imprisonment and an increased sedentarization: zones from which they cannot leave. Zygmunt Bauman has a compelling mediation when he asks, roughly, "What do we mean when we say this is a 'no go' area?" The obvious response is that this is an area which is dangerous and which you do not enter. Bauman suggests we flip this logic because what this actually means is that the people who live in these areas cannot leave, and this is becoming the case for the vast majority of the world's citizens. Through systems like mass incarceration and curfew, populations are becoming increasingly contained, rendered sedentary, insomuch as to move from where you don't belong is deemed to be dangerous. You can see this in the case of Hurricane Katrina, where the US government declared that they had an internal refugee crisis. Why would you designate or signify these people as refugees if you did not want to establish encampments to keep them where they belong? The one thing the American public didn't want was the victims of Katrina wandering around the so-called "land of the free." So, containment itself is a geospatial orientation, which is very racially and class determined.

TYLER J. POLLARD: Of course, we see this not just in exceptional instances like Katrina, but also ubiquitously in almost every major inner city area — New York, Chicago, Philadelphia, Detroit, and so on. We see this in the collapse of public education and the makeover of schools as prisons and warehousing spaces. The point really is not to allow these kids to create something better for the future; it really is to leave them in what João Biehl has referred to as "zones of abandonment."

BRAD EVANS: Yes. And to go back to an earlier question, when you're dealing with these zones of abandonment, you're also dealing with the pedagogical encouragement of resilience, and resilience is indeed about further entrenchment — the idea is that you stay in your environment and "bounce back" in your environment, learn to deal with your environment, which becomes pernicious in the further sedentarization of life. There's something profoundly unsettling happening here. A large part of the education of the city is directed towards encouraging people to survive in only their current environment, while elite institutions are encouraging the study of the liberal arts and are basically saying "free your mind, open yourselves up to the world of possibility," and so we have educational apartheid. If you work in the education system and you want to understand the relationship between power and politics, you need to ask why the liberal arts are good for the elite institutions of the world, and yet, we don't want to teach them in educational sectors where we would prefer to teach young people to be resilient.

TYLER J. POLLARD: Teach kids to get used to a world with little or no social protection, demoralized teachers with no unions, not enough desks, no art classes, no gymnasiums, no music programs, and of course, no thinking critically about inequality, the environment, politics, and so on.

BRAD EVANS: Yes, and education becomes not only a substitute for vocational training, but also a much cruder disciplinary setting, with kids forced to accept the catastrophe of their condition.

TYLER J. POLLARD: We've talked at length over the past week about neoliberalism, the emergence of corporate forms of sovereignty, and the ways in which power, in particular at a global level, has been disconnected from politics. While politics has been rendered local, power has been elevated largely into global corporate and economic spheres, where it has, in many ways, become indifferent to the specificity and practices of local political realities — for instance, the kinds of struggles facing young people in places like Greece, Spain, across North Africa and the Middle East, as well as in the US and elsewhere. In other words, politics no longer seems to exist in the spaces where we see power most visibly. Could you talk about this tenuous relationship between power and politics — the forces causing it, for instance — and about how this makes it particularly difficult but, of course, more necessary than ever, to find ways of challenging the complex forms of neoliberal violence bearing down on young people today? I wonder, how can local, grassroots forms of political organization ever hope to speak to a powerful elite whose scope seems to have become transnational?

BRAD EVANS: The idea that there has been a separation between power and politics resonates throughout the wonderful corpus of Zygmunt Bauman. Bauman eloquently argues that neoliberal power is global, and yet, the recourse to thinking about the political remains entrenched in the model of the nation state — that is, ways of acting politically or the orthodox assumptions around what politics means remain at the national level. We have yet to conceive of a global political consciousness or imaginary, or indeed a framework through which to really deal with the emerging political problems of our times. Some people might point to global organizations such as the World Health Organization or the United Nations development project, and so on, which resemble an already existing architecture for global governments, and I think that is partly right. However, much of what passes for a global political architecture is basically a hyperextension of the modern nation state — it's built on the shoulders of the modern nation state, which has now been reduced to a militarizing and policing function for the service of global neoliberalism and global capitalism.

So, the first question becomes: If there is this separation of power and politics, can the modern nation state still be a site for political emancipation? The simple answer, if you look at those young people who are reimagining the meaning of the political, is that the nation state doesn't matter. While we can place demands on the nation state, there is a real need to fundamentally reconceive not only what it means to be political but also the forms of organizations that are now required to transform the world for the better.

Young people can point to a real clear structural violence in place to prevent those organizations from producing precisely those political architectures that are required to challenge the way power operates today. This violence can be understood very much in terms of the containment zones, the physically embodied containments of the local struggles, which prevent everyone from connecting globally. The state can accept the protest of youth, provided it's regulated and doesn't upset the political status quo. The moment that protest starts to really play into the politics of the everyday, or if it becomes overtly militarized, you see the reversion to law and order.

Part of this emerging terrain about the political in the 21st century has to do with rejecting the idea that the political is about taking place in an electoral process once every four or five years. "Representative democracy" is not democracy, it's *representative*: in other words, it's an illusion. The political emerging is about new modes of subjectivity that are yet to exist. In this sense, it's a generational thing; it's a youthful project. The political, as the creation of new modes of existence, requires a new language, a new political vocabulary, and new political registers and terms of engagement and organization.

You understand this if you look at the ways youth are protesting and operating today. They are often lambasted for not having a recognizable political vocabulary, but that is precisely the point. They are emerging and constructing a new sense of what the political means, which we're still yet to formulate, we're still yet to make sense of. It's only really with the passage of time that political theorists will be able to make sense of and respond to the empirical reality that youth are constructing. Youth are constructing this new imaginary, and it's up to political theorists to catch up to the new empirical reality of the world. The great joy that I see when you look at these movements, (and it's not *a* movement, it's multiple movements), is how wonderfully affirmative, optimistic, and poetic they are. They don't resort to old dogmatic, positivist political vocabularies. There are those in the academy that will say these ways of thinking are immature, but others will say that this is a wonderful moment; that despite all the crises, these youths are actually willing to do something positive and affirmative and are not buying into the conceit that they have to accept the way things are. Also, if we accept the idea that youth are constructing new imaginaries, new political vocabularies, then they're not simply going to rest on their laurels and accept what was deemed to be emancipatory discourses over the past 20 or 30 years.

My early work grew out of those discourses, and I put a lot of intellectual purchase into those ideas — ideas of certain post-structural and postmodern theorists — and though sometimes those terms have been bastardized, there is still intellectually emancipatory potential that exists in those theorizations. But to assume that those ideas haven't already been reappropriated by power is, I think, what we might call "the ostrich theory of politics" — you stick your head in the sand, and no one can find you out. Foucault's ideas about the "care of the self" have been reappropriated, and military personnel have openly appropriated his language of war by other means. The ideas of Deleuze and Derrida have been appropriated by power. If we are going to take the ethics of these theorists seriously, then there is a need to move beyond them, and there is a need to accept very clearly that what they once called emancipatory is simply the way power operates today.

TYLER J. POLLARD: I wonder, then, what you think about the current nostalgia of many on the left for social democracies of the 20th century?

BRAD EVANS: Nostalgia is always a wonderfully powerful political tool — and a very dangerous road to go down. One of the most pernicious outcomes of the way power operates today is what Giroux characterizes as "the violence of organized forgetting." Everything now has become so instantaneous that we simply respond to the present; we simply learn to survive in the present. Part of this is that everything has now become "post" — post-racial, post-gender, post-class, as if the history of those struggles can simply be forgotten and collapsed into the present. We live in a kind of dystopian time where we're told everything is as good as it's going to get.

If we are going to take the political value of critical pedagogy seriously, then we have to still maintain a commitment to what Michel Foucault called the history of our present. History is only important insofar as it allows us to interrogate the political present, the political conditions that we have arrived in. History, in that sense, becomes important because it allows you to learn lessons from the past. If we learn from the empirical realities, from the history of our past and the conditions and ideas that shaped them, why on earth would we try to go back to, say, state socialism as it previously existed or, indeed, communism as it previously existed? The empirical realities of those projects were socially, intellectually, personally, and politically disastrous for the vast majority of the people who lived under them. This seems to be the dialectic operating — either we try to live with the current condition or we simply revert back to some old past — which in itself is a kind of war on youth because it says that we cannot think the political in a new way.

TYLER J. POLLARD: It's certainly a further denial of the emancipatory potential, which, as you noted earlier, is always embodied in young people.

BRAD EVANS: Absolutely. It denies the imagination of political ideas that are yet-to-come and that are already embodied in youth. As if it's only the present or the past that has the answers to the future. History is profoundly significant for doing some of the critical evaluation of what has always passed as emancipatory politics. A large part of my work is an open critique of the legacy of Immanuel Kant and precisely the false promises that Kantian politics has promoted, the way Kantian thinking lent itself to the moralization of biopolitics, the apparent racism in his thought. However, to my mind, it's not a case of forgetting Kant; quite the contrary, Kant is not read widely enough.

But this, of course, raises another significant problem: Who has the time in the modern condition to read? Even in the academic setting, the luxury of reading is increasingly being denied. If we are going to move forward, one of the weapons at our disposal is *temporality*. We have to reclaim time; we have to reclaim the value of time. Paul Virilio understood this 40 years ago; speed has conquered space, politics has sped up such that we have set about in a delirium. One of the temporalities that we should insist upon as a fundamental category for thinking about the political is time itself and how we can reclaim the meaning of time. We can link this back to (as Simon Critchley pointed out) the claim that Tony Blair makes, in the immediate aftermath of 9/11, that "this is the day the world changes forever;" and yet, 20 days later, we go to war. If truly 9/11 was a moment in history when the world changed forever, shouldn't we spend more time reflecting on the political and philosophical consequences of this? But modern politics doesn't lend itself to that kind of temporality.

TYLER J. POLLARD: The politics of time are also important to Larry Grossberg, who finds "the problematic of temporality" central to our ability to theorize the possibilities for the future. How might intellectuals today take up the question of the past in order to resist the intellectual violence of forgetting? What role must historical memory and public memory play in our engagement with questions about young people and the war on youth?

BRAD EVANS: The first place to start with this question around the future is to look at the historical conjuncture in which we operate, and when I talk about "we," I'm referring to the digitally connected liberal zones of affluence in the world. When we talk about global imaginaries of threat and governmentality, what we're largely referring to is a system of rule that privileges liberal zones of affluence. It's a small percentage of the world's population that is deemed to be under threat and under siege. The way the historical conjuncture that now operates within the liberal metropolitan zones — however equally precarious, with their own pockets of abandonment — is that ideas of space and time have no meaning. What used to hold the modern political project together was a clear sense of spatiality, where the world was literally carved up into boxes, and your sense of political belonging emanated from whichever box you happened to be born into. Any sense of time was also very utopian: everything was chronological, naturally unfolding, and teleological. Hannah Arendt understood all too well that this idea of spatiality has been in crisis ever since World War II. The idea that sovereign integrities now matter has been eviscerated from liberal zones of affluence. We live in an almost post-spatial setting in that all problems in a liberal society are global problems. That isn't to say that internal demarcations don't take place, just that the global imaginary and global powers have all but eviscerated any sense of the outside. Ideas of the inside and the outside no longer resonate.

Ideas of time, too, have been all but abandoned. Our politics and modes of governmentality present a catastrophic imaginary that has been politically disastrous. We cannot think about contemporary problems today without pointing to a future catastrophe. Of course, the connections to neoliberalism become all too evident here — it's a future market. It's all about predicting the future and acting on the future: quite literally, waging the destiny of the species of human life on its future political strategies.

TYLER J. POLLARD: It's a discourse and a politics that's speculating on death?

BRAD EVANS: Speculating on death, yes. Speculating on where the next catastrophe is going to arise, speculating on who has the freedom to leave and who is forced to stay in these catastrophic zones and who will learn to be resilient. We need to start from this fundamental premise of the collapse of the space-time continuum that once held modern politics together. Anyone who has a so-called smartphone knows this all too well. The smartphone is the clearest indication of this time–space collapse: you don't need to know where you are or what time it is because your phone will tell you. You don't need to be smart any longer because your device is smart for you. You don't need to travel anymore because the world comes to you. That's what globalization really means: *the world comes to you*. Instantaneously, you can know about every crisis that is happening in the world today. Quite literally, it's in the palm of your hand. The question, then, is what happens when our sense of space and time loses all meaning? Well, history becomes important only insofar as it reaffirms the crisis of the times and the catastrophe awaiting.

TYLER J. POLLARD: History evaporates into the present. It becomes, in a sense, evolutionary.

BRAD EVANS: Yes, it becomes neo-Darwinian. We have, we're told, always been on the verge of survival, we've always been resilient subjects. This becomes the natural unfolding such that where we are as political subjects today is where we were always meant to be — we just didn't really realize it. The task of criticality becomes how we can excavate an alternative history of our present, how we can attend more clearly to histories of nonviolence, how we can attend more clearly to a history of political subjectivity.

TYLER J. POLLARD: You make a key distinction between what you call *soft* and *hard* forms of militarism, which in many ways, I think, speak to Giroux's distinction between the *soft* and *hard* wars on youth. On the one hand, young people and the spaces they occupy are endlessly commodified and turned over to ethically vacuous forms of marketization, financialization, and so on. On the other hand, those young people who, for whatever reason, can't fit the liberal consumerist script are funneled into one of the multiple containment zones of the punishing state. That said, your notion of *soft* and *hard* militarism I think nicely addresses the ways in which militarization works throughout society on multiple levels — in the form of global, national, and domestic security, but also insofar as military language, logics, and affects have crept ubiquitously into our everyday lives through a forcefully militarized cultural apparatus.

BRAD EVANS: "The War on Youth": how do we look at the discursive provocation of saying there is a war on youth taking place? We've had some discussion around whether the term "war" itself is a metaphor or whether it is a diagnostic tool for really analyzing the conditions of the present. The question that is instantly raised is how the term "war" functions politically. Within military establishments, and certainly within the political environment on popular media, the proliferation of the use of the term "war" has not been anything unique. Throughout the 1990s, every form of social ill seemed to have a war waged on it — the war on poverty, the war on drugs. This goes into the War on Terror, which becomes an openly declared war on all fronts. I was watching Fox News yesterday, and they were talking about a war on Wal-Mart.

This language is emotive and functions in a certain political way. But it also reveals the way people diagnose the operation of power. A regime of power will say a war needs to take place upon this particular social problem, giving the word "war" a sense of moral and ethical imperative: action needs to be taken, and because the stakes are so high, there will be casualties — all wars produce casualties. An earlier, really sophisticated mediation on this appeared in Foucault's *Society Must be Defended*, where he really appreciates the idea that power has always taken life as its object, particularly since the beginning of modernity, and indeed, that war has always taken life to be its object. This resonates with the Nietzschean idea that war is the mode of modern societies such that nihilism is also the motive of modern societies.

If we take power at its word, then youth are quite literally inserted within a war paradigm. In the post-9/11 moment, youth overseas were deemed to be the troubling demographic, easy to radicalize and made into insurgents. Youth at home increasingly became profiled and analyzed for their radicalism. The complex of war, insecurity, and profiling has increasingly become normalized, and academia has become the front line of the war effort against youth with the most militarized and crude policing and monitoring of students — their attendance, performance, behavior, tendencies, and radical thoughts. We have openly talked for the last 10 to 15 years about this as a "war for hearts and minds." In other words, how could you even think to divorce education from a war for hearts and minds? It's an integral element for the war effort for a war that is, by definition, a war without end. There is no end to the catastrophic condition of our times.

TYLER J. POLLARD: This is what you mean when inverting Clausewitz; when you talk about politics today becoming a war by other means?

BRAD EVANS: Absolutely. And politicians have expressed this precise sentiment that we need to see politics as the continuation of war by other means. Why? Because conventional understandings of warfare have been all but eviscerated. There is no clear sense anymore of who are our friends and who are enemies, who is inside and who is outside, and when times of war and times of peace exist. These categories have been all but eviscerated because neoliberalism has collapsed the precise space-time continuum that once held modern politics together.

TYLER J. POLLARD: Which is why I think to deny that there is a war on youth is not just to misunderstand what's happening to young people today, but it's also to misunderstand the changing shape of war in the contemporary moment.

BRAD EVANS: Absolutely. And to misunderstand the ways in which war has become normalized — to deny the very terms that power uses. Power has openly declared a war upon youth, and any peace effort has to begin from the logical position that a war is taking place, a war that takes children as its object. Why does it take children as its object? Because some ideas are liberating some ideas are dangerous — this is a war effort that is taking place at a time when the military paradigm of society cannot be divorced from the civic. One of the inevitable outcomes of this has been the shift towards what we can call "entertaining militarism." Not only we do entertain the military as a central element of global civil society, but the idea that the military should simply exist in the barracks and be brought out during times of exceptional crisis has been gutted altogether. We had the military providing security for the London Olympics, we have the military parading on talent shows as if it's part of everyday entertainment, we have military personal openly recruited into education systems through Troops to Teachers programs, and so on. The lines between the military and the civic have been so eviscerated that it is impossible to distinguish between times of war and times of peace. Peace is now seen to belong to a bygone era, and war has become so normalized that the front lines exist everywhere, nowhere more than in terms of what types of subjectivities we are producing.

TYLER J. POLLARD: It seems that any logic of "towards perpetual peace" has become perverted into "towards perpetual war."

BRAD EVANS: Well, this is one of the real great ironies of the revival of thinking around perpetual peace because what we have quickly discovered is that through inaugurating perpetual peace, we've actually declared global war. Global war becomes the inevitable outcome of a peace that cannot be achieved other than through militarism. The question Foucault asked was what type of political subjects do you produce if violence is necessary for their production? Of course, the type of subjects you produce are subjects that have learned to accept the normalization of violence as integral to their very forms of life.

TYLER J. POLLARD: Subjects, in fact, which don't simply accept violence but which have been schooled into taking immense pleasure in violence.

BRAD EVANS: We have to look at the proliferation of spectacles of violence today to see how violence operates not only through the pleasure principle but also as the only way that you can truly find empowerment today. And yet, we demonize anyone who acts upon these precise messages, which popular culture deems the only way to find empowerment, pleasure, and desire in the present moment.

Originally published in somewhat different form in Review of Education & Critical Pedagogy.

Another War, Another Evil: Haven't We Learned that the Devil Cannot Be Slain?

Brad Evans

Friday, 26 September 2014

ONCE AGAIN, THE DRUMS of war are beating a familiar and inevitable tune.

Today's British Parliamentary recall, as to be expected, was mere formality. There is no real debate when there are evil beasts to be slain. What is at stake in the motion to take military action in Iraq represents more than some humanitarian commitment to save strangers from the terrifying rampage of ISIS. Unless we act now, we are told, what we see happening on the desert plains will soon become a feature of life on our streets. We must engage because it is our security that is on the line. Or at least, that is the official narrative.

All this sounds eerily familiar. In fact, it follows a very well-rehearsed strategy where, slowly but surely, the public is sold the idea of the need for violence to cure the world's ills. It begins with stories and images of people suffering. This leads to rightful condemnation of the violence and the disregard for human life.

Gradually, what takes place overseas is situated within a broader political frame as local violence is increasingly presented as a threat to global security, peace, and prosperity. The public can then relate to the plight, for now it is their lives and existence on the line. War thus becomes inevitable, though we'd prefer to call it by some other name, as declarations of war are fraught with all kinds of messy legalities.

Any moral concerns here can be easily overcome if the fight is presented in absolute terms. The war is necessary because it is against the forces of evil in the world. David Cameron reaffirmed this position in his respects to the horrifying beheading of British Aid worker, David Haines, calling the filmed atrocity a "pure act of evil."

Such reliance upon this all-too-theological expression has, in fact, become a hallmark of politics in the post-9/11 period. George W. Bush famously declared that he "wanted to rid the world of evil," whereas Barack Obama's Nobel Peace Prize acceptance speech read more as a treatise for war in the 21st century, noting the need for violence: "Make no mistake, evil does exist in this world."

None of this is incidental. The language of evil serves a very clear political function. As the wars on terror have demonstrated, narratives of evil effectively remove historical context, deny truly democratic debate about violence to be carried out in our names, and preclude serious discussion concerning revulsion for certain forms of violence and yet tolerance for more high-tech forms of slaughter.

Dealing with the violence of ISIS requires political contextualization and serious engagement beyond the imminent frame in which their spectacles of violence appear. However abhorrent we might find their actions, it is patently absurd for any leader not to recognize the historical context to this problem. That is not in any way to justify the violence or to seek to rationalize its occurrence. But if you continually bomb a people, invade a land, appropriate its resources, torture its children, imprison and humiliate its fathers, and tear apart the fabric of the social order, there is direct responsibility for the radicalization to follow.

Since the democratic vote continues to be denied — for it seems decisions of warfare are too important to be left to public deliberation — more searching questions need to be asked about the continuous use of violence in the name of creating better futures. Those politicians in favor of the actions will be quick to point out here that it is all about the protection of innocents. How can we stand by and watch the massacre of women and children? And yet, as a recent letter to *The Guardian* reminds:

> All the experience of the varied military action taken by the west in Afghanistan, Iraq and Libya shows that such interventions kill innocents, destroy infrastructure and fragment societies, and in the process, spread bitterness and violence. While we all reject the politics and methods of Isis, we have to recognize that it is in part a product of the last disastrous intervention, which helped foster sectarianism and regional division.

It is not in any way being suggested here that we should stand back and watch the vulnerable suffering a horrifying fate. It is, however, to recognize complicity, responsibility, and what Noam Chomsky calls the manufacturing of consent, which enables the perpetuation of violence by those on both sides who would have us believe that the world is neatly separated between the forces of good and evil. The slaughter of innocents is intolerable. That much we can agree upon. We must, however, be alert to the conscious politicization of suffering where the intolerable plight of the vulnerable produces a greater tolerance for violent retribution.

From the perspective of victims — whether they are willfully targeted or "collateral damages," to use that most dehumanizing of terms — there is no such thing as a "just war." In all wars, the logic of violence and militarism reigns supreme, and every war produces its casualties. The many casualties of the wars on terror are, from a humane, political, economic, or intellectual perspective, self-evidently shameful, and yet the violent forces of militarization carry on regardless. The idea that we might be able to transform the world for the better has been undone by the interventions of the last decade or so, but modalities of violence have adapted by developing ways for war to take place *at a distance*.

One is never entirely sure what monsters will be created through violence. ISIS proves to be a terrifying example of this. What is more, if history shows us anything, it is that you cannot bomb ideas (however abhorrent we might find them) out of existence. Violent ideas, in fact, thrive in violent conditions. Their outrage is fueled by a perceived sense of injustice and victimization compounded by each new death.

Countering this requires breaking the cycle of violence, not the endless resort to violence.

"The greatest trick the Devil ever pulled" wasn't "convincing the world he didn't exist," as *The Usual Suspects* paraphrased Baudelaire. The Devil's greatest trick was to convince us all that he might be slain. For as we seek to purge the evil of violence from the world, what takes its place is the necessity of good violence, by good warriors, with good planes, who drop good bombs, upon evil targets to make the world a more humane place. Humanity as such continues to be defined by the wars carried out in its name. It is only by challenging the inevitability of violence that we might even begin to take seriously the task of creating peaceful relations among the peoples of the world.

Originally published in somewhat different form in TruthOut.

Facing the Intolerable

Brad Evans

Tuesday, 11 November 2014

JACQUES RANCIÈRE'S *Figures of History* is the latest instalment from a serious thinker whose pioneering work engages with the politics of aesthetics in an attempt to reimagine the political as an art form. In *Figures of History*, Rancière offers an accessible introduction to the links between aesthetics and various regimes of power and the ways aesthetics is integral to thinking about who we are as people. He also provides a nuanced framing of the modern history of art, wrestling out the silenced and invisible from figurative enslavement. As Rancière writes,

> If there is a visible hidden beneath the invisible, it's not the electric arc that will reveal it, save it from non-being, but the mise en scène of words, the moment of dialogue between the voice that makes those words ring out and the silence of images that show the absence of what the words say.

Rancière's Anglo-American appeal is evidently on the rise: translations of his works are proliferating and his audience is growing in a broad set of academic disciplines. This has placed him in direct confrontation with two notable contemporaries: Giorgio Agamben and Alain Badiou. Rancière and Badiou both studied under the tutelage of Louis Althusser, and they both have affinities and animosities with Gilles Deleuze, although different ones. Badiou, for instance, largely rejects Deleuze's intellectual corpus, especially concerning the idea of "the event," which Badiou universalizes through his notion of fidelity to truth, including the truth of art, whereas Rancière does not. Deleuze, in fact, remains instrumental for Rancière in terms of his ongoing thinking of the political function of art through what he terms the "distribution of the sensible": aesthetics, for Rancière, is integral to the delimitation of spaces and times, including what is perceived as proper to thought.

Rancière's *Figures* embodies the tragedies of modernity. Our first glimpse of this appears on the cover, which features Larry Rivers's *Erasing the Past II*. Rivers's subtle erasure of the image of a Holocaust survivor (invoking all-too-evident connections with the cover art of the Abacus edition of Primo Levi's *If This Is a Man/The Truce*) captures the author's contention that we must approach all representations of historical events with scepticism — questioning what is memorialized, what is erased, what is being shown, what is being slowly forgotten. History, he claims, should be rethought by attending to the hidden traces. Rancière writes, "history isn't done yet with turning itself into stories," drawing upon a range of compelling examples from Francisco Goya, Otto Dix, Claude Lanzmann, and Zoran Mušič in order to draw particular attention to the victims of historical forces. This allows him to explain how "figures" represent the overt politicization of the truth of history while providing figurative displacements that allow for novel interpretations and the recovery of more complex narratives concerning histories of violence.

Every war produces its casualties. While these are often measured along some crude atrocity scale, as societies try to make statistical sense of the quantifiable levels of destruction (i.e., numbers of individual fatalities, economic costs of damage to infrastructure), it is the less immediate victims and the more intangible losses that often prove to have more devastating and lasting effects. This is particularly the case when dealing with the intellectual casualties of war. Time and again, the reductionist search for causes and lasting solutions tends to remove from the critical microscope more searching questions about the willingness to justify widespread slaughter and engage in acts of the most abhorrent dehumanization, regardless of political or ideological emblem. Hence, genuine debate about the raw realities of rendering entire populations disposable is silenced, and we see the marginalization and demonization of those political categories that might allow us to break the cycle of violence and the normalization of brutality.

Following the horrors of World War II, it was possible to identify three notable intellectual casualties. These included: (1) the politics of desire, or what is now commonly called "affect," in which this once liberating concept, as theorized by Spinoza and others, was cast aside as dangerous due, in part, to Nazism's manipulation and oppression of the masses (as identified, for instance, by Wilhelm Reich in his landmark text *The Mass Psychology of Fascism*), only to be colonized by marketers and PR consultants armed with usual sound-bite euphoria (from stage-managed theatricality of National Party Conventions that display the outpouring of emotionally charged patriotism onto the celebration of killings, as in the case of Osama bin Laden, where vitriolic displays on the streets of Manhattan had certain orchestration by elements of the mass media); (2) the politics of atmosphere, in which the ability to think about the positive manipulation of active living space became, until the advent of environmentalism, the sole privilege of military strategists who long since appreciated the value of "climatic conditioning"; and (3) the politics of aesthetics, in which the systematically orchestrated separation between art and politics rendered the aesthetic field dangerous in terms of symbolic decadence. This was especially true in the context of visible regalia of power directly linking fascist dressage with fetishistic and sadistic forms of behavior (portrayed in the most disturbing ways with Pier Paolo Pasolini's *Salò*) along with racial and gendered stereotyping; aesthetics was assumed to have nothing to say about the "serious business of politics" in the reasoned halls of established power — with our societies becoming more and more "image conscious" at the same time.

This dismissal of the politics of aesthetics interests Rancière, demanding an entirely new concept of the political. Much of what is presented in *Figures* will be already familiar to followers of the author's work. The book's central claim — that every image contains, within its framing, subaltern resonances and political traces that are capable of being deconstructed and open to further interpretation — is textbook Rancière. So, too, is the methodological style adopted as the author continues to show his keen ability to identify and dissect the political meaning of art in order to de-figure representational schematics. On this occasion, Rancière takes his readers on a compelling and disturbing journey via the "four senses of history," the "three poetics of modernity," and the "three forms of history painting" to provide tangible frameworks for critique.

What is significant about *Figures*, however, is the explicit linking of aesthetics to violence. As Rancière explains, in what is arguably the most compelling chapter of the book, "In the Face of Disappearance":

> The German word for the extreme form of that will, as we know, is *Vernichtung*, which means reduction to nothing, annihilation, but also annihilation of that annihilation, the disappearance of its traces, the disappearance of its very name. What is specific to the Nazi extermination of the Jews of Europe was the rigorous planning of both the extermination and its invisibility. It is the challenge of this nothingness that history and art need to take up together: revealing the process by which disappearance is produced, right down to its own disappearance.

Rancière ties this challenge for art to the extermination of the Jews and connects the vexed question of representation to extreme violence (a connection he has addressed elsewhere, most notably in *The Future of the Image*). As he notes in *Figures*, it is

> sometimes too easily drawn that the extermination is "unrepresentable" or "unshowable" — notions in which various heterogeneous arguments conveniently merge: the joint incapacity of real documents and fictional imitations to reflect the horror experienced; the ethical indecency of representing that horror; the modern dignity of art which is beyond representation and the indignity of art as an endeavor after Auschwitz.

Countering this problem of representing humanity's negation, Rancière resurrects what is, for many cultural theorists, an all-too-familiar (if unresolved) debate:

> So, we have to revise Adorno's famous phrase, according to which art is impossible after Auschwitz. The reverse is true: after Auschwitz, to show Auschwitz, art is the only thing possible, because art always entails the presence of an absence; because it is the very job of art to reveal something that is invisible, through the controlled power of words and images, connected or unconnected; because art alone thereby makes the human perceptible, felt.

Rancière's revision of the Adorno question should be taken seriously. Its purpose is to rethink the political function of art, and, in doing so, start the process that will allow us to reimagine a more artistic conception of the political — one that is not simply tied to perceptions of endangerment and the pure task of human survival.

In the powerful chapter on the "Intolerable Image" from an earlier volume on *The Emancipated Spectator*, Rancière turns specifically to the work of Alfredo Jaar, whose unique interplay between words, sounds, and aesthetics overturns "the dominant logic that makes the visual the lot of multitudes and the verbal the privilege of the few." He focuses in particular on Jaar's installation *The Eyes of Gutete Emerita*, which demands that the spectator first read about Emerita's experience of the Rwandan genocide before being confronted with the woman's concentrated and framed stare. Rancière acknowledges how the inversion of the gaze, the forced witnessing of the eyes upon the most horrendous acts, demands an appreciation of the way in which the intolerable can be turned into a recognition of humanity. As Rancière writes, instead of showing the mutilated bodies, Jaar's work "restores the powers of attention itself." The art historian and renowned cultural theorist Griselda Pollock notes the same, adding that Jaar's installation asks the question: "Will you too remember her eyes — eyes that look at you forever but forever see murder?" Jolting us "from the kind of consumption of the image that makes images out of atrocity without inducing a political response," Emerita's eyes register the experience that others had been obliged to witness. It is this element that marks the singularity of Jaar's work in creating encounters for the viewers far away from the event that force them to recognize the gap cut into a living person's life by proximity to atrocity, by the wound that is trauma: an event too shocking to be assimilated.

Violence should be intolerable. That is the point. And so, while the task of political discourse is to speak to the intolerable such that it becomes possible to confront injustice and subjugation in the world, the political function of art, as Rancière writes in *Figures*, consists in being faithful to the general task that art — figurative or otherwise — prescribed for itself once it stopped being subject to the norms of representation: showing what can't be seen, what lies beneath the visible, and invisible that is simply what ensures the visible exists. This entails "reserving for the rigor of art the power of representation," which for

Rancière demands more critical awareness of how we might reinscribe "the annihilation in our present."

Facing the intolerable provides a view into what we might term truly
"exceptional art," wherein violence is dutifully considered against the
terrifying normalization of mass productions. It also brings to the fore
the micro-subjective stakes: we relate the tragic reality of violence to
our own lived experiences. This requires us to identify forms of poetic intervention that speak directly to the problem of human disposability in a way that disrupts aesthetic regimes of mediated suffering.
Through that disruption, we can make visible what remains hidden in
plain sight, thereby opening up the space for reflection and rearticu-
lating the fundamental categories of the political. Judith Butler's important work on the "framing" of warfare and violence, and how this
allows for the mediation of suffering and mourning, is one example.

The Los Angeles–based artist Gottfried Helnwein can provide another
pertinent example here. As Kenneth Baker has noted, the artist's work
not only "mirrors of dark times but as counterthrusts to the aggressive reach of so much contemporary culture." The artist himself is fully
aware of the political function of art and its importance in the age of
the spectacle. "We are living," he writes,

> in the age where materialism has finally triumphed. The
> world has been purged of fairies, elves, witches, angels,
> enchanted castles and hidden treasures. Dreaming and
> fantasizing is nowadays considered a chemical imbalance
> in the brain of the child. For reasons of national security
> there are no realms of imagination anymore in which to es-
> cape — children are held in the merciless headlight of the
> adults level-headed, common-sense-madhouse: a world of
> stock-markets, war, rape, pollution, television-moronism,
> prozak [sic], prison-camps, miss universe-competitions, ge-
> netic engineering, child pornography, Ronald McDonalds,
> Paris Hilton and torture.

Importantly, for Helnwein, art responds to the violence of the world
by raising the right type of questions and not colonizing the imaginary
with fixed interpretations. As he told Yuichi Konno in 2003, "My art is
not an answer, it is a question." Helnwein's *Disasters of War 13* is a compelling example of this. This unsettling and provocative image depicts

a blood-soaked, innocent, young white girl. Given the artist's definition of the function of the work, we might ask what questions this image raises. Consciously disrupting familiar representations of casualties of war, the questions we might hear arising from the work include: What if it was your child? What if this was your daughter? What if this was your neighbor? What if this was you? This is not about shocking the spectator into submission. Nor is it simply the mirroring of experience to bring about empathy or produce a shallow and sensationalist response. It is to bring about a forced assimilation with the unassimilated — to face the intolerable — so that it viscerally registers as such. As Helnwein further explains:

> When I look at a work of Art I ask myself: does it inspire me, does it touch and move me, do I learn something from it, does it startle or amaze me — do I get excited, upset? And this is the test any artwork has to pass: can it create an emotional impact on a human being even when he has no education or any theoretical information about art? […] Real art is self-evident. Real art is intense, enchanting, exciting and unsettling; it has a quality and magic that you cannot explain. Art is not logic, and if you want to experience it, your mind and rational thinking will be of little help. Art is something spiritual that you can only experience with your senses, your heart, your soul.

Helnwein shows how facing the intolerable is not simply about revealing the raw reality of injustice in the present. It's about transgressing the limits of mediated suffering. Or as Rancière might explain, it reveals precisely "the critical project of art" as it "eliminates its own lie in order to speak truthfully about the lie and the violence of the society that produces it." By confronting the spectacle of violence with a more imaginative response, aesthetics now offers a damning indictment of the contemporary moment and, in doing so, reveals the hidden order of (in)tolerance that is less about the violence itself than about what the very act of its revealing means for established relations of power and privilege.

How might the politics of aesthetics allow us to challenge the spectacles of violence to which we are witness? Rancière would suggest that as we seek to liberate the past, we need a more critical sense of our historical present. Nevertheless, it remains a shame that he doesn't connect his historical figures to more contemporary modalities of violence, such as the kind Hollywood, network television, and video games render on a daily basis. Questions might also be raised about whether Rancière allows for a broader and more transformative discussion on the art of the political. His aesthetics certainly leaves itself open to claims that it is too narrow in conception or still premised upon some identifiable separation between the distinct spheres of aesthetics and politics instead of seeing aesthetics as integral to a concept of the political, which from the outset should be recognized as a creative and imaginative process — an art for living tasked with the creation of better futures and peoples to come.

What would happen if we started our understanding of art in terms of its potentiality to prefigure aesthetics and its modes of distribution, if we restore to art the power of imagination and creativity that doesn't simply find its meaning in relation to what is apprehended? As our world seems to continually move from one catastrophe to the next without a credible governing leadership, authors like Rancière, despite whatever reservations we may have about them, force us to conceive of politics differently. What might the future study of politics look like if classes on "American Presidents" or "Theories of Government" and "Liberal Democracy" were replaced by courses on "The Art of Politics," "The Power of Imagination," and "Poetics of Resistance"? Perhaps, then, we might be able to take seriously Michel Foucault's majestic demand:

> From the idea that the self is not given to us, I think that there is only one practical consequence: we have to create ourselves as a work of art [...]. We should not have to refer the creative activity of somebody to the kind of relation he has to himself, but should relate the kind of relation one has to oneself to a creative activity.

Originally published in somewhat different form in the Los Angeles Review of Books.

The Eyes of the World

Brad Evans

Friday, 16 January 2015

INITIAL PUBLIC REACTIONS to violent and traumatic events are understandably driven by a range of emotions, from grief to outrage. Ideally, of course, we would have time to sit back and reflect upon the philosophical significance and political stakes to such moments before committing ourselves to matters of interpretation — long before the question of "what is now to be done?" is raised.

In the age of 24-hour broadcast news, this luxury of reflectively contemplating is denied us. Not only does the imminent nature of global digital and media broadcasting demand immediate interpretations and responses, the organization and function of politics today is a massive exercise in the governance of emotions — from "feel good" indexes to the construction and manipulation of shared anxieties and fears to further certain political rationalities.

The response to the Charlie Hebdo massacre proves to be no different in this regard. Let's be clear from the outset: the violence witnessed on the streets of Paris was abhorrent. Like all forms of violence that are primarily driven by uncompromising political attitudes, it should be rightly condemned and seen for what it is — a vicious act that claimed the lives of people who were armed only with their pencils.

Let's also be clear, however, that this is not about freedom of expression. It is about the freedom of particular forms of expression. While the "I am Charlie" campaign, for instance, was presented as a shared universal commitment to, well, condemnation, it is far from the case that its calling is for a level discursive playing field in matters of public critique and ridicule, let alone the outright condemnation of violence in all its forms.

It has become common currency to suggest that this violence was an attack upon our most cherished of values — the freedom of the right to say what we like.

But really?

Power is manifest in modern societies precisely through the conscious politicization of language and discourse, rendering some thoughts and words worthy of public attention while castigating others as irrational, immature, dangerous, treasonous, and in some cases, worthy of incarceration based on its provocative content. Santiago Slobadsky offers a provocative rebuttal to what he describes as "civilizational blackmail" of the manufactured campaign:

> In the midst of the Arab uprisings, the now famous magazine Charlie Hebdo published one of their traditional satirical covers. They titled the issue "Killings in Egypt" and drew the figure of a Muslim religious activist who was riddled with bullets. The subtitle was more than eloquent: "The Koran is a piece of shit," the agonizing Muslim was made to say, because "it does not stop bullets."

Charlie, as the collective became known around the world in the aftermath of the (unequivocally condemnable) shooting, had no problem laughing about the bloodshed in Egypt. Yet, one could only wonder what would happen if critical voices were to reproduce the same cover that Charlie offered a few years ago with the portrait of the murdered director of the newspaper. [Editor's note: at least two versions of this parody have now been made and can be found on Twitter.] It could be titled "Killings in France. The Pencil is a piece of shit. It doesn't stop the bullets" and tweeted/facebooked under the hashtag #Iamtheth-irdkouachi. Indignation — rightful indignation — would inundate the Western press and public sphere. The fact is that Charlie's right to create a satire is protected under freedom of speech. But its alternative would be considered in bad taste and an insult to the solemnity of the tragedy. This double standard makes us question what is veiled when the discussion is framed in terms of liberal rights.

We would also do well to remind ourselves here that it is precisely the power of words — most notably apparent in oxymoronic novelties such as "humanitarian war" and its concordant "collateral damages" — deploys the language of freedom and rights to author the most brutal forms of violence, enslavement, torture, and humiliation upon Muslim and other populations. Natasha Lennard has captured the hidden order of politics at work here brilliantly:

Any keen surveyor of hypocrisy will note that the 3.7 million-strong Parisian rally in support of the massacre's victims did not exactly attract the world's greatest defenders of free speech. Israeli Prime Minister Benjamin Netanyahu — forecloser of Palestinian freedom and speech — walked alongside Saudi Arabian Ambassador to France Mohammed Ismail Al-Sheikh, whose country regularly flogs and jails journalists. Russian Foreign Minister Sergey Lavrov, a popular target of harsh Charlie Hebdo satire, marched too in what journalist Jeremy Scahill rightly called a "circus of hypocrisy." Thirty-three journalists have been murdered in Russia, allegedly for their work, since 2000. The list of hypocrites who came out for Charlie is long.
Violence needs to be understood as something much more than a singular act or atrocity. Political violence always has a history.

As John Pilger recently reminds us, just as we cannot understand the emergence of genocidal organizations such as the Khmer Rouge without accounting for the willful devastation and destruction wrought on Cambodia during the US bombing campaign of 1969–73, when the equivalent of five Hiroshima bombs were dropped from the sky, we cannot understand fundamentalism and the dystopian violence of groups such as ISIS without the violent and brutal interventions in Afghanistan and Iraq. Again, this is not to in anyway justify the violence. It is, however, to raise more difficult and searching questions regarding culpability and what drives politically motivated outrage.

As Tithi Bhattacharya and Bill Mullen observe in a historically sensitive reading (noting, in particular, the Algerian context to the violence):

It is as if we are watching a rerun of the Battle of Algiers, with one thing missing. In this alternate universe rerun of the film, we have in place the looming arc of French/ Western imperialism; the poverty and racism contaminating working-class lives in the colonies and elsewhere; a state ready to pounce upon the figure of the migrant and the marginal and incarcerate him/her. We have all that in place. Except we don't have a mass political movement led by the FNL [National Liberation Front], which rocked imperialism. Unfortunately, this rerun is not in an alternate universe. For the conditions that produced the first are woefully similar to those that produced the second. Indeed, more than 40 years after the end of 'formal' French colonial rule in Algiers—from which the Kouachi brothers and their families migrated — fully 60 percent of the prisoners in French jails are Muslim.

What particularly marks out violence in the contemporary age is the precise way it is organized and packaged for public consumption. Violence is now a global media event. Consciously so! That is to say, not only have digital and news media changes transformed the relationships between the specificity of an event and its public display by making local events accessible to a global audience, they also usher in an era of increasing awareness — the age of the spectacle — in which screen culture and visual politics create spectacular events just as much as they record them. The symbolic nature of violence as such tells us a great deal about the ways people understand questions of oppression, injustice, and persecution in the contemporary moment. As Zygmunt Bauman has acutely observed:

> On September 11, 2001, political assassinations were directed not against specific, identifiable, and named political "personalities" in the political limelight, or for that matter, against people held personally responsible for the wrongdoings the assassins pretended to punish, but against institutions symbolizing the economic (in the case of the World Trade Center) and military (in the case of the Pentagon) power. Notably, a center of spiritual power was still missing in the combined political operation... [O]n 7th January, 2015, political assassins fixed a highly media-visible specimen of mass media. Knowingly or not, by design or by default, the murderers endorsed — whether explicitly or obliquely — the widespread and fast gathering public sense of effective power moving away from political rulers and towards the centers viewed as responsible for public mind-setting and opinion-making.

Our societies are undoubtedly "image conscious." This doesn't simply refer to the fetishization of aesthetics or the way personal success is so often matched by a carefully fitted image profile. Consciousness is now shaped and defined by the complex interplay of signs, images, and narratives that, due to the contemporary onslaught of continually changing storylines endangering us from every possible angle, only add to our sense of anxiety about a world that increasingly appears insecure by design.

Not only does this raise important questions regarding the political power wielded by those in charge of the corporate media landscape, it demands a fundamental reassessment of the political function of art and aesthetics — especially in terms of their ethical privileges and responsibilities.

Writing in his usual sardonic style on the massacre, the author Will Self rightly observed:

> The memorial issue of Charlie Hebdo will have a print run of 1,000,000 copies, financed by the French government; so, now the satirists have been co-opted by the state, precisely the institution you might've thought they should never cease from attacking. But the question needs to be asked: Were the cartoonists at Charlie Hebdo really satirists, if by satire is meant the deployment of humor, ridicule, sarcasm, and irony in order to achieve moral reform? Well, when the issue came up of the Danish cartoons, I observed that the test I apply to something to see whether it truly is satire derives from H.L. Mencken's definition of good journalism: It should "afflict the comfortable and comfort the afflicted." The trouble with a lot of so-called "satire" directed against religiously motivated extremists is that it's not clear who it's afflicting or who it's comforting.

Self is evidently concerned here with the ethical responsibilities of artistic critique by those in positions of privilege. Can, indeed, we call it "satire" if the ridicule is focused on those who see themselves as the persecuted victims of recent history? Surely, when ridicule takes aim at the downtrodden and the already demonized, it becomes something altogether different: no longer an art form committed to the critical function of art; no longer attending to the contours of power and violence. The cartoonist Joe Sacco has illustrated his concerns with these issues and how they connect to the ethical subject of violence in this context.

There is another dimension that needs to be addressed here that relates to all of us who are now "global witnesses" to events beyond our control. For those of us who live in sites of relative digitalized privilege, we are all bearing witness in one way or another.

Technology, in fact, has redefined the very nature of globalization, as smartphones quite literally put the world into our hands. Such witnessing is not, however, a neutral and objective process. What we "witness" is highly policed through aesthetic regimes of mediated suffering, which encode that some lives are more important than others and reduce complex historical questions to crass reductionist interpretations. How else can we account for the continued attention given to Samuel Huntington's dreadful *Clash of Civilizations*, which remains one of the most racist and oversimplified texts written in living memory?

Part of our task today is to remain alert to the overt politicization of tragic events when they are repackaged back to us, making what initially appeared intolerable the moral vehicle upon which further violence is sanctioned and authorized. We should hold onto the sentiment that what happened on the streets of Paris, how their families felt, was intolerable — just as we should recognize that an innocent taxi driver brutally violated in Abu Ghraib or a child facing the bitter winter in a Syrian refugee camp is also intolerable.

Integral to these concerns is the need to expose the sheer poverty of contemporary political imagination when dealing with the problem of violence. Nowhere was this more shamefully apparent than the political hijacking of the Unity march in Paris by a political class whose participation was nothing more than a stage-managed photo opportunity.

How far removed are these self-serving mediocrats from the likes of Martin Luther King Jr., who understood that to stand up for your beliefs required showing true solidarity with those on whose behalf you speak, not parading within the comforts and securities of a militarized enclave? We can still hear them echo now: *Where is the unity, we must lead it, all our futures depend upon it!*

The politicization of the solidarity march risks turning any appreci-ation of the intolerable situation into something that works against its nonviolent impetus. Indeed, the political appropriation of "I am Charlie" outrage has disturbing parallels to the way the widespread protests over the deaths of Eric Garner and Michael Brown in New York in December 2014 were quickly countered by the narrative of the po-lice as the victims, fueled by the shootings of officers Wenjian Liu and Rafael Ramos.

On both occasions, there is a conscious public relations effort to pres-ent definitive "truths about the event" so that any demands for sys-tematic and historically sensitive analysis become displaced by the motives of individuals, which absolves the system of any guilt and confirms the idea that our societies are under siege from people of ei-ther a distinct cultural background or racial profile.

And yet, we must not lose sight of the fact that those who continue to take to the streets and call for nonviolence, the respect for human dignity, and togetherness should be applauded. It is too easy in this contemporary moment to buy into the dystopian realism peddled by liberal governments and their narrative about the violence of fanatics across the world.

People continue to show they will resist and stand up against what they find to be patently intolerable. They also refuse to be cast as some docile mass for whom the burdens of history and the complexities of the contemporary condition (as notably presented on corporate news platforms peddling their parade of daily endangerments) render them incapable of action.

Likewise, the art of JR (based on Eric Garner's eyes in New York City and Stéphane Charbonnier's eyes in Paris), inspired by the earlier work of Alfredo Jarr, offers a counter-spectacle that affirms the ambitions to look beyond any sense of passive spectatorship, reminding those who would abuse and render human life disposable that the eyes of the world are watching. And so, we must continue to bear witness to violence while condemning the shameful politicization of tragedy in all its forms.

Originally published in somewhat different form in TruthOut.

Challenging a "Disposable Future,"
Looking to a Politics of Possibility

Brad Evans, Henry A. Giroux &
Victoria Harper

Sunday, 10 May 2015

VICTORIA HARPER: Let's begin the discussion of your book, *Disposable Futures: The Seduction of Violence in the Age of Spectacle*, by asking, what do you mean by "disposable futures"?

BRAD EVANS & HENRY A. GIROUX: Our starting point for this book was to try and provide an incisive and timely critique of the state of global politics, especially the unequal distribution of power, wealth, and opportunity most apparent in the world today. It is within this historical conjuncture and the current savagery of various regimes of neoliberal capitalism that we conceived the need to develop a paradigm that focused on the intensification of the politics of disposability.

For us, this required taking our analysis beyond 20th century frames of analysis to look at the ways in which more and more individuals and groups are now considered excess, at least by the onslaught of global forces that no longer offer the possibility of alternative futures. In the book, we advance an older Gramscian notion regarding the concept of historical conjuncture. We argue that the morbid anxieties of the age do not simply represent a fusion of mass violence, politics, and power, but signify a new historical conjunction in which violence has become a defining political moment and framing device, and which points to a historical shift, a new historical configuration.

As the subtitle suggests, this politics of disposability demanded new conceptual vocabulary and demanded a fundamental rethinking of the problem of violence. Mass violence, we maintain, was poorly understood as it continued to be referred to as casualties on battlefields or framed through conventional notions of warfare. We understood the alternative need to interrogate the multiple ways in which entire populations are rendered disposable on a daily basis. This seemed crucial if we were to take seriously the possibility of justice and the meaning of global rights and citizenship in the 21st century.

Violence operates not on the periphery of society, but at its center as an organizing idea that legitimates a culture of perpetual anxiety and surveillance while serving as a primary form of mediation in addressing major social problems. Violence is the principal recourse and default for those societies in which the social state is under attack, even as the traditional state becomes the corporate state. Under such circumstances, an ever-wider range of behaviors are criminalized, everyday relations are militarized, knowledge is weaponized, and daily life now resembles what is akin to war by every means.

We are arguing in the book that thinking through the politics of disposability not only makes visible the expanding populations now relegated to the status of the precariat and subjected to new forms of violence; such a politics also highlights a form of global capitalism in which the financial elite live in an immune culture of self-regulation and personal enrichment, whether they are the corrupt hedge fund managers and bankers who caused the recent economic crisis, CIA operatives who tortured people and were not prosecuted, or the police in the US who have no qualms about assaulting and killing black men and, for the most part, are acquitted of their crimes.

Such an enquiry is no doubt timely. For the past year or so, we have begun memorializing what was often termed the "century of violence," which included the 20th anniversary of the Rwandan genocide, the centenary of World War I, the 70th anniversaries of the bombings of Hiroshima and Nagasaki, and the 40th anniversary of the "killing fields" in Cambodia, each of which should force us to confront the suffering of the past. The suffering, however, continues in novel and no less devastating ways. Indeed, while there is no doubt a need to collectively memorialize traumatic and horrifying world events, it is irresponsible to use this as an opportunity to claim that we now live in more secure and peaceful times.

Even in terms of conventional warfare, we still seemed incapable of connecting individual deaths with broader questions of mass violence and policies of systematic abuse. In the five years of the Obama drone policy, for instance, we are nearing comparable figures to the horrors of September 11, 2001. Even if we accept that a significant number of these are, in fact, combatants, the policy of assassination denies us any recourse to verifiable modes of justice. And how many innocents are to die before this violence is explained in comparative terms? This says nothing to the broader questions of endemic gun crime or the mass incarceration of people of color in the United States — numerically comparable to forced imprisonment witnessed during the global slave trade.

Neither does it speak to the socially engineered conditions of extreme poverty and inescapable despair so commonplace throughout the world. Not only has violence become more widespread, interconnected, and extreme in its visibility, it seems to have completely detached itself from any sense of social and ethical responsibility. Violence now inhabits not just the repressive apparatuses of law and order; it has become a form of public pedagogy parading as entertainment, immersing global publics in a media-cultural saturation of celluloid violence, all of which points to the power of the spectacle to normalize the most vicious underside of neoliberalism.

The book as such is not about these memorialized "exceptional moments in history" but speaks instead to those contemporary forms of disposability that have become normalized, where the burden of guilt is placed on the shoulders of the victims while the most pernicious of systemic abuses continue to hide things in plain sight. We hope that it offers and enables a critical angle of vision that goes well beyond the mere authentication of lives as simply born vulnerable to question the systemic design for oppression and exploitation that produces humans as some expendable category.

VICTORIA HARPER: The subtitle of the book evidently is inspired by Guy Debord and other authors who look to the importance of the media in shaping our notions about social relations. In the section of the book focused on George Orwell, you propose that these authors should be approached in a different way if they are to have any critical value today. How is that?

BRAD EVANS & HENRY A. GIROUX: Part of the problem with a lot of critical scholarship today is the tendency to appropriate 20th century concepts and apply them to the 21st century terrain as if the structures of power were still the same. We live in an entirely different political moment to the likes of Debord, Orwell, and the many other critical voices that reverberate throughout our text.

Take Debord, for example. He couldn't have possibly envisaged the types of digital broadcasting we are both continually and immanently subjected to with devices that quite literally put a mediated world into our hands. Neither could Orwell have understood the breadth and depth of the contemporary surveillance state and the subtle yet pernicious way it works precisely by getting its users to willfully give over information about all aspects of their lives. Nor could he have imagined that in addition to repressive surveillance techniques, new regimes of terror could emerge that supplemented the regime of Big Brother.

Repression is now matched by modes of dystopian governance in which the production of subjectivity, consciousness, identity, and agency become the stuff of continued oppression, depoliticized through cultural apparatuses that render people civically illiterate, reduce agency to an act of consumption, and parade freedom as the exclusive domain of self-interest. Still, for us, what's going on here is much more than a question of technology; it is the way technological change is a mere enabler to broader power dynamics, which in the name of advancement both depoliticizes and renders more and more populations disposable.

Contemporary liberal societies are undoubtedly, as Debord started to appreciate, saturated by images and representations of violence. From 24-hour news coverage and the extreme torture of Hollywood blockbusters to increasingly brutal gaming formats, the realities of violence have arguably never been so embedded in our cultural, economic, and social fabric. Some might even argue that violence has become so normalized today that it is reaching the point of the banal as its entertainment value supersedes any considered political and ethical questioning.

Our aim has been to take this realization and open some discussion by specifically dealing with the question of violence in the age of the global spectacle. Broached this way, it is possible to critique the spectacle as a means by which we can understand some of the defining features of modern liberal societies. For example, from terror to extreme weather and everything in between, what contemporary spectacles of violence evidenced to us are the following:

1. We live in an age of radical interconnectivity that has collapsed all notions of space and time. As a result, the realms of inside and outside, along with past, present, and future, are rather meaningless for us.

2. This has had a profound impact upon notions of threat, as the very idea of endangerment parades under the rubric of a universal law and encompasses all of life on a global scale. There is, as such, no sanctuary anymore. There are no sites of refuge. Everywhere is a site of potential hostility and violence.

3. The outcome of this has been the collapse of all modern demarcations — of friends and enemies, times of war and times of peace, and citizens and soldiers — as we enter into what Giorgio Agamben might call a "zone of indistinction."

4. With security (not least social security) all but abandoned, vulnerability assumes a scale of magnification that transforms individual fear into the fundamental principle underwriting modes of governance today. One consequence is the normalization of the idea that all things are fundamentally insecure by design. The doctrine of resilience is the most purposeful expression of this, and we are all encouraged to partake in a world that is deemed to be catastrophically fated.

5. Power operates upon this terrain by foregrounding the politics of catastrophe as the inescapable fact of the human condition. Life as such appears everywhere endangered and subject to forces outside of politics and change.

6. Within this terrain, all forms of catastrophe now appear part of a complex and networked topography of danger that

reaffirms at every turn the insecure sediment of existence. Threat has become ubiquitous and part of the everyday fabric of our societies. Such threats redefine fear as an individual register concerned with attacks on the body and on one's comforts and are defined solely within the register of personal fears. Lost here are those modes of insecurity and fear that point to the suffering that comes from a lack of social provisions, poverty, a culture of cruelty, and a society in which politics becomes an extension of war.

7. We live in an age that is fixated by spectacles of violence that continue to harvest our attention. Those of us who live in liberal zones have all become global witnesses to events that are presented to us as beyond all measures of control.

8. Not only does this normalize the violence of the present. It ties logics of rule to the inevitability of catastrophe and the promise of violence to come. The prospect of a violent death as such has already taken life itself hostage without fortune.

9. As a result, our politics is best described as a state of dystopian realism. The very idea that we might be able to transform the world for the better is denied us. The best we can hope for is to bounce back and be more prepared for the next catastrophe on the horizon.

Integral to this state of dystopian realism are highly mediated aesthetic regimes of suffering, which serve to authenticate the meaning of lives by rendering certain forms of violence tolerable for public consumption while delegitimizing others through various forms of public censorship. The spectacle has produced a carnival of violence produced through the ideological and affective spaces of neoliberalism, in which violence is evoked as a source of pleasure and entertainment, reinforcing what can be called violence with a fascist edge. Violence not only has become normalized as the face of gratuitous pleasure; it also contains what Rustom Bharucha has called "an echo of the pornographic." This has led us to put forward the following definition, which, worth repeating here, we believe captures the contemporary logic of spectacles of violence:

The spectacle of violence represents more than the public enactment and witnessing of human violation. It points to a highly mediated regime of suffering and misery, which brings together the discursive and the aesthetic such that the performative nature of the imagery functions in a politically contrived way. In the process of occluding and depoliticizing complex narratives of any given situation, it assaults our senses in order to hide things in plain sight. The spectacle works by turning human suffering into a spectacle, framing and editing the realities of violence, and in doing so renders some lives meaningful while dismissing others as disposable. It operates through a hidden structure of politics that colonizes the imagination, denies critical engagement, and pre-emptively represses alternative narratives. The spectacle harvests and sells our attention while denying us the ability for properly engaged political reflection. It engages agency as a pedagogical practice in order to destroy its capacity for self-determination, autonomy, and self-reflection. It works precisely at the level of subjectivity by manipulating our desires such that we become cultured to consume and enjoy productions of violence, becoming entertained by the ways in which it is packaged, which divorce domination and suffering from ethical considerations, historical understanding, and political contextualization. The spectacle immerses us, encouraging us to experience violence as pleasure such that we become positively invested in its occurrence, while attempting to render us incapable of either challenging the actual atrocities being perpetrated by the same system or steering our collective future in a different direction.

VICTORIA HARPER: You seem to be saying in your book that we need to rethink the history of the present through the spectacle? What does that mean for the role of the public intellectual?

BRAD EVANS & HENRY A. GIROUX: Our concern with the spectacle of violence extends to a concern with intellectual violence. They cannot be separated. Both bring us directly to the closing down of historical memory and public spaces as the multiple experiences of political events are subsumed within a singular, allegedly true narrative. Take the events of September 11, 2001, for instance. They demonstrated how imposing a uniform, master truth as an explanation resulted in a profound failure of political vision and a curtailment of the radical imagination.

Indeed, one of the greatest casualties of the war that followed was intellectual — namely, the idea that it is still possible to transform the world for the better and rely on any unimpeachable truth, any statement rooted in the discourse of certainty. The spectacle thus works precisely by closing down critique and dissent while erasing any vestige of thoughtfulness and any mode of inquiry that matters. It demands and celebrates a violent response to the recourse to the violence now figured as business as usual.

If the first order of politics in the age of the spectacle is to colonize the imaginary, then it is our task to expose more fully how the merging of the spectacle, extreme violence, and politics represents a form of violence to thought. A theatrical politics of the visceral has replaced the more measured and thoughtful commentary on human suffering bequeathed by a post-World War II generation of intellectuals, artists, and others. Representations of fear, panic, vulnerability, and pain increasingly override narratives of justice, and spectacle shapes and legitimates social relations. Violence is no longer viewed or experienced merely as a side effect of warfare and criminal exclusion; it has become a deliberate mediating strategy of representation, marked by the careful policing of violence, in which the spectacle is central to a species of political rebirth that puts life back into a social order where only an economy of violent relations reigns supreme.

Violence has become a fundamental pedagogy and politics for assigning identities, modes of agency and thought itself. Thoughtlessness has moved from what Hannah Arendt once called the center of totalitarianism and banality of evil to an all-embracing attack on the very notion of critical agency, on the care of others, and on democracy itself. The contemporary dystopian imaginary takes this to its logical conclusion: militaristic values colonize visions of the world, while subjects willing to serve the corporate and financial elite benefit from the violent wreckage produced by spectacle. At the same time, political and economic power are willing to serve the spectacle itself, bypassing even the minimal democratic gesture of gaining consent from the subjects whose interests are supposed to be served.

Nevertheless, the course of history is far from certain. Unfolding experiences of trauma and loss can actually bring people together in a fragile blend of grief, shared responsibility, compassion, and a newfound respect for the power of common purpose and commitment. The translation of such events into acts of public memory, mourning, and memorializing are ambivalent and deeply unsettling. They offer no certainty. But we must recall that they do not only bring about states of emergency and the suspension of civil norms and order: they can, and often will, give birth to enormous political, ethical, and social possibilities. Currently, we see instances of such possibilities in the outpouring of rage and protest against police brutality and violence against black men in Ferguson, Missouri, New York City, and Baltimore, Maryland.

Can public mourning neutralize the violence of organized forgetting and the spectacle of violence? Memory can be an instigator of both despair and hope, blurring the distinction. Such uncomfortable moments of consciousness provide the basis for a form of witnessing that refuses the warmongering, human rights violations, xenophobia, and violations of civil liberties that take shape under the banner of injury and vengeance.

VICTORIA HARPER: One of the most challenging political ideas you address in the book is the concept of "dystopian realism." Could you explain what you mean by this and why this is important in terms of rethinking politics in the 21st century?

BRAD EVANS & HENRY A. GIROUX: Dystopian politics has become mainstream politics. The practice of disposability has intensified, and more and more individuals and groups are now considered excess, consigned to "zones of abandonment," surveillance, and incarceration. The widespread destruction and violence produced by the politics of disposability can be seen in the ever-growing armies of individuals and groups whose existing and future prospects remain bleak. This includes those lacking basic necessities amid widening income disparities, the reckless imprisonment of immigrants, the school-to-prison pipeline, and the widespread destruction of the middle class by new forms of debt servitude. Terminal exclusion, disappearance, proliferating forms of social death, and the use of the prison as a default solution serves to both address the major social problems of the day and to contain, depoliticize, and remove from the polity poor minorities of class and color. Citizens, as Gilles Deleuze foresaw, are now reduced to data, consumers, and commodities and, as such, inhabit identities in which they increasingly become unknowables with no human rights and with no one accountable for their condition.

There is something, however, more at stake here than the contemporary plight of those millions forced to live in intolerable conditions. What makes the contemporary forms of disposability so abhorrent is precisely the way they shape disposable futures of endemic catastrophe and disorder, from which there is no viable escape except to draw upon the logics of those predatory formations that put us there in the first place.

Frederic Jameson's claim, then, that it is easier to "imagine the end of the world than it is the end of capitalism" is more than a reflection on the poverty of contemporary imaginations. It reveals the nihilism that forces us to accept that the only world conceivable is the one we are currently forced to endure: a world that is brutally reproduced and forces us all to become witnesses to its spectacles of violence and demands we accept that all things are ultimately insecure. The notion that one has to think otherwise in order to act otherwise has become a form of dangerous thinking, subject to censorship at best and prison in the worst-case scenario, as in the case of protesting students and whistleblowers. The unbridled concentration of power in neoliberal societies relies not merely on the repressive state apparatuses but also on symbolic and intellectual forms of violence that kill the radical imagination, kill any vestige of the politics of possibility.

Critical theorists are, of course, well aware of the intellectual stakes here. Dogmatic advocates of "political science" and "analytical philosophy" often accuse critical thinkers concerned more with the irreducible qualities of the human condition of being too abstract or esoteric. This has led to the marginalization, subjugation, and outright discrimination against those who argue for an emancipatory pedagogical force. And yet, as Arendt understood all too well, for the most part, political violence is not carried out by irrational monsters. It is reasoned, rationalized, calculated, and premised upon all-too-scientific and analytical claims that some lives are worth killing for the greater good.

Representations of human suffering are now essential parts of the machinery of consumption: sensationalist images designed to excite, stimulate, and offer the lure of intense sensations. This is especially true for spectacles of violence, many of which are stylistically extraordinary, grotesque depictions of the culture that produces them. Spectacles of violence provide an important element in shaping a market-driven culture of cruelty that merges an economy of pleasure with images of violence, mutilation, and human suffering.

This is not to suggest that the only images available in contemporary liberal societies are those saturated with violence and pain, but to emphasize that alternatives to such violence seems to be disappearing. And it is not to suggest that images of violence can only produce sadistic pleasure or can be reduced deterministically to one reading and point of view; our argument is simply that under a neoliberal regime, we are immersed in a media-saturated culture that inordinately invests in and legitimizes a grim pleasure in the pain of others, especially those considered marginal and disposable.

VICTORIA HARPER: Some would say that you look to the future with a real sense of pessimism. How do you avoid being thought of as just another political critic of our times? How do we break down the distinction between spectacles of violence and political passivity?

BRAD EVANS & HENRY A. GIROUX: We began writing this book with a remarkable sense of faith and optimism for our collective futures. We take heart from the fact that people will resist what they find patently intolerable. We also understand that no regime for power can be totalizing. Human beings have this remarkable capacity to reimagine the world and show remarkable love for their fellow citizens, despite the catastrophes and horrors of the times. We must keep hold of that all-too-human sensibility or else the battle is truly lost. What nihilism is, after all, is a willingness to succumb to the idea that the world can no longer be politically and ethically transformed for the better.

Central to our notion of resistance and educated hope is the belief that agency is a product of education, and that at the heart of any viable notion of politics is the recognition that politics begins with attempts to change the way people think, act, feel, and identify themselves and their relations to others. There is more to agency than the neoliberal emphasis on the "empire of the self" with its unbridled narcissism and unchecked belief in the virtues of a form of self-interest that despises the bonds of sociality, solidarity, and community. Truth erupts in the pedagogical awakening, the moment when the rules are broken, when taking risks becomes a necessity, when self-reflection narrates its capacity for critically engaged agency and thinking the impossible is not an option but a necessity.

Dystopian realism, the spectacle of violence, and the normalizing of catastrophe can only be addressed through a politics that is educative, one that is willing to use the tools of belief, persuasion, and pedagogy as a way of changing how people view the world. It is precisely by making the political more pedagogical that pressing the claims for economic and social justice can be made possible and movements for change can be developed. Educated hope can develop a language of critique and possibility.

Many theorists, including Jacques Rancière, have been critical of the presumption that horrifying images alone are sufficient enough to mobilize us into political action. And he is right. Many of the images witnessed today are policed by a highly mediated regime of suffering which overtly politicizes the captured moment, leading to the suffocation of alternative political meanings. Nonetheless, just as we recognize no separation between political action and poetic intervention, we also refuse to condemn artistic interventions because they aren't immediately quantifiable for "impact assessment."

None of us can anticipate or indeed measure the true quantity and scale of a creative political moment, whether it is witnessing Rosa Parks sitting on a forbidden seat or the works of Isaac Cordal and Gottfried Helnwein whose remarkably potent and politically charged aesthetics disrupt, unsettle, and transform our image of the world. Both are important "events" in the memory of our imagination as they seize hold of the best of our desires, holding the possibility that passivity might be turned into affirmative witnessing of a history that is now being steered in a different and more liberating direction.

As Deleuze wrote:

> In every modernity and every novelty, you find conformity and creativity; an insipid conformity, but also "a little new music"; something in conformity with the time, but also something untimely — separating the one from the other is the task of those who know how to love, the real destroyers and creators of our day.

Originally published in somewhat different form in TruthOut.

Self-Plagiarism and the Politics of Character Assassination: The Case of Zygmunt Bauman

Brad Evans & Henry A. Giroux

Sunday, 30 August 2015

IN A RECENT STUDY published in *The Times Higher Education Supplement*, the world-renowned sociologist Zygmunt Bauman was charged with repetitive counts of "self-plagiarism." As Peter Walsh and David Lehmann of Cambridge University claimed to have discovered, following an alleged meticulous reading of some 29 of Bauman's works, "substantial quantities of material … appear to have been copied near-verbatim and without acknowledgement from at least one of the other books sampled. Several books contain very substantial quantities of text — running into several thousands of words, and in the worst case almost 20 thousand — that have been reused from earlier Bauman books without acknowledgment." This recycling of prose, they argue, constitutes a monstrous "deception" on the part of the author, undermining one of the fundamental pillars of credible scholarship — the ability to cite with authenticating safeguards.

But what is really the charge here? Why would an emeritus reader at Cambridge University and doctoral student spend so much energy investigating and attempting to reveal repetition by another scholar? There was no doubt a personal agenda at work here, and Walsh had already leveled accusations about Bauman's work before. That much is clear. This sordid affair, however, speaks more broadly to the tensions and conflicts so endemic to the neoliberal university today. It strikes at the heart of what passes for credible intellectual inquiry and scholarship and reveals more purposefully the shift from engaging with the ideas that embody a life — especially one rooted in a quest for political and economic justice — to the penchant for personal attacks that seek to bring into question the character and credibility of respected authors. This is more than simply the passing of judgment from a moral position upheld by histories of elitism and privilege. It is tantamount to intellectual violence wrapped in objective scholarship, a violence that plagues the academy. Within the neoliberal university, not only has the personal become the only politics that matters (when politics is even addressed), it has also become a strident form of careerism in which getting ahead at any costs mirrors the market itself.

Anybody who is familiar with Bauman's corpus will appreciate the repetition in his narrative and prose. This is especially the case in his later works with his deployment of the metaphorical term "liquid," which has been purposefully applied to many of the various facets of late modern societies — from economy, terror, and climate to social and personal relations. The concern here, however, is not one of repetition as an act of plagiarism, as if the latter term is the only category to employ in this case. It's what Bauman embodies as a public intellectual and critical scholar, one who is less concerned with hierarchy and deference than he is with offering a fundamental challenge to established doctrine. But then again, this is a methodological assault, one that is purposely designed to camouflage both the authors' politics and what actually counts in the relationship between scholarship and the need to address broader social issues.

Personally, we have never once felt "deceived" by any of Bauman's important works. Yes, there is repetition. By why is that such an issue? There is, of course, much to be said for reading the same ideas with a different angle of vision and in a different context. But there is even something more critical at stake here: namely, the formation and subsequent authentication of "thought processes" and "regimes of truth." Citations are deemed essential to academic practices because they establish authoritative sources for factual claims and give due credit to the labors of others. Leaving aside well-established concerns with the need for authorization, as if this process were objective and certain (with the evident racial, gender, and class bias this invariably reproduces), what is being further demanded here is the need to give due credit to oneself. Bauman is thus seen as guilty of not citing, well, Bauman! He is not authorizing himself! Why, we might ask, is this necessary, if not to simply further authenticate a system of intellectual propriety and policing that is less concerned with pushing forward intellectual boundaries than it is in maintaining what is right and proper to think. The lesson here is clear. For thinking to be meaningful, it needs to conform to the set parameters and rules of the game. As Walsh openly admits in his defense, "Age and reputation should not exempt anyone from the normal standards of academic scholarship." There is a curious and revealing silence here regarding the history of power relations that define alleged "normal standards of academic scholarship." After all, left theorists have been punished for decades in the academy for publishing either controversial political work or for not publishing in "acceptable" academic journals or publishing houses — outlets that are often extremely conservative and mirror the reigning ideology and corporatized professionalism of the academy.

Any student of the history of intellectual forms of violence will no doubt appreciate the discursive move being deployed here. The invocation of "the norm" is the surest way to suffocate different ways of interrogating and thinking about the world. Often sanctified in some universal regalia (as recycled here by Walsh's all-too-familiar insistence), as if to indicate the natural and uncontroversial order of things, normalization is the mask of mastery for those who have a vested interest in maintaining the status quo. What becomes proper to thought as such is already set out in advance, hence framing in a very narrowly contrived way what it means to think and act with a conformist diligence.

Might we not insist here that the accusers follow their own demands for scientific veracity? Maybe they ought to conduct a qualitative study of his readership to see how many actually feel "misled" in the way they take as conclusive? Personally, we feel privileged to have come to know Bauman and his work. That he still has the energy, dedication, and fight to challenge oppression and injustice should be the source for affirmation and not critique. We are not suggesting here that Bauman's ideas should not be put under the critical microscope. They certainly should. Even twice! But we need to be mindful of much greater deceptions. The recycling of ideas and passing them off as original by claiming some positivist ascription of an "objective reality" is problematic enough. The pride taken by some in academia today in conducting forms of public shaming that are tantamount to a Stasi witch hunt is deplorable.

For what we elect to term the "gated intellectuals" of consumer capitalism — for whom every thought has to be new and packaged in a glittering endnote, preferably with a shiny display of what might be called the culture of positivism or empiricist hysteria — Bauman has been charged with the alleged insidious crime of repeating some of his own work. Of course, we all repeat ideas in our writing, and theorists such as Slavoj Žižek even make such repetitions central to how they define their work. We would argue that what Bauman presents is a perfect case of strategic repetition. But according to the academic police squad at Cambridge University, he has plagiarized his own work. We have read almost all of Bauman's work, have taken endless notes on it, and always learn something, even if some issues are reworked. Who doesn't rework important themes in their work?

Of course, in the world of the orthodox empiricist, such questions are only discussed in terms that are quantified, not thought through in order to ask how such work further deepens and layers complex ideas, concepts, and paradigms. The real task is not to count repeated ideas but to ask how an author's work gains in meaning over time as it is understood in terms of earlier interventions and evolving changing contexts. Reading an author's work in terms of its assemblage of formations, especially with regard to how it articulates with larger issues that are evolving over time, is a crucial critical task but not one empiricists are concerned about. They are bean counters who eschew substance for the reification of method. They now inhabit the academy and mimic the work of accountants who inhabit the small rooms of factories making No. 2 pencils.

First, strategic repetition is important not only to mediate the overabundance of information that people confront, but also to reach as many audiences as possible. Strategic repetition is all the more necessary in a world in which there is an immediate access to an abundance of digital-visual information, making it all the more difficult for readers to pay attention to and follow the development of a logically connected argument. Bauman's use of strategic repetition makes it easier for the reader to follow his narratives, focus on the argument, and reflect on the material being read. Second, the apostles of data mining and reductionistic instrumentality abhor Bauman's kind of critical argumentation; their interests are in reducing the value of scholarship to the trade in information because only that provides useful predictions for corporations and the Defense Department. Grasping ideas — thinking through them carefully — is less the result of merging empirical methods with arid calculations than it is an attempt to encourage acts of translation, awe, and insight. Bauman's scholarship attempts to expand the imagination and to elevate language to an act of resistance — resistance to the dumbing down of intelligence and the idea that data is all that matters — and this is precisely what Bauman has mastered with his use of strategic repetition.

Bauman once explained how his writing is like walking into the same room through a different door. This metaphor illuminates how he is not tirelessly repeating his work, he is building on it, expanding it, and endlessly trying to reassess its implications under changing circumstances. The charge of plagiarism is truly despicable, a reactionary ideological critique dressed up as a discourse about method and indebted to the tired legacy of depoliticized empiricism. What these guardians of orthodoxy really are afraid of is hearing his ideas over and over again, recognizing that they are reaching more and more audiences while modeling not what is euphemistically called scholarship but the role scholars might play as public intellectuals who address important social issues. Needless to say, self-plagiarism of ideas is a preposterous idea. The willful plagiarism of policing methods to authenticate what is proper to thought is what reproduces intellectual servitude. Now that's a problem that demands our vigilance and needs to be critiqued!

This point is stressed by J. P. E. Harper-Scott, who, writing in *Open Democracy*, notes that the real charge against Bauman is that his "self-plagiarism" ultimately constitutes a "sin against capitalism, one of whose doctrines is that there must always be new things to sell so that the consumer can buy with confidence." As Harper-Scott rightly observes, it is, then, part of a broader intellectual shift that cannot be divorced from the changing institutional settings in which such personal attacks originate and assume the status of a "public concern," even though at their ideological core is a desire to annihilate the commons.

We are not suggesting here that the demands for previously unpublished originality are unimportant in certain contexts. We appreciate that academic journals demand this consideration. Bauman is actually exemplary in this regard — his repetitions are directed beyond the academy. Students are also subject to the same criteria, as self-plagiarism is deemed problematic by most academic institutions in assessment criteria. This requirement is designed to expand student awareness and critical insight, not to limit understanding, knowledge, and its dissemination. What is more important here is precisely the "standardization" (a term Walsh refers to) of critical thinking and public engagement. Bauman understands better than most that no piece of work can speak in a universal language. There is a need, in fact, to write the same ideas in different ways in order to be respectful of the audience and not assume homogeneous readership. The problem, of course, is that Bauman doesn't conform to the standardization of thought as set out in normalized academic protocols. In short, there is a profound failure here to grasp that he fully understands the value of writing in different media, for different audiences, with varying languages and critical insights. Bauman exemplifies a conceptual persona who has truly broken out of the ivory tower and its outdated insistence that academics simply write for academics or established forms of power. That's what really perturbs his attackers.

We are also mindful here that there is a danger of countering a pernicious critique with a more authenticating position to hyper-moralize critical thought. Anybody can be a critic. That's not in question. What concerns us is the ethics of critical engagement, especially the difference between those who invoke a critical position in order to set out the parameters of thought against those whose critical dispositions are tasked with liberating what it means to think and act in the world with ethical care and political awareness of the consequences of both. We could do no better here than cite Bauman's final words from his wonderful book *Collateral Damages*:

> Dialogue is a difficult art. It means engaging in conversation with the intention of jointly clarifying the issues, rather than having them one's own way; of multiplying voices, rather than reducing their number; of widening the set of possibilities, rather than aiming at a wholesale consensus (that relic of monotheistic dreams stripped of politically incorrect coercion); of jointly pursuing understanding, instead of aiming at the others defeat; and all in all being animated by the wish to keep the conversation going, rather than by a desire to grind it to a halt.

Given that Bauman has no interest in being part of some quantifiable research assessment exercise (which has notably led to the valorization of positivist methodologies in the United Kingdom), these concerns with "self-plagiarism" only really matter in an age where thought has to become quantifiable like any other property. It is worth reminding, in a discussion about intellectual property, citation, and quotation, that none of us own our ideas. They are always the product of many conversations that too often go unacknowledged. Ideas in this regard always belong to the commons. Objectifying and commodifying thought — and pretending that all previous thoughts and ideas are thereby obsolete — is a much greater deception. Demands for "rigor" often have less to do with understanding the contested genealogies of complex thought systems than with referencing a domesticated term, one so often deployed to validate methodological approaches that it ends up ensuring that work conform to the status quo. The parallels with Eric Dyson's criticisms of Cornel West are all too apparent. (To elaborate on this, we could insert the piece here, but instead we will just direct the reader to Henry A. Giroux's "The Perils of Being a Public Intellectual."

There is a bankrupt civility at work here, disingenuous in its complicity with the intellectual forms of violence it authors and yet blinded to the moral coma it attempts to impose. What is abandoned in this particular case is the very notion that the public intellectual might have a role to play in resisting authoritarian politics and the tyrannies of instrumental reason, which promote isolationism over collegiality. This is the civility of authoritarian voices that mask their intellectual violence with weak handshakes, apologies for their necessary assassinations, forced smiles, and mellowed voices. Like the punishment dished out to a recalcitrant child through instrumental rulings or outright public shaming, more "mature" ways of thinking about the world (the authoritarian default) must eventually be shown to be the natural basis for authority and rule. In this instance, intellectual violence undermines the possibility for engaging scholarship through the use of rigorous theory, impassioned narrative, and a discourse that challenges the unethical grammars of suffering produced by neoliberal modes of instrumental rationality that have overtaken the academy, if not modernity itself. What we are dealing with here is a kind of neoliberal violence that produces what Frank B. Wilderson III called, in his *Red, White, and Black*, "the discourse of embodied incapacity."

Such character assassinations should not therefore be viewed in isolation or removed from political struggles. They point to the neoliberal assault on global academia that is now so pervasive and potentially dangerous in its effects that it must be viewed as more than a "cause for concern." While the system in the United States of America, for instance, has been at the forefront of policies that have tied academic merit to market-driven performance indicators, the ideologically driven transformations underway in the United Kingdom point in an equally worrying direction as the need for policy entrepreneurship increasingly becomes the norm. The closures of entire philosophy programs signify the most visible shift away from reflective thinking to the embrace of an evacuated approach to humanities education that has no time for anything beyond the objectively neutralizing and politically compromising deceit of pseudo-scientific paradigms.

Instrumentalism in the service of corporate needs and financial profit now dominates university modes of governance, teaching, research, and the vocabulary of consumerism used to describe students and their relationship to each other and the larger world. One consequence, as the Bauman Affair shows, is that discourses, ideas, values, and social relations that push against the grain, redefine the boundaries of the sensible, and reclaim the connection between knowledge and power in the interest of social change too often become inconvenient enough that they rapidly are redefined as dangerous. Since there is little appetite to engage ideas at any substantive level beyond the superficial, criticism turns instead — following an all-too-familiar move — to questions of individual pathology and character deficiencies. This is a textbook power play. This is a form of intellectual violence that empties words of their meaning and takes on the mantle of shaming.

Intellectuals are continually forced to make choices (sometimes against our better judgments). In truth, there are no clear lines drawn in the sand. And yet, as Paulo Freire insisted, one is invariably drawn into an entire history of struggle the moment critical ideas are expressed as force and put out into the public realm to the disruption of orthodox thinking. There is, however, a clear warning from history: our intellectual allegiances should be less concerned with ideological dogmatism. After all, no force is more micro-fascist or intellectually violent than the self-imposed thought police who take it upon themselves to be the voices of political and intellectual purity. Bauman's pedagogy has always insisted that the task of educators is to make sure that the future points to a more socially just world, a world in which the discourses of critique and possibility, in conjunction with the values of freedom and equality, function to alter, as part of a broader democratic project, the grounds upon which life is lived. This is hardly a prescription for intellectual short cuts or taking the easy road: it embodies a lifelong commitment to a project that as Stanley Aronowitz observed in his introduction to Paulo Freire's *Pedagogy of Freedom* continues to give education its most valued purpose and meaning, which in part is "to encourage human agency, not mold it in the manner of Pygmalion."

Figures such as Bauman remain important as ever. This is especially the case in the current conjuncture, as neoliberalism arrogantly proclaims that there are no alternatives to its hegemony. Such an ethical disposition, as Foucault critically maintained (in his preface to Gilles Deleuze & Felix Guattari's *Anti-Oedipus: Capitalism and Schizophrenia* and elsewhere), requires waging an ongoing fight against fascism in all its forms: "not only historical fascism, the fascism of Hitler and Mussolini — which was able to use the desire of the masses so effectively — but also the fascism in us all, in our heads, and in our everyday behavior, the fascism that causes us to love power, to desire the very thing that dominates and exploits us": precisely, in other words, the types of petty punishments and normalized practices of public shaming that take direct aim at the dignity and value of a fellow human.

Academics and public intellectuals have an ethical and pedagogical responsibility to unsettle and oppose all orthodoxies, to make problematic the common-sense assumptions that often shape students' lives and their understanding of the world. But we also have a responsibility to energize students to come to terms with their own power as individual and social agents. Higher education, as Bauman continually reminds us, cannot be removed from the hard realities of those political, economic, and social forces that both support it and consistently, though in diverse ways, attempt to shape its sense of mission and purpose. Politics is not alien to the university setting — politics is central to comprehending the institutional, economic, ideological, and social forces that give academia its meaning and direction. Politics also references the historical conflicts that mark higher education as an important site of struggle. Rather than the scourge of either education or academic research, politics is a primary register of their complex relation to matters of power, ideology, freedom, justice, and democracy. None of these are raised as issues in this latest intellectual assault.

To get a sense of the full absurdity of all this, just imagine for a moment a reworking of the United Kingdom's *The Independent* newspaper's headline, "World's leading sociologist accused of copying his own work," but instead of referring to Bauman the sociologist, we wrote of Van Gogh, Francis Bacon, Barbara Kruger, or Pablo Picasso. Our indignation at the claim (which could be rightly made if one considers the use of the same techniques and repetitive imagery) would require no further justification on account of its patent idiocy and sensational provocation without any grasp of the form. Critical thinking is no different. Indeed, as Bauman himself acknowledges in his aptly titled book *The Art of Life*, one of the most deceptive claims regarding politics, sociology, and philosophy has been their reductionist assignation to the realm of "social science." These fields of inquiry should instead be seen as art forms that are integral to the creation of new ways of thinking about the world and its poetic and creative modes of existence. They cannot be so easily reduced into a quantitative matrix without stripping life of its all-too-human qualities.

The hidden structure of politics in the charge of plagiarism is the refusal of the gated surveillance academics to use their time figuring out how capitalism and its empiricist acolytes recycle the same dreadful ideologies about the market over and over again. Unlike Bauman's work and its strategic repetition, the methodological embrace of citations and the obsession with repetition in "normal science" amounts to what Marcuse once called "scholarshit" — truly a crime against justice and social responsibility.

In sum, this despicable charge against Bauman is a reactionary ideological critique dressed up as the celebration of method and a backdoor defense of a sterile empiricism and culture of positivism (and *nota bene*: we know we are repeating ourselves). This is a discourse that enshrines data, correlations, and performance while eschewing matters of substance, social problems, and power. As Murray Pomerance points out, plagiarism is a form of theft, and since we cannot steal what we own, we can't steal our own work. On the contrary, we expand its reach and build on it, thereby making it more relevant as the contexts that produce it change. What these guys really are afraid of is hearing his ideas over and over again, recognizing that they are reaching more and more audiences. Theft has nothing to do with strategic repetition in the interest of clarity, expanding and deepening an issue, or building upon one's own work. On the contrary, theft is about claiming false ownership, allowing power to steal one's integrity, and engaging in those corrupt practices that erase any sense of justice.

In the world of gated intellectuals who thrive in a university landscape increasingly wedded to data banks, thought itself becomes another casualty of disposability. Metrics now merge with a business culture that has little time for anything that cannot be quantified. Matters of identity, justice, power, and equality — if not freedom itself — are reduced resources for generating data, developing surveys, and measuring intellectual output. The value of what an intellectual such as Bauman writes or says is irrelevant to a neoliberal world in which personal smears parade as scientific understanding and the stripped-down discourse of empiricism is presented as truth. Scholarship, intellectual output, and engagement with social problems are all interventions that travel in a variety of forms. It is the richness of the forms and the substance of the arguments that matter. The Cambridge surveillance team seems to have missed this point — or is it more that they willfully buried it? Utilitarianism has always shared an easy space with contempt for intellectual and politically insightful work, or what Richard Hofstadter once called the "life of the mind."

Maybe what is really at stake here is not the reworking of ideas but a kind of hostility to critical pedagogy and modes of writing that push against the grain not once but over and over again. A kind of toxic ideology is at work in this charge against Bauman — one that not only trivializes what counts as scholarship but also elevates matters of surveillance and policing to a normalized standard of evaluation.

Certainly the authors of the pernicious article about Bauman could do with reading Deleuze's *Difference and Repetition* to have a modicum of philosophical appreciation here — or better still, at least to be honest about their own methodological plagiarism, which, since the dawn of the humanities, has continued to produce self-anointing thought police, micro-fascists policing what is acceptable to think, their all-too-political agendas less concerned with the quality of the work than with condemning those who provide a fundamental challenge to their sense of privilege and their self-imposed illusions of grandeur. Thus, a reality check is needed for the likes of Walsh and Lehmann. You are not standing on the shoulders of giants. You are but one entry in the employment inventory of an intellectual surveillance apparatus.

Originally published in somewhat different form in Counterpunch.

How Do We Tell Our Children About the Violence in Paris?

Brad Evans

Monday, 16 November 2015

MANY OF US STILL feel a real sense of helplessness, anger, outrage, resignation, and disbelief at the violence we witnessed on the streets of Paris a few days ago. The images were intolerable and devastating, just as the suicidal terror that ripped apart communities in southern Beirut a day before demanded equal condemnation. French President François Hollande has now called for a "pitiless war" in response, as if we have somehow emerged from an age of compassion and human togetherness?

Such tragedies compel us to write, trying to make sense of the sense-lessness, hoping to gain some insight into its randomness, which only reaffirms the insecure and fragile nature of our times. Words continue to fail us. And yet, I have been haunted by the comments of a dear friend who, writing of her family's safety in Paris at the time, added, "so I'll now go home. And think tomorrow about how I shall explain this all to my children." This personal reflection speaks volumes. It should be at the forefront of our attentions. How do we tell our children about this violence?

Maybe it would offer us some comfort to explain to them, as some will do, that unfortunately the world is simply full of "irrational monsters." And we could tell them that in the end, what is good always triumphs over what is evil.

That too, however, would be a deception. The world is certainly full of dangerous people. But, like Paris, for the most part it is those who reason, rationalize, and calculate with a sure clarity of mind and purpose that pose the greatest threats. Our violence is no different than the violence being inflicted upon us: murder is murder, injury is injury. We, too, seem incapable of answering the question, "When is too much killing enough?" We just act as if there is justice to be had through violent retribution.

And yet, don't we already teach our children to think about the importance of forgiveness? Why then don't we heed such counsel when facing the cycle of violence and its inevitable ruinations? I am reminded here of Simon Critchley's "impossible demand" a decade after the violence of September 11, 2001. As Critchley wrote in a prescient tome:

> What if the grief and mourning that followed 9/11 were allowed to foster a nonviolent ethics of compassion rather than a violent politics of revenge and retribution? What if the crime of the September 11 attacks had led not to an unending war on terror, but the cultivation of a practice of peace — a difficult, fraught, and ever-compromised endeavor, but perhaps worth the attempt?

What might such a politics of forgiveness look like today? How can we instill this compassion in our children in the political hope that they might steer history in a different direction? All violence has a history — that much is clear. One option is to talk to them about the different forms that violence takes, without purposefully or even accidentally affirming to them that some lives matter more than others.

Children and youth are being exposed to forms of violence borne of an age of new media technologies. This places difficult and challenging demands upon parents and educators who rightly want to protect them from the raw realities of suffering and violence. But what does this mean when they are continuously exposed to its occurrence, or worse still, in the firing line? Maybe we can begin by reaffirming that the rights of children should be at the forefront of all political discussions, while stressing the importance of the arts, humanities, and other fields in producing critically minded and ethically astute generations to come — in other words, fighting against the current cutbacks in education.

Social media have notably been awash the past few days with what we might term "hierarchies of grief." We mourn Paris, but not Beirut. Many of us are, of course, already aware of why this should not be so. That doesn't, however, diminish our outrage at this intolerable event. Violence should be condemned in all its forms. To argue that some victims are more or less important than others is to fall into the trap set by those who argue that some casualties are justifiable — the militaristic myth that some casualties create more peaceful relationships in the long run.

Politics and ethics are not located at their ends; they should be judged as if the means *are* the ends. The recourse to violence is certainly no exception in this regard. We know what motives are created through the violence of historical forces and what historical forces motivated those who devastated Paris. Isn't it about time we taught our children less about the virtues of nationalistic regalia and more about our own history and what it has wrought in the world? Less about grief and rage and more about engaging in peaceful relations with peoples by extending a hand of friendship and taking seriously the politics of love? We know, after all, where the alternative leads us.

As I walked around New York City's Columbia University campus on Sunday, I thought of my beautiful little daughter back home in England, thankfully protected against the violence of historical forces. I also thought of her a few years ago, walking around the campus here in New York and rushing over to kneel before the replica sculpture of Rodin's *The Thinker* situated outside the philosophy department. Confronted by *The Thinker* again, though, now against the backdrop of the violence witnessed in the past few days, I was reminded of the importance of the power of education and critical pedagogy in order to break the cycle of violence.

Rodin's *The Thinker* at Columbia appears on a contemplative and isolated plinth. In this setting, *The Thinker* might be thinking about anything in particular. We just hope it is something serious. And yet, in its original 1880 form, *The Thinker* appears situated kneeling before the gates of hell. This seems tragically apt today. What does it mean to think in the presence of the raw realities of violence and suffering? How, in the face of such wretched acts and the widespread militarization of everyday societies, can we challenge the spectacle of violence and the forced witnessing it creates? How can we explain to our children the virtues of pacifism in a world that seems to have forgotten them?

Looking at the sculpture, I imagined, as some have argued, that the figure in this commission was Dante — the poet — who is contemplating the circles of hell as narrated in *The Divine Comedy*. I was reminded of the importance of this in the context of Edward Said's claim that with Dante, Orientalism truly begins to assume a monumental intellectual force. I thought of the need for a more somber and honest reflection of our shared histories of violence — including our complicities. And I thought of the books I hoped my daughter would someday read, from Eduardo Galeano's *Open Veins of Latin America* to Frantz Fanon's *The Wretched of the Earth*.

The idea that the future belongs to our children now seems perilous and fraught. We live in an age of dystopian realism, where entire populations can be rendered disposable, only for the bodies of their children to end washed up on the planetary shores. All the while groups such as ISIS have now mastered the spectacle, humanizing violence to devastating political effect, making the human — the progressive liberal, the aid worker, the journalist, the homosexual — now appear as a set of sacrificial categories. And yet, we must not lose sight of the most important questions our children should be demanding of us in this bleak contemporary moment: namely, what might it mean to break down the distinction between spectacles of violence and political passivity? How might the world be transformed for the better?

If the first order of politics in the age of the spectacle is to colonize the imaginary, it is our task to educate our children so they can offer more measured and thoughtful commentary on human suffering while still finding reasons to believe in the future. This requires us to develop modes of critical reflection for them, which not only forces us to be alert to the ways in which our attentions might be harvested by the seduction of violent images, but how we might be co-opted by forms of depraved aesthetics that debase us as political subjects. It is to present to them alternative images of the world that are not destined to be littered with corpses of violence to come.

In Rodin's original commission, *The Thinker* is actually called *The Poet*. *The Thinker* was initially conceived as both a being with a tortured body — almost a damned soul — and yet a freethinking human, determined to transcend his suffering through poetry. We continue to teach our children that politics is a social science and that its true command is located in the power of analytical reason. Such continues to be the hallmark of reasoned, rationalized, calculated violence in the name of political change. Never have we more urgently required a new political imagination that can take us out of the cycles of violence into which we are immersed.

Our children's futures don't need to be violently fated. Those who wish to condemn them to its spectral destiny cannot deny them the ability to imagine better worlds. They have the power of the imagination at their disposal. We need to give them the confidence to believe that imagination itself is the starting point for rethinking politics. Only then might we reclaim our collective futures. Our task is to speak with them about such tragic events and to affirm the devastating futility of violence in ways that encourage more compassionate relationships and thus move us beyond the recourse to violence. We are tasked with creating more peaceful futures.

Originally published in somewhat different form in TruthOut.

The War on Terror is a War on Youth: Paris and the Impoverishment of the Future

Brad Evans & Henry A. Giroux

Tuesday, 24 November 2015

> There's a nagging sense of emptiness. So, people look for any-
> thing; they believe in any extreme — any extremist nonsense is
> better than nothing.
>
> — J. G. Ballad

THERE IS A REVEALING similarity between the attacks on September 11, 2001 — when airplanes were flown into the Twin Towers, killing thousands of people — and the attacks in Paris, in which over 130 people were killed and hundreds wounded. Yet, what they have in common has been largely overlooked in the mainstream and alternative media's coverage of the more recent terrorist attacks. While both assaults have been rightly viewed as desperate acts of alarming terrorism, what has been missed is that both acts of violence were committed by young men. This is not a minor issue because unraveling this similarity provides the possibility for addressing the conditions that made such attacks possible.

While French President François Hollande did say soon after the Paris assault that "youth in all its diversity" was targeted, he did not address the implications of the attacks' heinous and wanton violence. Instead, he embraced the not-so-exceptional discourse of militarism, vengeance, and ideological certainty: a discourse that turned 9/11 into an unending war — a tragic mistake that cost millions of lives and ensured that the war on terrorism would benefit and play into the very hands of those at which it was aimed. The call for war, retribution, and revenge extended the violent landscape of everyday oppressions by shutting down any possibility for understanding the conditions that gave birth to the violence committed by young people against other innocent youthful civilians.

Hollande channeled the Bush/Cheney response to an act of terrorism and, in doing so, further paved the way for the emergence of the mass surveillance state and the collapsing of the state-army distinction, all the while legitimating a culture of fear and demonization that unleashed a wave of racism and Islamophobia. There is a hidden politics here that prevents a deeper understanding, not only of the failure of the government's responses to the Paris attacks, but also how such warlike strategies legitimate, reproduce, and quicken further the acts of violence, moving governments closer to the practices of a security state. Under such circumstances, fear becomes the foundation for producing both regressive and vindictive policies and for producing subjects willing to accept violence as the best solution to address the conditions that cause such fear. Judith Butler is right in arguing in *Truthdig* that the fear and rage at the heart of such responses "may well turn into a fierce embrace of a police state."

A War Waged on Youth and by Youth

While politicians, pundits, and the mainstream media acknowledged that the Paris attackers largely targeted places where young people gathered — the concert hall, the caf , and the sports stadium — what they missed was that this act of violence was part of a strategic war on youth. In this instance, youth were targeted by other youth. This incident was part of a larger war waged on youth and by youth. For ISIS, the war on youth translates into what might be called hard and soft targets. As hard targets, young people are subject to intolerable forms of violence of the sort seen in the Paris attacks. Moreover, there is a kind of doubling here because once they are lured into the discourse of extremism and sacrificial violence, they are no longer targeted or defined by their deficits. On the contrary, they now refigure their sense of agency, resentment, and powerlessness in the image of the suicide bomber who now targets other young people. The movement here is from an intolerable sense of powerlessness to an intolerable notion of violence defined through the image of a potential killing machine. In this instance, the hard war cannot be separated from the soft war on youth, and it is precisely this combination of tactics that is missed by those Western governments waging the war on terrorism.

The soft war represents another type of violence, one that trades in both fear and a sense of certainty and ideological purity borne of hyper-moral sensibilities, which writes off the victim as a mere necessity to the wider sacred claim. As symbols of the future, youth harbor the possibility of an alternative and more liberating worldview, and in doing so, they constitute a threat to the fundamentalist ideology of ISIS. Hence, they are viewed as potential targets subject to intolerable violence — whether they join terrorist groups or protest against such organizations. It is precisely through the mobilization of such fear that whatever hopes they might have for a better world is undermined or erased. This constitutes an attack on the imagination, designed to stamp out any sense of critical agency, thoughtfulness, and critical engagement with the present and the future.

The use of violence by ISIS is deftly designed to both terrorize young people and to create a situation in which France and other governments, influenced by structural racism and xenophobia, will likely escalate their repressive tactics toward Muslims, thereby radicalizing more young people and persuading them to travel to Syria to fight in the war effort. Put differently, when Hollande calls for pitiless vengeance, he is creating the warlike conditions that will enable an entire generation of Muslim youth to become sacrificial agents and the pretext for further violence. When violence becomes the only condition for possibility, it either suppresses political agency or allows it to become either a target or the vehicle for targeting others. War is a fertile ground for resentment, anger, and violence because it turns pure survivability into a doctrine and produces subjects willing to accept violence as the best solution to addressing the conditions that cause an endless cycle of humiliation, fear, and powerlessness.

But the soft war does more than trade in a culture of fear. It also relies on a pedagogy of seduction, persuasion, and identification. ISIS also capitalizes on the desperation, humiliation, and loss of hope that many young Muslims experience in the West, along with an endless barrage of images depicting the violence waged by Western nations against Iraq, Syria, Afghanistan, and other Middle Eastern nations. The spectacle of violence is its defining organizational principle. Many young people in the West are vulnerable to ISIS propaganda because they are constantly subject to widespread discrimination, and, because of their religion, continue to be harassed, dismissed, and humiliated. Much of this is further exacerbated by the expanding Islamophobia produced by right-wing populists in Europe and the United States. All the while, these youths' suffering and impoverishment are ignored, while their resentment is dismissed as a variant of ideological and political extremism devoid of both historical force and personal experience. Heiner Flassbeck rightly argues that ISIS is particularly adept at highlighting the conditions that produce this sense of resentment, anger, and powerlessness, and how it strategically addresses the vulnerability of Muslim youth to join ISIS by luring them with the promise of community and support and visions of an Islamic utopia. He writes:

> For as much as we know, they grew up in human and social conditions that few of us can even imagine. They grew up fearing attracting attention to themselves and being branded as potential terrorists if they were a bit too religious (in the eyes of the West) or frequented Arab circles a bit too often. They also saw that the West shows little reservation in bombing what they considered their "home countries" and killing hundreds of thousands of innocent people in order to guarantee the "safety" of its citizens.... The sad truth is that thousands of young men grow up in a world in which premeditated killings take place on an almost daily basis when army personnel from thousands of miles away push a button. Is it really surprising that some of them lose their wits, strike back and create even more violence and the death of many innocent people?

When the conditions that oppress youth are ignored in the face of the ongoing practices of state terrorism — the attacks waged on Muslim youth in France and other countries, the blatant racism that degrades a religion as if all terrorists are Muslims, or the willful ignorance that all religions produce their own share of terrorists — there is little hope to address the conditions that both impoverish and oppress young people. To expect them to develop the insight and vision to address such conditions before they erupt into a nihilistic form of rage is a tall order. Abdelkader Benali gives credence to this argument when he writes:

But I know from my own experience that the lure of extremism can be very powerful when you grow up in a world where the media and everyone around you seems to mock and insult your culture. And European governments are not helping fight extremism by giving in to the Islamophobia cooked up by right-wing populists. What I see is a lack of courage to embrace the Muslims of Europe as genuinely European — as citizens like everyone else.

Very few voices are talking about the terrorist attacks in Paris as part of what can be called the war on youth. The terrorists in this latest case targeted places where young people gather, sending a message that suggests that young people will have no future unless they can accept the ideological fundamentalism that drives terrorist threats and demands. This was an attack not simply on the bodies of youth, but also on the imagination — an attempt to kill any sense of a better and more democratic future. When this script is ignored or derided as an unrealistic fantasy, war, militarism, violence, and revenge define the only options for governments and young people to consider — a binary forged in a complex friend-enemy duality that erases the conditions that produce ISIS or the conditions that make possible the recruitment of young people to such a deadly ideology.

The Seeds of Terrorism

The seeds of terrorism do not lie simply in ideological fundamentalism; they also lie in conditions of oppression, war, racism, and poverty; in the abandonment of entire generations of Palestinian youth; in the dictatorships that stifle young people in the Middle East; and in the racist assaults on black youth in urban centers in the United States. Youth are now the subject and object of a continuous state of siege warfare, transformed either into suicide bombers or the collateral damage that comes from ubiquitous war machines. There are few safe spaces for them anymore, unless they are hidden in the gated enclaves and protectorates of the globally enriched.

In an age of extreme violence, civil wars, and increasing terrorism, it is crucial for those wedded to a democratic future to examine the state of youth globally — especially those marginalized by class, race, religion, ethnicity, and gender — in order to address the underlying forces that produce the conditions of violence as well as ideological fundamentalism, militarism, and massive political and economic inequalities. This is a crucial project that would also necessitate analyzing and distinguishing the ever-expanding global war machines that thrive on violence and exclusion from those governmental processes that might offer a transformation for the better.

Surely, there is more to the future than allowing young people to be killed by drones while sitting innocently in a café or, for that matter, for their spirit to be crushed or misdirected by impoverishment of body and mind. Maybe it is time to ask important questions about the choices different youth are making: Why are some youth joining and supporting violent organizations? And what has led others to resist state violence and terrorism in all of its forms, framing this violence as an indecent assault on individuals, groups, and the planet itself?

Maybe it is time to ask ourselves what it means when a society ignores young people and then goes to war because they either engage in terrorist acts or are its victims. One thing is clear: there will be no sense of global safety unless the conditions that produce young people as both the subjects and objects of violence are addressed and eliminated. Safety is not guaranteed by war, militarism, and vengeance. In fact, this response becomes the generative principle for more violence to come, thereby guaranteeing that no one will be safe. These young people have been initiated into a culture of violence that precedes them: they are the product of a world we have created. As Flassbeck rightly argues:

> Safety cannot be guaranteed. Airplanes, public buildings, and politicians can be protected, but there is no way to guarantee the safety of citizens. Those who oppose the "system" that, in their eyes, constitutes a destructive and life-threatening force may strike anywhere. To them, it makes little difference who dies as long as their actions create death, destruction, fear and, of course, more violence as a reaction. Safety can only be achieved if we start to realize and admit to ourselves that these angry young men are a product of our world. They are not just strangers that are driven by some perverted ideology. They are the result of a long series of misjudgments from our part and from our callousness when

it comes to identify potential suspects and hit them with bombs and drones in order to restore "order" and "safety."

Western powers cannot allow the fog of violence to cover over the bankruptcy of a militaristic response to an act of terrorism. Such militaristic responses function largely to govern the *effects* of acts of ISIS terrorism while ignoring its wider systemic dimensions. Dealing with the violence of ISIS requires political contextualization and serious engagement. However abhorrent we might find their actions, it is patently absurd for any leader involved with the ongoing acts of violence constantly recorded and made available on the internet not to recognize that one strategic assault posed by ISIS is to deploy the production values and aesthetics of Hollywood films and video games to project images of subjugation and power — much like those produced by US military media operations in Guantánamo Bay at the outset of the terror wars.

John Pilger ventures to take this a step further by noting the historical parallels with the Khmer Rouge, which terrorized Cambodia. As Pilger writes, this movement was the direct outcome of a US bombing campaign:

> The Americans dropped the equivalent of five Hiroshimas on rural Cambodia during 1969-73. They leveled village after village, returning to bomb the rubble and corpses. The craters left monstrous necklaces of carnage, still visible from the air. The terror was unimaginable.

The outcome was the emergence of a group largely made up of radical young men driven by a dystopian ideology, dressed in black, sweeping the country in the most violent and terrifying of ways. The historical comparison is all too apparent: "ISIS has a similar past and present. By most scholarly measures, Bush and Blair's invasion of Iraq in 2003 led to the deaths of some 700,000 people — in a country that had no history of jihadism."

If a nation continually bombs a people, invades and occupies their land, appropriates their resources, harms their children, imprisons and humiliates their families, and tears apart the fabric of the social order, there is direct responsibility for the inevitable backlash to follow. It actually produces the very conditions in which violence continues to thrive. The rush to violence kills more innocent people, is strategically useful only as a recruiting tool for terrorists, and further emboldens those who thrive on a culture of fear and benefit from creating a surveillance state: a lockdown society and a violently determined order based on the principles of limitless control, managed forms of social and political exclusion, and privilege — including the privilege to destroy.

But the rush to violence does more than perpetuate a war on youth; it also eliminates what might be called a politics of memory, the legacy of an insurrectional democracy, and, in doing so, furthers the registers of the militaristic state. The call for lethal violence in the face of the murderous attacks in Paris eviscerates from collective consciousness the mistakes made by President George W. Bush who, in Mary Kaldor's words, "declared a 'War on Terror' after 9/11, a statement that led us to the Patriot Act, the invasions of Afghanistan and Iraq, and Guantánamo." The consequences of that rush to judgment and war are difficult to fathom. As Bret Weinstein observes, Bush responded in a way that fed right into the terrorists' playbook:

> The 9/11 attack was symbolic.... It was designed to provoke a reaction. The reaction cost more than 6,000 American lives in the wars in Iraq and Afghanistan, and more than $3 trillion in US treasure. The reaction also caused the United States to cripple its own Constitution and radicalize the Muslim world with a reign of terror that has killed hundreds of thousands of Iraqi and Afghani civilians.

How different might our futures look now had an alternative response been sought at that particular moment? Continuing the cycle of violence and revenge, the response ramped up the violence and, as Kaldor notes, derided anybody who called for "addressing some of the social, cultural, and economic problems that create a context for extremism." The Soviet occupation of Afghanistan, the failure of the US war in Vietnam, the failure of the Western invasion of Iraq, and the futility of the military attacks on Libya and Syria all testify to the failure of wars waged against foreign populations — especially people in the Middle East. As Peter van Buren dryly observes:

> We gave up many of our freedoms in America to defeat the terrorists. It did not work. We gave the lives of over 4,000

American men and women in Iraq, and thousands more in
Afghanistan, to defeat the terrorists, and refuse to ask what
they died for. We killed tens of thousands or more in those
countries. It did not work. We went to war again in Iraq, and
now in Syria, before in Libya, and only created more failed
states and ungoverned spaces that provide havens for terrorists and spilled terror like dropped paint across borders.
We harass and discriminate against our own Muslim populations and then stand slack-jawed as they become radicalized, and all we do then is blame ISIS for tweeting.

The "War on Terror" and the ethos of militarism that has driven it into
the normalized fabric of everyday politics is seen by many of its victims
as an act of terrorism because of the dreadful toll it takes on noncom-
batants — and who can blame them. When President Obama uses
drone strikes to blow up hospitals, kill members of a wedding party,
and slaughter innocent children, regardless of the humanitarian sig-
natures, the violence becomes a major recruiting factor for ISIS and
other groups. When the practice of moral witnessing disappears, along
with the narratives of suffering on the part of the oppressed, politics
withers, and the turn to violence and terrorism gains ground — especially among impoverished youth. When the West forgets that, as
biochemist Dr. Gideon Polya has shown, analyzing UN data, "Muslim
avoidable deaths from deprivation in countries subject to Western
military intervention in 2001–2015 now total about 27 million," such
neglect serves to create more fear of the "other" and to generate more
resentment and hatred by those who are relegated to the shameless
and morally reprehensible status of collateral damage.

The call for war eliminates historical and public memory. The pedagogical dimensions embedded in its practice of forgetting ensure that
any intervention in the present will be limited by erasing any understanding of the past — a past that might otherwise cultivate a renewed
sense of political identification, social responsibility, and those forms
of ethical and political commitment that bear on the immediacy of a
world caught in the fog of war and the thoughtlessness of its conditioning. As such, those who forget the past ignore precisely the similarities mentioned above whether we are discussing the Western actions
that created Pol Pot and his Khmer Rouge or the histories of violence
that created ISIS. Chris Floyd is right to remind us:

Without the American crime of aggressive war against Iraq — which, by the measurements used by Western governments themselves, left more than a million innocent people dead — there would be no ISIS, no "al-Qaeda in Iraq." Without the Saudi and Western funding and arming of an amalgam of extremist Sunni groups across the Middle East, used as proxies to strike at Iran and its allies, there would be no ISIS. Let's go back further. Without the direct, extensive and deliberate creation by the United States and its Saudi ally of a worldwide movement of armed Sunni extremists during the Carter and Reagan administrations, there would have been no "Won Terror" — and no terrorist attacks in Paris.

Joseph G. Ramsey is also correct in insisting that those who focus only on the immediate and the shocking images of the suffering and trauma of those young people killed and wounded in Paris while failing to acknowledge the broader historical context out of which this intolerable violence emerged, "neither do justice to the situation, nor do they help us to achieve a framework for response, in thinking or in action, that can, in fact, reduce rather than escalate and increase the dangers that these terrible events represent, and that they portend."

One way in which such violence can be escalated is by giving free rein to the cheerleaders of racism, denouncement, and militarism. This is the "bomb first and think later" group that not only makes a claim to occupy the high moral and political ground but also refuses adamantly to consider any alternative narrative addressing the underlying causes of terrorism — especially what we are calling the war on youth. Unfortunately, as Deirdre Fulton points out, the gospel of fear and sensationalism is being encouraged by mainstream corporate media outlets, especially the cable news networks, which, in their search for higher ratings, shamelessly spread moral panics, fuel anti-immigrant sentiment, and encourage warmongering by providing coverage that lacks any historical context or complex and informative coverage of terror.

How Fear Turns to Fascism

As Rabbi Michael Lerner has brilliantly argued, fear and the desires it generates are the moving forces of fascism. Fear undermines historical memory due to its appeal to intense emotions and quick reactions steeped in violence. And, as Lerner writes, fear also guarantees that

> fascistic and racist right-wing forces will grow more popular as their anti-immigrant policies are portrayed as "common sense." In doing so, the politics of fear will inevitably lead to the empowering of domestic intelligence forces who are eager to invade our private lives and adamant in their call to receive greater support from the American public in the name of a disingenuous commitment to security. The call for tighter security and the allocation of increasing powers of surveillance to the government and its intelligence agencies will be supported by liberal leaders who seek to show that they too can be "tough."

Violence borne of such viscerally felt moments is always rooted in a pedagogical practice that mobilizes fear, embraces emotion over serious deliberation, and serves to legitimate a discourse that drowns out historical memory and ethical considerations. This is a discourse that is mobilized as a public pedagogy spread through a number of cultural apparatuses and favors the pundits, intellectuals, politicians, and others who benefit from the continuation of violence and the normalization of insecurities, thereby using it to promote their own shameless political agendas. At work here is a particularly pernicious discourse embraced by many in the West who want to use any major catastrophe to restrict civil liberties and impose a surveillance state in the name of security. In France and Belgium, for example, top government officials have now called for new sweeping security bills, expanding the anti-terrorism budget, new powers for the police, and the use of wiretaps.

Capitalizing on the recent terrorist attacks in Paris in a way that is nothing more than an act of political expediency, John Brennan, the head of the CIA, has now criticized those who had exposed the illegal spying activities of the National Security Agency. *The New York Times* claimed he was using the tragedy in Paris to further his own agenda and had resorted to a "new and disgraceful low." The *Times* also stated that Brennan was, in fact, a certified liar and that it was hard to believe anything he might say. James Comey, the head of the FBI, made a similar case suggesting that the encryption messages used by Apple and Google customers were benefiting terrorists and that these companies should "make it possible for law enforcement to decode encrypted messages."

There is no evidence that the Paris attackers used encryption. While the mainstream media's criticisms of this call for expanded surveillance powers were well placed, they nevertheless failed to report when airing the comments of both Brennan and Comey that the US government was not simply spying on terrorists but on everyone. But there is more at stake here than sacrificing civil liberties in the name of security. In the wake of the Paris attacks, security takes another turn in the direction of practices associated with totalitarian states. We hear it in the words of Nicolas Sarkozy, the former French president, who wants to put Syrian immigrants in detention camps. Marine Le Pen, the leader of France's most popular right-wing party, referred to the new migrants as "bacteria," according to Marina Jimenez writing in *The Star*, and called "for the country to annihilate Islamist fundamentalism, shut down mosques, and expel dangerous 'foreigners' and 'illegal migrants.'"

Intensified Bigotry in the Republican Party

The return to such fascistic language is also evident in the various ways in which the discourse of bigotry has become a major and manipulative tool of politicians in the United States. They empty politics of any viable meaning, substituting in its place an anti-politics that feeds on fear and mobilizes a racist discourse and culture of cruelty. The Republican Party's leading presidential candidates have resorted to racist and politically reactionary comments in the aftermath of the Paris killings that would seem unthinkable in a country that calls itself a democracy.

When asked about Syrian refugees, Ben Carson referred to them as "rabid dogs," as reported by David A. Fahrenthold and Jose A. Del Real in *The Washington Post*. Donald Trump echoed the Nazi practice of registering Jews and forcing them to wear a yellow star when he stated

that, if elected president, he would force all Muslims living in the United States "to register their personal information in a federal database."
He also called for shutting down mosques in the United States. Marco
Rubio, another leading Republican presidential candidate, went even
further, Kay Steiger reports, arguing that he would not only shut down
mosques but would also shut down "any place where radical Muslims
congregate, whether it be a café, a diner, an internet site — any place
where radicals are being inspired."

Carson and Rubio have also called for policies that would eliminate
abortions, even for women whose lives are at risk or who have been
raped. The roots of antidemocratic practices reach, in this case, deeply
into US society. Of course, all of these polices will do nothing more than
legitimate and spread insidious acts of racism and xenophobia as an
acceptable political discourse while normalizing the forces of oppression and violence. How else to explain the rabid racism expressed by
Elaine Morgan, a state senator in Rhode Island, when she stated in an
email that "the Muslim religion and philosophy is to murder, rape, and
decapitate anyone who is a non–Muslim." As Esther Yu-Hsi Lee writes,
Morgan also proposed putting Muslim refugees in "camps."

Intellectual Efforts to Legitimize
Militarism and Racism

Of course, it is not just Carson, Trump, Rubio, and virtually the entire
Republican leadership who trade in warmongering and racism. Bigotry is also to be found in public intellectuals such as Bernard-Henri
Lévy and Niall Ferguson, who provide intellectual legitimacy to the
marriage of militarism and racism. Lévy, a right-wing favorite of the
mainstream media in France and the United States, argues that it is
necessary in the face of the Paris attacks to think the unthinkable,
accept that everyone in the West is a target — allegedly, because of
our freedoms — and, reluctantly, to go to war! For Lévy, caught in his
own fog of historical denial, the greatest failing of the West is Western
leaders' aversion to war; he goes as far as to claim that the aversion to
outright war in these times is democracy's true weakness.

The real weakness is that Lévy finds genuine democracy dangerous
while refusing to recognize the antidemocratic intellectual violence

he practices and supports. Lévy's militarism is matched by the historian Niall Ferguson's contemptuous and despicable claim in a recent *Boston Globe* op-ed. Channeling Edward Gibbon, he claims that the Syrian refugees are similar to the barbaric hordes that contributed to the fall of Rome. Unapologetically, he offers a disingenuous humanitarian qualification before invoking his "war of civilizations" theses. He states the following regarding the Syrian refugees:

> To be sure, most have come hoping only for a better life. Things in their own countries have become just good enough economically for them to afford to leave and just bad enough politically for them to risk leaving. But they cannot stream northward and westward without some of that political malaise coming along with them. As Gibbon saw, convinced monotheists pose a grave threat to a secular empire.

Ferguson also calls Western countries weak and decadent for opening their gates to outsiders. Effectively inverting the humanitarian mantra of saving strangers, these types of comments reinforce a vision of a deeply divided world, demanding continued militarism and the insatiable call for war. Devoid of political imagination, such an analysis refuses to address the violence, misery, suffering, and despair that, in fact, create the conditions that produce terrorists in the first place.

To End the Violence, We Must Eliminate Militarism

Eliminating ISIS means eradicating the conditions that created it. This suggests producing a political settlement in Syria, stabilizing the Middle East, and ending Western support for the various antidemocratic and dictatorial regimes it supports throughout the Middle East and around the world. One obvious step would be for the West to stop supporting and arming the ruthless dictators of Saudi Arabia and others who have been linked to providing financial support to terrorist groups all over the globe. It also demands understanding how the "War on Terror" is, in reality, a war on youth who are both its target and the vehicle for targeting others. Zygmunt Bauman's metaphor "Generation Zero" thus becomes more than an indication of the nihilism of the times. It becomes the clearest discursive framing as "0" symbolizes those who are targeted based on their hopes and future aspirations.

The forms of violence we witness today are not only an attack on the present; these forms of violence also point to an assault on an imagined and hopeful future. As a result, youth connect directly to the age of catastrophe — its multiple forms of endangerment, the normalization of terror, and the production of catastrophic futures. Vagaries in the state of war cannot only be understood by reference to juxtaposed temporalities — present horror as distinct from past horror or anticipated horrors to come. Rather, they must be addressed in terms of their projects and projections, their attempts to colonize and, failing that, eradicate any vestiges of the radical imagination. War is both an act of concrete violence and a disimagination machine; that is why the present landscape is already littered with corpses of the victims of the violence to come. The cycle of violence already condemns us to walk among the ruins of the future.

We must also not forget the plight of the refugees who are caught in the strategic crossfires. As usual, it's those who are the most vulnerable who become the scapegoats for calculated misdirection. The refugee crisis must be resolved not by simply calling for open borders, however laudable, but by making the countries that the refugees are fleeing from free from war and violence. We must eliminate militarism, encourage genuine political transformation, end neoliberal austerity policies, redistribute wealth globally, and stop the widespread discrimination against Muslim youth. Only then can history be steered in a different direction. There will be no havens anywhere in the world until the militaristic, impoverished, and violent conditions that humiliate and oppress young people are addressed. As Robert Fisk writes with an acute eye on new radically interconnected and violently contoured geographies of our times:

> Our own shock — indeed, our indignation — that our own precious borders were not respected by these largely Muslim armies of the poor was in sharp contrast to our own blithe non-observance of Arab frontiers ... Quite apart from our mournful Afghan adventure and our utterly illegal 2003 invasion of Iraq, our aircraft have been bombing Libya, Iraq, and Syria along with the aircraft of various local pseudo-democracies for so long that this state of affairs has become

routine, almost normal, scarcely worthy of a front-page headline ... The point, of course, is that we had grown so used to attacking Arab lands — France had become so inured to sending its soldiers and air crews to Africa and the Middle East to shoot and bomb those whom it regarded as its ene- mies — that only when Muslims began attacking our capital cities did we suddenly announce that we were "at war."

A global system that inflicts violence on young people all over the world cannot be supported. As Michael Lerner has argued, not only must the iniquitous and dangerous structural conditions for econom- ic, political, and cultural violence be eliminated, but the subjective and psychological underpinnings of a hateful fundamentalism must also be addressed and challenged through a public pedagogy that emphasizes an ethos of trust, compassion, care, solidarity, and jus- tice — the opposite of the self-serving, survival-of-the-fittest ethos that now dominates the political landscape.

Young people cannot inherit a future marked by fear, militarism, and suicide bombers — cannot inherit a world in which the very idea of democracy has been emptied of any substantive meaning. Or if they do, then the destructive forces of nihilism and resentment will have truly won the political argument. Creating alternative futures requires serious and sustained investment in attesting to the cycle of violence and imagining better futures and styles for living among the world of peoples. It is to destroy the image of a violently fated world we have created for ourselves by taking pedagogy and education seriously, harnessing the power of imagination, and equipping global youth with the confidence that the world can be transformed for the better.

Originally published in somewhat different form in TruthOut.

Can We Leave the Atrocity Exhibition?

Brad Evans

Thursday, 23 March 2017

WRITING WITH CONSIDERABLE FORESIGHT, the author J. G. Ballard coined the term "The Atrocity Exhibition" to emphasize the changing influence the media was having on all human relations, especially the ethical challenges faced when witnessing tragedy. As Ballard famously wrote:

> The media landscape of the present day is a map in search of a territory. A huge volume of sensational and often toxic imagery inundates our minds, much of it fictional in content. How do we make sense of this ceaseless flow of advertising and publicity, news and entertainment, where presidential campaigns and moon voyages are presented in terms indistinguishable from the launch of a new candy bar or deodorant? What actually happens on the level of our unconscious minds when, within minutes on the same TV screen, a prime minister is assassinated, an actress makes love, an injured child is carried from a car crash? Faced with these charged events, prepackaged emotions already in place, we can only stitch together a set of emergency scenarios, just as our sleeping minds extemporize a narrative from the unrelated memories that veer through the cortical night.

Contemporary life is largely shaped by the digitalization of such atrocities, which now exhibit in real time a continuous stream of violent occurrences directly into the palms of our hands. This is how many of us have come to see and relate to the world. Consciousness itself is now atrocious.

Turned into producers of content and forced witnesses to human suffering on a daily basis, our sleeping minds are often violently interrupted as if we are continuously playing out the awakening scene from Hitchcock's *Vertigo*. We awake from nightmares, night after night, only to realize that nightmare *is* the present condition.

I am writing this in the cold light of morning following more violence on the streets of London yesterday. Once again, it seems, we are shown the willful disregard some have for the basic value of human life. For British Prime Minister Theresa May, this was not simply an act of psychopathic disregard for the suffering of others. She described the "lone wolf" attack as a strike against "the heart of our capital city where people of all nationalities, religions, and cultures come together to celebrate the values of liberty, democracy, and freedom of speech."

Reiterating how "these streets of Westminster," which, "home to the world's oldest parliament, are ingrained with a spirit of freedom that echoes in some of the furthest corners of the globe," May insisted that the voices of hatred and evil would not succeed in driving people apart.

But isn't that exactly what the politics of fear achieves? It not only creates all-too-real divisions between humans based on the fearful suspicion of others but also co-opts us all into its logics whose visceral effects are palpable. The politics of fear makes us play its game even if we are already exhausted.

Terror is not the fear of the unknown. It is borne of the fear of things ordinarily taken for granted. It is located in the weaponization of the everyday. And as a result, it sends everything into flux, for nothing holds certainty anymore. Neighbors become potential enemies. Zones of safety are filled with anxiety. Automobiles are turned into weapons of destruction.

Terror is also imagined. That is not to say it is somehow unreal. On the contrary, it is viscerally felt in the hearts and minds of people often far away from the event itself. Everyday terrors are, in fact, played out in the minds of watching citizens who change their behaviors as a result, thereby eviscerating the very notion of being some innocent bystander.

But if we know that terror reinforces a politics of fear — co-opting us all into its violent logics, which in turn often leads to further violence and retribution — might we not ask of our own culpabilities in perpetuating its fearful imaginary?

Where is the door actually located so that we might leave this Atrocity Exhibition?

I want to turn to the role of the media in all this, for, as Ballard intimated, they are principle narrators in setting out emergency scenarios. The British Broadcasting Corporation (BBC) is significant in this regard, for, despite its claim to political impartiality, in practice, it shows a notable penchant for the sensational in ways that reveal clear formulistic tendencies more often associated with the allegiant right-wing presses.

This is not about laying down definitive truths about such violence. Certainties are, after all, comforting and make people feel secure. Reporting on terror works in accordance to a paradigm that brings every emotion into play, from the extreme to the absurd, the serious to the comic, the exceptional to its veritable normalization.

Let's just take the sequencing of the reporting yesterday from the BBC to get some sense of this.

As the news of some tragedy started to appear on various newsfeeds across social media, the BBC immediately opted to describe the incident as an "attack" even though it could alternately have been read as a tragic "accident" before any of the facts were established. The Metropolitan police subsequently reiterated this pre-factual position. Terror was something that needed *ruling out*. In these terrifyingly normal times, it is the media default for all things atrocious.

What followed was the release of various cell phone videos from people filming whilst fleeing the scene so viewers could actually get a sense of and intimately connect to the panic, confusion, and terror in closer proximity. All this was periodically overlaid with announcements for the public to remain calm and let the security services do their work.

We might argue that, at the level of public consciousness, it doesn't really matter whether the event, in the end, turned out to be intentional or not. It was already framed and registered as yet another chapter in the psychic life of all things terrifying to which we have become accustomed.

Since the event was immediately diagnosed as a terror incident, all too quickly, various sensational superlatives appeared such as "attack on the heart of the capital." The scale of the violence was thus quickly amplified and extended to bring every single resident into the orbit of endangerment. And since the "heart of the capital" is also the heart of the nation, this language implies that nowhere is actually safe from harm.

I am not in any way underplaying here the tragic loss of life and suffering. But one of the first casualties of terror, from both sides, is to deny us any meaningful sense of perspective. Instead of focusing on the local facts on the ground, what followed was the effective trans-historicizing and internationalization of the event as commentators started drawing comparisons to previous atrocities in the capital, such as the coordinated bombings on the British transport system that took place over a decade ago on July 7th, 2005, resulting in 52 fatalities to more comparable events (in respect to the methods used) as witnessed in truck attacks in Nice and Berlin.

Geography, it seems, is secondary in this epic drama of sequential violence.

We know that digital technologies have obliterated the modern time/space continuum. While everything is immanent, thereby denying us any time to reflect, there is no longer any "outside" or place to find refuge. But what we didn't foresee were the ways in which people on the street would feed into the various media machines to reinforce dominant narratives and sensational scripting.

That the public provided the sensational interface between the watching viewers and the scene of the crime further allowed commentators to technologically connect the violence to recent events, like the killing of off-duty British Army soldier Lee Rigby in 2013 by two men who described the killing as retribution for the killing of Muslims by the British armed forces. This was brought up in a number of the commentaries, showing how the technological nature of the spectacle of violence is also capable of flattening, or perhaps even completely circumventing, what might be seen as more tenuous linkages.

It didn't take too long, however, before just a little comedy started to surreptitiously enter the discursive arena. No sooner had Londoners and the nation been put into a heightened state of insecurity consciousness, the BBC informed us that "MPs are locked in the Chamber" of Parliament: a message that could be taken either with extreme seriousness or a certain hilarity depending on your political disposition.

What followed were a series of mixed messages whose differing tonalities only added to the blurring between the serious and the absurd for any slightly informed and politically cognizant listener. These ranged from the assertive declaration that "Theresa May is safe" (spoken in a way which suggested civilization depended on it); to a more conciliatory indication "Donald Trump is being kept informed" (okay, perhaps you should be slightly worried about this development); onto "President Trump had now spoken with Theresa May," without any further details or content provided on the nature of this conversation. (One could only assume that we should keep an eye on Trump's Twitter feed for full details.)

Throughout the day, various terrorist "experts" were summoned to add clarity to the background noise of sirens and flashing lights. As we were presented with images of bodies on the ground, so the mantra about this being a "sophisticated and coordinated attack" was repeated to the point of monotony. One is left to wonder what exactly is sophisticated about someone plowing an automobile into a group of innocent bystanders?

Shutting down the digital infrastructure that powers the City of London would be sophisticated. What we witnessed on Wednesday was not.

Violated bodies are always overlaid with overtly politicized discursive ascriptions. That the term "catastrophic" was used to describe the injuries sustained by the survivors was not incidental. Ours is an age of catastrophe wherein the dominant political imaginary is one of "dystopian realism." There is always another inescapable catastrophe, in waiting, on the fateful horizon of future possibility.

As the day moved on, the line of questioning invariably turned towards asking how such an event could possibly happen. Commentators were drawn to ask about all the investment in counterterror strategies such as the official Prevent doctrine. Talking heads like Michael Clarke of the Royal United Services Institute appeared to remind us this was the attack the experts had actually been expecting. Despite all the preventative strategies, what we must accept is that our societies are fundamentally insecure by design.

The official government line reiterated by the media is to tell us — the population — that we must remain "vigilant" in this heightened state of emergency. But how is one expected to be vigilant when the source of the terror is ubiquitous? One cannot possibly be vigilant against something that appears to come out of nowhere and yet potentially resides everywhere in the fabric of a vibrant city.

What takes its place is a general state of anxiety and inertia borne of the mutually assured sense of vulnerability. All of this ultimately plays into the hands of the "alt-right," whose allegiances blend Huntington's *Clash of Civilizations*, white supremacy, Islamophobia, and anti-Semitism with a general desire for political stardom by those seeking to fill the void left by the fallen Milo Yiannopoulos.

As the evening wore on, the BBC's flagship evening news broadcast program, *Newsnight*, turned into a special edition dedicated to the day's atrocities. Here, we encountered a heady mix of reinforcing narratives, which went from emphasizing the "exceptional" nature of the violence to enumerating the ways our society needs to come to terms with this as part of the "normalized" fabric of unending threats in these dangerously uncertain times.

This only adds to the confusion as the exceptional and the normal, the friend and the enemy, the secure and the insecure, and truth and fiction blur into what the Italian philosopher Giorgio Agamben has termed a "zone of indistinction." Nothing upon this terrain can be located with any certainty.

It was left to the columnist and writer Simon Jenkins to provide a rare voice of reason. Lambasting the BBC on its *Newsnight* program, Jenkins took direct aim at the levels of coverage and prominence being afforded, which he explained was culpable of "aiding and abetting" extremism. The politically ill-equipped presenter, Evan Davis, was left to defend a decision from a position of evident bodily discomfort. Not even he seemed to believe it when questioned.

And so, as I now sit here, staring into the screen of my handheld device, I find myself scrolling through the various news items the BBC news site has to offer. None of them seem to offer any indication about how we might actually break the cycle of violence. The doors to this Atrocity Exhibition seem to be closed; they just forgot to let everybody out beforehand.

My suspicion is that the answers are to be found behind a different door in another venue.

Originally published in somewhat different form in TruthOut.

Remembering the 43

Brad Evans

Saturday, 9 September 2017

IT'S NEARLY THREE YEARS since the fateful attacks upon college students in Iguala, Guerrero state, Mexico. Following a coordinated assault by unidentified gunmen upon five coaches, the violence left six dead, 40 wounded, and 43 forcibly disappeared. Their whereabouts still remains unknown; but with each passing day and the continual finding of mass graves in the region, most inevitably fear the worst for the innocent young men from Raúl Isidro Burgos Rural Teachers' College in Ayotzinapa, Guerrero. And so, as mothers, fathers, brothers, sisters, friends, and loved ones continue to live in a cruel limbo of hope and despair, it is important we remember the "43" and, in the fight for justice and all-too-human dignity, ask searching questions in their names.

Despite my historical interest in the region, like many academics, I first became aware of this event following an email circular from one of my Mexican students. It was a powerful call for solidarity yet written with an emotional desperation and urgency coming from the heart. It was full of typos and often capitalized, no doubt, as it was hastily put together through a stream of tears. And yet, the day after the occurrence, despite what we might have expected to be global outrage and condemnation, the incident was notably absent from mainstream media headlines. This must have only added to the sense of helplessness. The United Kingdom, in particular, was more interested in the launch of airstrikes and the legitimated use of violence in new offensive against ISIS in Iraq, along with the glitzy wedding of George and

Amal Clooney in Venice, and Chelsea giving birth to the next in the Clinton dynasty.

The fact the victims of this horrifying event were students immediately resonated. Those who endured what *The New York Times* called a "night of terror" were most likely full of the same radical idealism — that the world could be changed for the better — as the students I have the privilege of speaking and debating with on a daily basis. This was Saturday. On Monday, the voices of the disappeared appeared to me in the presence of the students waiting for me to give my first lecture of the new semester on the theme "What is Political Violence"? I briefly mention this to suggest relationship between political and personal stakes. The study of violence, for me, has never been about abstract theorizing. It must begin with the raw realities of suffering.

I was outraged, angry, and deeply saddened by this incident in Guerrero. Maybe it was because I could find some relationship in the eyes of my new cohort of students. Trying to compose myself, I simply asked my students to reflect upon the fact that, for many people outside of zones of relative affluence, politics truly is a matter of life and death. I was thinking at that moment about the harrowing fate of Julio Cesar Mondragon, whose tortured and dumped body was found like a throwaway object the morning after the attacks. His facial skin and muscles were torn from his fractured skull and his internal organs severely ruptured. There were ineluctable limits to what I could achieve in this moment. How could I possibly do justice to this ongoing atrocity in the safety of a classroom environment, trying to get students to emphasize and relate to those students born in a different part of the world — students who were visible in our thoughts and hopes only due to their murder and absence and the "mystery" that surrounded their fate?

Critical narratives that followed invariably focused on state corruption, the influence and power of narco-trafficking in one of Mexico's poorest and most violent states, how local elected leaders operated like mafia captains by controlling their fiefdoms through violence and intimidation with the help of the state apparatus, the blurred lines between the authorities of the state and private guns for hire revealing the complicated lines between official law enforcement and violence of a more clandestine and extrajudicial nature. This is not a bad place to start. Such developments are important in terms of identifying responsibility and holding people to account for their actions. Nor would I wish to cast doubt on the fact that some state authorities have consciously tried to do everything possible to hide the truth of what happened. I have nothing but admiration for those family members, journalists, human rights advocates, and activists who insist upon finding out the truth of what happened. Without these continued efforts, nothing can possibly change.

There is also one more important qualification to mention here. I do not claim to be an "expert" in Mexican politics, even though I have spent some time in the country and have taken a vested interest in its revolutionary movements. It is not my place to speak on behalf of Mexicans about their struggles and demands for justice. There are many brilliant authors from that country already doing tireless work in ways far exceeding my capacities, so to do so would also be disingenuous. As an educator on violence, invariably influenced by Mexican students and friends, my concern is to try to ask alternative political and philosophical questions about the nature of the violence without appropriating the victims or generalizing the real horror of the atrocity.

But I am not only a political philosopher who has spent far too long reading about the worst of the human condition. I am a father and concerned citizen of the world. And while I am admittedly overprotective of my daughter, I would still hope to instill in her the ideas and ethical beliefs that it is important to stand up for deeply held principles, it is dignified to fight against injustice, it is honorable to put the plight of others ahead of yourself, and it is important to recognize the rights and equality of all the world's peoples — the very ideas the students of Ayotzinapa paid the ultimate price for with their lives.

So, how can we begin to do justice to the memory of the "43" on the third anniversary of their absence? I would like to begin by dealing with the question of memorialization. We know a sinister hallmark of all great tyrannies is what Henry A. Giroux calls the "violence of organized forgetting." Disappearance is the most potent and devastating example of this as it quite literally denies access to the truth. And yet, politics is all about a battle for memory. This especially includes open contestation concerning truths about the violence of the past. Such memories do not exist in time capsules neatly placed in some historical archive. The way we narrate the past is integral to how we imagine the present and how we come to perceive the future. But how do we memorialize the tragic loss of lives, which are now absent? How can we resurrect the memory of a life that has vanished without a trace?

Memorialization takes many different forms. It is a complex question and open to various interpretations. Indeed, unlike the familiar memorialization of military generals and political elites, who are often immortalized in cast iron form across the capital cities of the world, the memorialization of the expendable, the downtrodden, and historically forgotten necessarily requires a more human form. It is often family and friends who bring their otherwise absent loved one back to life through candlelight vigils and intimate stories about their lives, idiosyncrasies, hopes, and brutally shattered dreams. There is a human dimension to memorialization, which speaks to the human in all of us. And so, the human in all of us should be compelled to listen.

Absent any public recognition of the importance of the disappeared lives, it is common to try to coalesce and mobilize around alternative symbols, which can focus the attention. Often, we see this in the form of a numerical symbolism — "43" — as if to both emphasize the scale of the atrocity and serve as a potent symbolic reminder. But such numerical concentration also has its limitations; namely, it can lead to some of the most remiss comparisons (as in the work of Steven Pinker) between different atrocities as the quantitative number of victims becomes more important than the uniqueness of each horrifying act. It is all too easy to lose sight of the fact that we are not just dealing with 43 victims. What happened in Iguala was the violation and wanton destruction of a wonderful life full of promise and ambition, 43 times over, as well as the other six people who died that night.

Another question we need to invariably ask concerns global media interest — or lack of it — when dealing with these disappeared students. Again, this is not incidental. While the impact of media events has a significant political bearing in terms of influencing the demands for justice and political response, it also reveals the politics of disposability and the ways some lives are seen as more valuable — hence more worthy of living — than others. As I was delivering the lecture to my students on that Monday afternoon, I couldn't help imagining how differently they might have reacted if I was discussing a violent and forced disappearance of British or American students. This is not a commentary on the levels of compassion, dignity, and empathy many of my students showed when hearing about the atrocity. It is simply to acknowledge much broader questions of power when it comes to the politics of mourning and who gets to have what Judith Butler calls a "grievable life."

For Butler, to ask the question of what lives are publicly grieved is to also ask about the importance and value attributed to a life. Grief or its denial is, therefore, a political act, which opens us to various hierarchies of suffering. Furthermore, it is a point of entry into the logics of power as it exposes more fully what a society is willing to protect at all costs against those elements of society, which, as we know in this case, can vanish without any consequence. The Ayotzinapa students were already inserted into a diminished hierarchy of importance within a country that should have been nurturing their potential instead of seeing them as something altogether meaningless. Within global power structures built upon the colonial architectures of which Mexico has historically been an integral part, their relative value in relation to the white Anglo-Saxon of European descent is painfully reductive.

Defenders of the corporate media might argue the reason why such violence doesn't register is due to its unexceptional and all-too-familiar frequency of its occurrence. As Eduardo Galeano pointed out, Latin America is so soaked in the blood of history it even looks like an ailing and weeping heart on a map. The media certainly has a fixation with what is deemed to be the exceptional, and it took this mass disappearance to be unexceptional. What passes for the exceptional often revels in a certain fetishized aesthetics with the spectacular — images of exploding towers capture the attention, but disappeared bodies are less compatible with the format of "image conscious" societies. It seems we would rather confront the realism of the spectacle, which also removes the body from actual depictions of violence, than dwell on the horrors of a problem that demands more sustained reflection.

But there are a number of points that we do need to address here. What passes for an "exceptional" event is filtered through racialized filters. Now, of course, some events are so spectacular they cannot possibly be ignored. Nevertheless, the media can often take two very comparable events in terms of aesthetic qualities and the scale of its devastation (often of a lesser scale in terms of "our" relatable suffering) and mediate its importance. The media works with its culture's calculus of disposability.

This is why the notion of the exception is so dubious. From the perspective of the victims, Ayotzinapa was a truly exceptional and unique event — even in a state in which violence has become normalized. Hence, the reduction of this event to the vocabulary of the normal is also part of a politics of memorialization and its hierarchies of grief. After all, it is far more difficult to critique something that appears to be normal than exceptional.

History teaches us time and time again that political violence is not simply carried out by irrational monsters. It is very often rationalized, reasoned, and calculated. It is also purely subjective. I am not simply referring to the fact that some forms of violence are seen as necessary or righteous while others are found truly abhorrent, intolerable, or the personification of evil. Violence is all about inscribing itself upon the desecrated body markers of identity. The subject of violence in the act of violation cuts away at the existing qualities of a life in order to undermine and negate its very existence. So, what were the subjective dimensions to the violence in Ayotzinapa? What, in other words, was put on trial, found guilty, and executed without any concern for the rights, dignity, or value of those lives?

We know rural colleges in Mexico have a long history of radical political activism and socialist sympathies. The temerity to question can often be the source of a great deal of endangerment, which reveals something about the logics of violence. Violence is not the excessive abuse of power. Violence occurs when power is impotent. The recourse to violence shows the persecutor can no longer rely upon the power of ideas and the possibility of their persuasion. Those armed with historical memory thus become dangerous because they offer sustained reflection on the abuse of power along with memories of resistance, collective struggles, and a legacy of troubling knowledge. They carry the education that is crucial to any viable notion of justice and peaceful cohabitation. The conscious targeting of students is, therefore, precisely an assault on the very idea that society should be actively producing critically informed subjects who, having the confidence to question authority, represent a beacon of hope in a situation that appears naturally fated.

Given the importance and centrality of the subjective dimensions to violence, what follows is the inevitable "character assassination" of the victims. This represents a double wounding of their existence. For if they are to be remembered, they must reappear as recalcitrant even though they are now unable to defend themselves. In other words, the victims must share some responsibility and partial guilt for the violence that inexorably finds them. Their activism is recast as the original confrontational moment that leads to the violence that follows. Such claims are often banal, as in the case of the students of Ayotzinapa and the alleged issue of stealing local buses for a trip to Mexico City — a student tradition of many years tolerated by local authorities. Had they not followed this ritualistic tradition, none of this would have happened! We know such claims are preposterous. You do not take the decision to willfully slaughter so many lives in such a calculated and organized way on account of some minor felony. Violence didn't simply find them. It sought them out and executed its plans.

It is often tempting to make comparisons with different forms of violence in order to try and identify logical commonalities and similarities in their performativity. While it is important to insist upon the uniqueness of each atrocity committed so that we don't fall into the dubious ethical quagmire of gauging acts of violence of more or lesser importance (i.e., each should be condemned on its own terms), there is nevertheless the need to situate all violence in a broader historical and systemic context. Very little violence is randomly carried out. It is part of a longer historical process, which reaches into the depths of radicalized and class-based forms of oppression and persecution. All political violence has a historical temporality that needs to be acknowledged.

But such temporalities are also politically fraught and subject to interpretation. How far back in history, for instance, do we begin to date the assault? Do we go back to recent history, or should we demand a broader, even colonial, assessment? Often, what stands out here are important historical events, which are fully loaded with their own symbolic memory and resonance. That the students were planning a trip to Mexico City to mark the anniversary of the Tlatelolco Massacre in which a large number of students were also killed by the state has evident, if tragic, poignancy in this case. "68" holds special meaning in the calendar of radical politics. Aside from the student massacre during the increasingly corporatized Olympic Games of 1968, the year also witnessed the assassination of Martin Luther King Jr.; the brutalities of the Tet offensive in Vietnam that resulted in serious self-reflection about the imperialism of the West; along with widespread protests in Paris and on many university campuses, such as Columbia University and the University of California, Berkeley. Hence, to connect to "68" is not simply about paying respects to other groups of fallen idealists who put their bodies on the lines. It is also to connect with a global spirit of revolution and the possibility of challenging inequality and injustice, both in Mexico and elsewhere.

There is something truly terrifying about the act of disappearance. Such abductions are not in any way new and have often been favored by authoritarian regimes, notably by military juntas and their paramilitary attachés in Latin America. But it is wrong to see the act of disappearance as some anti-spectacle or even as a form of violence devoid of communication. The spectacle of potential absence is projected onto the bodies of the living — those who now live in fear of their lives — just as the message speaks in a haunting language through their silent screams, which can be deafening. That anybody could disappear at any given moment just for believing in a certain set of principles, for reading troublesome books, or even just for having a friendly relationship with somebody who happens to be politically active, points to a genuine ecology of violence — a true climate of fear — which is both physically real and has a life independent of its actual occurrence. The act of disappearance takes us into the realm of the unknown: a mental space of anguish, torment, and imagined possibilities. It is part of the psychic life of violence, which turns imagination into an enemy of the self.

This is why disappearance is much more than simply the denial of a person's right to be on the earth. The memory that such people once walked amongst us serves as a warning to others they might suffer a similar fate and be forgotten without a trace. It is, therefore, not only the denial of life but also an assault on the very idea that a meaningful life, no matter how foreshortened, will at least find dignity in death. Disappearance, then, is a form of violence against the future. It immobilizes. Through the negation of life, it openly recruits the haunting memory of ghosts in order to impose a tyranny over the will of the living. And in doing so, the bodies of the disappeared reappear in the very act of denial, in miscommunications, in a sense of injustice, and in the contraction of some nightmare resolution that, eventually, the remains might at least be located.

So where does this leave us? Countering all forms of political violence demands both short-term action in terms of establishing responsibility and longer-term processes of instigating genuine political transformation. Short-term strategies must focus on bringing the perpetrators of this crime against humanity to justice. It is important that people are held accountable for their actions, and the violence must be condemned internationally in the strongest terms. But for the longer term, there are no simple solutions to the complexities of systemic violence whose tangled global lines connect to histories of political persecution and histories of violence. This is not a problem that can be "solved" by any single individual. It demands a new, radical conception of justice, which is not simply about bringing perpetrators of the most heinous crimes to account. It is about engaging in a shared conversation at local and global levels so the question of justice is realized in the dignity afforded to every human life. Such a call is not about doing away with the raw emotions many still feel. It is, however, to ensure that such anger, outrage, sadness, and despair becomes the catalyst for at least de-escalating the cycle of violence and steering history in a different direction.

I cannot possibly imagine what it must be like to go to bed every evening and wake every morning wondering what happened to your child, whose only crime was to believe in a better future. It must be all-consuming and the pain beyond comprehension to anyone who has been lucky enough not to live with such a loss. How do you even begin to cope when turning on the television or opening the daily newspaper, deeply conflicted by the wish to find the missing so a serious investigation can finally begin, all the while knowing that well-meaning claims about the need for closure will never bring any comfort or happiness? If solidarity means anything, surely it is for others to carry some of this burden and take up what must be a truly exhausting fight?

I'd like to conclude by offering a personal reflection on the problems faced when writing about such atrocities. I sent an earlier draft of this essay to someone born and living in Mexico whose opinion I deeply respect. While they were appreciative of the fact I had decided to write this piece and show my solidarity, they were nevertheless critical of its focus and direction. Such criticisms were not about what the essay actually said, which they largely agreed with; rather, they were concerned with what was being left out of the narrative. There is just as much to learn from the unsaid as there is the spoken word. Initially taken aback, what they were invariably asking me to consider was my own privileged status and relative comforts and the security from which I could engage. I cannot deny any of this. But rather than focus on the way they politely highlighted "limitations of the narrative," what I have further come to realize in dealing with these critiques, is that such limits are ultimately self-imposed. Or, to put it another way, instead of talking about permissible boundaries and restrictions in which we necessary operate, there is always a need to be mindful of our own shameful compromises with power, which can diminish the message we seek to communicate. The violence suffered by the 43 shames us all. And since they cannot speak, it is up to us to give them some voice, to hear their silent cries, to demand justice in their name, and to insist upon the need for a new radical imagination. This is not simply about pushing back against forces of injustice. It is to break out from the image of the world that continuously annihilates human lives.

Originally published in somewhat different form in BLARB, *the blog of the* Los Angeles Review of Books.

An Open Letter to Mara Fernanda Castilla

Brad Evans

Friday, 22 September 2017

Dear Mara Fernanda Castilla:

I have just read about your story, and, once again, I feel the shame of being a man. I never met you; nor will we ever meet in this lifetime. Like too many young women, your life was tragically and brutally cut short. As a father of a young girl, I cannot possibly imagine what your parents are living through at this moment. I just hope they find some solace and comfort in the solidarity the brave women of your country are showing right now, marching and demanding justice in your name.

I want to be honest with you. I feel our global society (if such a thing exists) owes you honesty. I only became aware of your disappearance and death as a result of the social media feed of a Mexican friend. I then wanted to learn more and found a few media reports, though in the United Kingdom these were relatively thin. I was tempted to say you shouldn't take this personally, but in truth, it's as personal as it gets. Violence against women is often hidden away, and the "center" ignores the "periphery."

As I read the reports, I was horrified to be confronted by the statistics. In your country alone, five women are killed every single day, and over 60 percent of women and girls over the age of 15 suffer some form of physical violence and abuse. I have no words for this epidemic. Except to say, of course, your life was always more than a statistical measure. You know that, and your loved ones know it. My media doesn't seem to know it, and I promise not to forget it.

You were a student with an interest in political science, and I teach politics at a university. At 19, you probably had the same enthusiasm and passion for life as the students now starting a new term here. The man who felt he had the right to take away your right to exist stole yet another life of promise and ambition. It didn't matter to him what you could have, would have become.

I lived in Puebla for a time. I remember that, before I visited, I heard about the nation's problems, its violence, the narco-trafficking and the need to be "vigilant." Yet, as a white male, I must admit I found the place that took away your life, the place you called "home," completely safe. Then again, the realities of safety are always dependent upon the bodies we occupy.

I also have a confession to make. As an author, I often write about the worst of the human condition. I can, therefore, also become too often fixated on exceptional violence. And even while I wrote a piece about the 43 missing students in your country recently, I have never written specifically about the problem of femicide. This has been a profound failure on my part.

Latin America's "machismo" culture is too easy an explanation for what happened to you. Aeschylus's *Oresteia* tells the story of King Agamemnon who, in order to appease the gods, needed to sacrifice his innocent daughter, Iphigenia. It's a metaphor really, but the tenor and the vehicle are one. The history of the human condition is one of men destroying the lives of innocent women.

I am not exactly running out of words to say — I could write books about this — but I am feeling in this moment how badly my words are falling short, how they could never do justice to your memory.

So, I would like to part by offering my heart-felt apology — not just on behalf of every man who thinks it's acceptable to denigrate, humiliate, and violate the body of any single woman. I would like to apologize not just for every man who has compensated for their own inadequacies by taking away the lives of innocent young girls, as that man did yours. I would like to apologize not just for every man who thinks women are some sexual and disposable object for their own deluded pleasures. I would like to apologize for my own shameful compromises with local and global systems of power, my own blindness — blindness which has continued to recreate gendered violence on a daily basis across the world.

It is my sincere hope you find some rest in peace,

Brad Evans

Originally published in somewhat different form in BLARB, *the blog of the* Los Angeles Review of Books.

Old pains, New Demons:
Critical Insights into Torture and Dignity

Brad Evans interviewed for the
International Committee of the Red Cross

Friday, 7 July 2017

RED CROSS: In your work, you have highlighted how public attitudes and discourses about violence have shifted since 9/11 with violence being increasingly accepted as a legitimate means to pursue national security goals. The ICRC has also recently highlighted people's general increased acceptance of torture. How, in your view, should humanitarian organizations respond to this?

BRAD EVANS: We need to begin by recognizing that violence is not some abstract concept or theoretical problem. It represents a violation in the very conditions that constitute what it means to be human as such. Violence is always an attack upon a person's dignity, their sense of selfhood, and their future. It is nothing less than the desecration of one's position in the world. It is a denial and outright assault on the very qualities that we claim make us considered members of this social fellowship and shared union called "civilization." Violence is both an ontological crime, insomuch as it seeks to destroy the image we give to ourselves as valued individuals, and a form of political ruination, which stabs at the heart of the human togetherness that emerges from the ethical desire for worldly belonging.

What defines the human condition is not simply that we live with a capacity to be wounded. We also have the capacity to think and imagine better worlds. So, this is what is really at stake here. To accept violence is to normalize the wounds that tear apart the bodies of the living. That is why violence — especially torture — is so pernicious as it becomes justified and more socially accepted. Through the subtle intimacy of its performance, it brings everything into its orbit such that the future can only appear to us as something that is violently fated. Every scar left upon the body of the individual is another cut into the flesh of the earth.

But the temporality of violence works in another direction, one that is just as insidious and intellectually colonizing. Not only does violence beget violence continuously, endlessly. As we also know, the memory of violence can have such a hold over us that the ways we come to read the past are filtered through the most brutal lens. The very concept "humanity" is subject to this historical assay. While the term has a complex and politically fraught history, we know that it really becomes significant after the horrors of World War II, especially when confronting the reality of the Holocaust. Humanity, in this regard, emerges as an ethical and juridical problem out of the realization of the very worst that humans were capable of doing to one another. Organizations such as ICRC thus respond to this reality — a reality where humanity itself is always figured or embodied as a violated and historically persecuted form.

This should raise profound questions for us, both in terms of dealing with the torturous legacy of human affliction and the continued capacity for us to violate the bodies of others; alongside the way we are to respond to these tragic conditions so that we might rethink the very concept of humanity in more affirmative, spiritual, and dignified terms.

RED CROSS: You also stress that, in contemporary society, many phenomena — from popular culture to the representation of terrorist groups and the ongoing terror wars in mass media — can desensitize people to violence. The spectacle of violence and torture has become banal. Are people becoming immune to the horrors of this world?

BRAD EVANS: In order for violence to be accepted, there is a need for normalization. Such normalization depends upon immunization, like a surgical strike penetrating the body with such ruthless efficiency we no longer see it as being violent. While we might see the cruelty as something painful, we can reason beyond this — hence, beyond the violence itself — for some greater political good. The violence, in this regard, is overlaid with a certain metaphysical cloak whose mask of mastery veils the desecrated body with a virtuous blood soaked robe.

But we also know that violence is always mediated by specific dichotomies of permissible and impermissible actions. Some forms of violence, as in the case of "collateral damage," can be fully rationalized while others clearly go beyond the tolerance threshold.

Let's connect this directly to the problem of torture. We have witnessed since 9/11 a notable public shift in the modalities of violence from spectacular attacks (in which humans were often removed from representations of the crimes) towards violence that is more intimate and individualizing. Such violence seems to actually be more intolerable for us as the intimacy works on a different register. While both are abhorrent, images of exploding towers are arguably easier to deal with than the more focused types of suffering we now witness from digitalized recordings of sacrificial terrorist violence to little children washed up on the shores of the Mediterranean or images of Abu Ghraib. There is something about the raw realities of intimate suffering which affects us on an all-too-human level.

Now, it is, of course, clear that such intimacy has also fed into (and in many ways been reinforced by) the pornographic violence of popular culture. Movie franchises and video games in particular excel in using the intimate realities of violence for entertainment value alone. It is also the case that our societies are so overwhelmed by images of suffering it's as if we are continuously walking through an interactive version of what the author J. G. Ballard called "The Atrocity Exhibition."

And yet, I think it would be far too reductive to say that people are simply immune to such violence. The fact that people may turn away from the violence or try to switch it off is arguably an all-too-natural reaction to its forced witnessing. Violence should be intolerable. What I think is more a problem is how to find meaningful solutions to the raw realities of violence that don't simply end up creating more anger, hatred, and division. People are certainly frustrated that the daily exposure to violence doesn't become a catalyst to steer history in a more peaceful direction.

RED CROSS: Conflicts around the world are changing and evolving. There is an undeniable global component, which we can see clearly in recent attacks claimed by ISIS. Conflict is no longer contained in the war zones where the ICRC is working but spilling over in cities around the world. What does this mean for the laws of war, and how can the ICRC respond to this spilling over of violence?

BRAD EVANS: I have always been skeptical of the term "laws of war" as the victors always write such laws. What I think is a more appropriate phrase is the "wars of law," which not only end up recreating global relations of power, but also, in the process, continue to mark out justifiable versus unjustifiable or tolerable versus intolerable forms of violence. Hence violence that is waged by high-tech smart weaponry is somehow legitimized whereas other forms of violence are deemed barbaric or pure evil. Does that mean we shouldn't see war as a criminal problem? Absolutely not! But we need to have a better ethical approach prior to any legalistic framing of war and its consequences.

Now, in terms of the changing conduct of war, you're correct to point out that everywhere has now become a battlefield. And, as a result, we can no longer make meaningful distinctions between friends and enemies, the inside as a place of sanctuary and the outside as a place of lawlessness, along with the ability to identify times of war from times of peace. We find ourselves engaged in a global civil war, which has become so normalized the very term "war" is no longer even declared. Are we still actually in a war on terror, for example? Politicians no longer feel the need to say it, and yet, nobody has actually declared it to be over. Such a condition cannot be attested by retreating back in some retro-topic way into 20th century paradigms. It demands new global ethical thinking in which organizations such as the ICRC must have a considered and represented voice beyond the juridical pale.

RED CROSS: When it comes to conflict and violence, social media is playing an increasing role in how armed groups or politicians address the world, not to mention on-line bullying and trolling. Violence seems to be going viral. How can society respond to this?

BRAD EVANS: "Going viral," like "immunization," is a term that is evidently fitting when thinking about the human as a mortal and biological form. It speaks directly to what political theorists call biopolitics — namely, the foregrounding of life itself as a political category. When we say something has gone viral, it immediately invokes notions of contagion, which has the capacity to spread throughout the body politic like an infectious disease. Now, one of the defining features of modern life has been the speeding up of all social relations, largely as a result of technological advance. While this is often seen as enabling, it has also had devastating philosophical consequences.

We might think here about the seemingly impossible task of controlling the "outbreak" of various spectacles of violence, which, once released, take on a life of their own such that their affective currency (their emotional impact) far exceeds the nature of the attack. It only takes, for example, the willful killing of a number of individuals today to create the image of a global security crisis of epic proportions. But more important still is how we might proactively respond to these outbreaks. In order to critique the world and think it anew, there is the need for sustained reflection. This is especially the case when it comes to breaking the cycle of violence. Such reflection is denied to us in a world, which demands immediate responses.

So how do we account for this? Too often, we produce technologies before considering their ethical implications. This is the case whether we are talking about the advent of communications technologies that radically alter social relations or the considerable investment that goes into newly designed weapons of war whose violence is claimed to be more "intelligent" and more "surgical" in their targeting of enemy combatants and "collateral," disposable persons. But we cannot focus on regulating the technology alone without asking more pressing questions about the seduction of violence. To my mind, it is less a problem of technological production and its very reductive and rather abject notions of what we mean by "human progress" than broader ethical points regarding the ways humans live with each other on this shared planet. Why, we need to keep asking, do we only seem to respond to suffering once it appears extreme or exceptional?

RED CROSS: What are the new trends in violence today? How can an international humanitarian organization like the ICRC respond to this in your view?

BRAD EVANS: What is troubling in the contemporary moment is the notable liberation of prejudice on all sides. I have already spoken of the advent of the catastrophic individual who is now capable of being the author of widespread devastation and slaughter. We cannot simply deal with this violence by responding to its consequences. What is required, and where the ICRC might make a truly positive intervention, concerns the yet to be answered question about how we begin to educate about violence today with proper ethical care and political consideration for the subject. This requires a sustained global conversation among many actors who know firsthand the realities of violence and the way it truly destroys any humanitarian claims.

RED CROSS: Given the new trends in violence, do you think that humanitarian organizations still have a role to play? What should that be in your opinion?

BRAD EVANS: Education. I am not denying the need for on-the-ground responses to deal with the legacies of war and the individual and social traumas of violence they produce, which undeniably require sustained engagements by multiple professional organizations. This work is important. But unless we start to develop the necessary educational tools, which bring together international organizations, advocates, community leaders, academics, artists and cultural producers, and everyday citizens, then we will continue to see violence justified for the furtherance of political goals.

Originally published in somewhat different form in Humanitarian Law & Policy: International Review of the Red Cross.

A World Without Books

Brad Evans & Phil Treagus

Saturday, 1 July 2017

PHIL TREAGUS: When someone asks you "what do you do for a living?" how do you respond?

BRAD EVANS: My response tends to be along the lines of "a political-philosopher and writer who works on the problem of violence and education," though I often complement this by mentioning my eight-year-old daughter's description who, when once asked what her daddy does for a living, responded, "He's a doctor of violence who makes up words in the hope they make sense." I still can't convince her I didn't invent the term "pedagogy."

PHIL TREAGUS: What are you reading at the moment?

BRAD EVANS: *Sculpting in Time.* It's a remarkable set of reflections by the late Russian film director Andrei Tarkovsky. I have always been completely in awe of his work, especially his ability to disrupt the aesthetic field of perception. It's like he brings the world of Nietzsche to life, and it's beautifully haunting. As the title suggests, Tarkovsky also understood better than anybody the importance of time. Everything, for him, is framed by time — including love, life, and our encounters with death, though not in any reductive chronological sense to which we have become accustomed. Time is differential, which means the experiential nature of life is defined by a more complex understanding of its temporalities. I am also completely taken by his understanding of interpretation. To quote: "A book read by a thousand different people is a thousand different books." I fully agree with this sentiment. Every book needs to live and have the ability to break out of the entrapments of its author.

PHIL TREAGUS: What's your earliest memory of reading?

BRAD EVANS: I recall my parents bought me a collection of stories by Hans Christian Anderson. It had these wonderfully detailed illustrations accompanying many of his classic stories. Though, to be honest, I only used to flick through its pages from time to time. My love for reading didn't really develop until I was about 15 years old. Stephen King's *Salem's Lot* is the book that stands out from this period. Growing up in the isolating former mining valleys of South Wales, it was a book that resonated on so many levels. Indeed, although I had already been scared witless by the movie — the first horror film I watched — especially the scene of the floating child at the window, it was this book that taught me that words on pages are simply a point of entry into the more enriching and sometimes more terrifying life of the mind.

PHIL TREAGUS: If you could encourage young people to read one book in particular, what would it be?

BRAD EVANS: *Alice in Wonderland.* I maintain it is the best book of political theory ever written. Lewis Carroll is such a captivating thinker, and he manages to break down the false and unhelpful binaries that set apart poetic and technical modes of thinking. *Wonderland* is a timeless book; I mean, is there a better character to capture the politics of Trump than the Queen of Hearts — she utters, therefore it's true? The way the book deals with questions of power, arbitrary violence, and the transformation in subjectivities is truly exceptional. Moreover, Carroll allows us to rethink the very terms of resistance and revolution, for what are Alice's greatest weapons, after all, if not the power of her imagination? If we lack resistance to the present, it's precisely because we don't have an alternative vision of the world.

PHIL TREAGUS: What is the worst job you've ever had?

BRAD EVANS: When I was around 16 years old, I worked for four weeks in a factory that built overhead projectors. On a production line, my responsibility was to attach the projector's metal arm to the base, over and over, countless numbers, each day. The only thing that broke the tedium of this mind-numbing task was to either watch the large, slowly moving clock situated on the factory wall (talking about the relativity of time) or to engage in conversation with the worker sat next to me who had been in his position for over a decade. This guy was an avid fan of *Star Trek*, and every five to six minutes, he would turn to me (being the new recruit) and begin "Did you know...," followed by yet another fact about the franchise. By the end, I didn't even respond, although that didn't stop him from carrying on enlightening me with the most random facts about something I'd never actually watched. I don't regret the experience. It was one of the catalysts in my decision to go into education.

PHIL TREAGUS: Do you read as much as you'd like to?

BRAD EVANS: One of the tragedies of modern life has been the veritable speeding up of all aspects of our existence. The problem, for me, is less about the volume of books or articles we can read but more about the time to reflect. Having the ability to positively critique the present in a meaningful and considered way demands a slowing down and not speeding up of our reflective engagements with the various knowledge-based productions — especially intellectually challenging books — we encounter. So, as with all aspects of life, maybe less is more — if less means developing more intimacy with every single sentence.

PHIL TREAGUS: What books do you feel are important reading for people on your career path?

BRAD EVANS: I have never really seen myself on a "career path." There has never been a clearly defined road I have tried to map out or had signposted before me. I just try to stay principled to the work I feel is important, trying as best I can to speak to multiple audiences through various mediums. Though I have been very fortunate to have the guidance of a number of truly brilliant mentors along the way, who have each instilled in me the idea that no book should ever be written unless it moves, disrupts, and challenges preconceived ideas — including my own.

But if I had to single two books out, they would be Paulo Freire's *Pedagogy of the Oppressed* and Gilles Deleuze and Felix Guattari's *A Thousand Plateaus*. The importance of Freire is to teach us that education is always a form of political intervention. It's never value neutral or objective. In this regard, education is not simply about introducing students to core "subjects." Education is always a regime of power, which produces certain subjectivities and is integral to the authentication and disqualification of lives. At its best, the power of education is to encourage and help liberate what it means to think and act in the world. *A Thousand Plateaus* develops this idea like a conceptual cluster bomb, disrupting the very idea that a book should have a logical structure and flow, thus allowing for a less structured and formalised understanding of critique. It is a truly original exercise, which, reflecting the complex layering of human realities, disavows any privileged intellectual hierarchies. And in the process, it shows how everything can be potentially political in its effects. The book also importantly represents a continuation in the on-going fight against fascism in all its forms.

PHIL TREAGUS: Is there a book that you've read more than once? What is it, and why did you revisit it?

BRAD EVANS: Dante's *Inferno*. It is brilliant and troubling. Dante shows in this poem how the very same text can be used to uphold the most formidable regimes of power yet reveal subtle revolutionary insights. While there is always something new to take from *Inferno*, I am actually less interested in the figure of Dante than Virgil. Virgil is not only a guide and tutor. He is seemingly the master of all things literary. And more importantly still, he is a poet who Dante recognised to be a witness of history and a maker of new worlds. Dante captures the poetic in ways we are yet to fully comprehend and appreciate. It's a poem that continually calls you back. The beginning of Canto 28 stays with me:

> Who could ever, even in straight prose
> And after much retelling, tell in full
> The bloodletting and wounds that I now saw?
>
> Each tongue that tried would certainly trip up
> Because our speaking and remembering
> Cannot comprehend the scope of pain.

Words often fail us. And in this regard, I disagree with Jacques Derrida. There is a world outside of language — a world of love and pain, shared hopes and tragedies, imagination and ruination, which remains irreducible to prose. That doesn't mean books are less important than we imagine. On the contrary, I like to think of books, like *Inferno*, as a key to open different gateways into these all-too-human experiences.

PHIL TREAGUS: What book have you recommended the most to friends and family?

BRAD EVANS: Mathias Enard's *Zone*. It's one of the most brilliant books I have read in a very long time. Enard's literary style alone is exhausting. But the subject matter he deals with — war and violence — should take us to this point. There is more depth in this book than any dry chronology of the history of warfare and its consequences.

PHIL TREAGUS: What's your favorite genre of book?

BRAD EVANS: I try not to privilege any genre of book. Though, often, I find there is more realism in literary styles than any so-called objective and scientifically validating study into the political and social nature of human beings. I am not anti-science. But I am anti-positivist. I believe the tendency to parcel the world of intellectual enquiry into neat boxes so we might retreat back into disciplinary purities — especially those under the reductive guise of quantifiable dogmatism — is counter-intuitive to the idea that the political should be tasked with creating better futures. I try to therefore keep my horizons as open as possible in this regard.

PHIL TREAGUS: What do you think a world without books would be like?

BRAD EVANS: Dead. I don't mean death in terms of the extinction of all things, but death in the terms of the killing of an element that makes us uniquely human. If you don't have libraries, you end up having prisons. If you don't provide people with the intellectual tools to empower critically minded subjects, you end up with incarcerated minds. A world without books is a world foreclosed. Every great tyranny begins by declaring a war upon the imagination and the appropriation or imprisonment of those deemed to be its most creative. Why? Imagining other worlds runs counter to the fascistic impulse to impose a forced unity upon a people. Tyrants always try to suffocate and replace the richness of the human condition with dogmatic images of thought. Such is the reason why books are often banned and outlawed by those who fear their contents. They are one the most powerful mediums in which the political can be reimagined and new styles of living developed. But we need to be vigilant. And as we also know, the burning of books can take many different forms.

PHIL TREAGUS: Is there an author whose writing you're such a fan of that you'll read everything they release?

BRAD EVANS: There are two, for entirely different reasons. The first is Henry A. Giroux. I have had the distinct privilege to collaborate with Henry on a number of occasions. Henry has such a brilliant and courageous ability to get beneath the surface of social myths and constructions — to expose us to the raw realities of power and its human consequences. What is more, his commitment to the ethical importance of public education is tireless, and everything he writes is done with compassion, sincerity, and dignity.

The second is Simon Critchley. The brilliance of Simon is to make complex philosophical ideas resonate. Whether he's writing about Oscar Wilde, *Hamlet*, or David Bowie, his books seamlessly move from the complexity of philosophical enquiry onto the ways the ideas shape and influence everyday life. This, I believe, comes from his particular approach to philosophy and the arts, which is about providing readers with a new angle of vision on a set of issues. I have also been enormously influenced by his stylistic promiscuity, learning to write for different audiences with different styles. This has been an important lesson for me. There is no such thing as a universal language.

PHIL TREAGUS: Do you think digital books will ever completely replace real books?

BRAD EVANS: I hope not. There is something quite magical about the material form of the book. And besides, the digital world is far more precarious than we care to imagine. As Paul Virilio has noted, we still don't know what a virtual accident looks like.

PHIL TREAGUS: What book do you feel humanity needs right now?

BRAD EVANS: One that takes us beyond the contemporary impasse in which we are simply presented with two visions of the world: the fated catastrophic imaginary of liberalism or the retro-topic and overtly fascistic visions of political realism. If only Nietzsche were alive to write it.

PHIL TREAGUS: What is the book that you feel has had the single biggest impact on your life?

BRAD EVANS: Primo Levi's *If This is a Man*. This is so much more than a book. It's a testimony to the worst of the human condition. It profoundly altered how I understood the relationship between history and its claims to civilization and human progress. And it also placed certain ethical and political demands upon me as a writer, as it should do with everybody who reads its harrowing pages. As Gilles Deleuze noted, it's a book that asks us all to continually question our own shameful compromises with power.

PHIL TREAGUS: Are there any books you haven't mentioned that you feel would make your reading list?

BRAD EVANS: Anything by Franz Kakfa. He is another of the great political and philosophical minds who understands the power of literature.

PHIL TREAGUS: What books or subject matter do you plan on reading in the next year?

BRAD EVANS: I am currently working on a number of projects, one of which is taking me into some obscure and fascinating places. It's also allowing me to focus more on the life and work of Frida Kahlo, who, to my mind, is one of the greatest revolutionary figures of the 20th century.

PHIL TREAGUS: If you were to write an autobiography, what would it be called?

BRAD EVANS: I would like to write some kind of autobiography someday — not about me (my life is not that interesting), but about the conditions of life growing up in a working-class community with all its hopes and desperations. Though the title is yet to be decided. Maybe I'll call it that: *Yet to Be Decided*. It needs to be optimistic.

Originally published in somewhat different form in The Reading Lists.

Recovering from an Addicted Life

Brad Evans & Russell Brand

Thursday, 9 November 2017

BRAD EVANS: We all know any book is the outcome of months and sometimes years of procrastination. What really compelled you to write this book at this moment in your life?

RUSSELL BRAND: I felt that anybody who is in recovery has an experience where the initial attempt to tackle addiction — in my case crack and heroin — ends up being utilized in every aspect of your life. Working through and following the same principles can alter all behaviors and all forms of destructive attachments. So, what I felt was I'd reached a point in my life where I have gone through so many layers of disillusionment — with sex, fame, Hollywood, and the rest — and the recovery lens through which I live my life offered something.

Don't get me wrong; disillusionment is a good thing. After all, who wants to be bloody illusioned! Now, I by no means do it perfectly. Far from it! But I have seen the techniques which I followed change lives. So, I wanted to expound these to offer a counterweight to the prevailing addictive ideologies of our times, which is a determined and yet unconscious self-centeredness.

BRAD EVANS: When reading the manuscript, I was trying to figure out what type of book it actually was. Ironic, I know, for a so-called postmodernist! I think, in an affirmative way, it's like an "Anti-Self-Help-Book." And what I mean is: the central message I see jumping off the pages is that it's precisely the self-centered, individualistic, fuck-the-world-and-its-loving-sentiments attitudes which gets you into the fix in the first place. Hence, it's not about self-help; rather, it's all about a sober and truthful cry for human connection.

RUSSELL BRAND: I think our culture and our biochemistry can collude to become our worst allies. They can create a kind of chronic individualism. And I feel the natural conclusion of a secular rejection of the mystical leads us to the point that we are just individuals. We are only here for ourselves, surviving alone, and learning how to dominate certain situations so we can fulfill our own impulses and desires.

When I try to find personal fulfillment in my life, I still often find myself in a sort of peculiar despair. I start to feel lonely and disconnected. Then I remind myself. Hence, why I feel qualified to write about addiction — my life is like a map of addicted lines from money, crack, fame, sex, relationships, and seeking out other people's approval. I see this phenomenon appearing again and again in my life. Maybe the label addiction itself is too confining, and what we are actually dealing with is the human condition in motion.

We live in a culture that uses as its fuel this will to acquire and possess. But the tragedy is: such a desire to possess things ends up possessing us. This makes for a constant battle. Every day, I wake, and I am bewitched and hypnotized by the seductive lure of materialism. And yet, I know that when I go and help other people, sometimes in blatant sub-Princess Diana ways, or even on a more basic human level by just listening to other people's problems, that's when I feel genuinely fulfilled and my life has meaning and significance. There is an indescribable energy there when you begin to help somebody else. It's a kind of elevated sense of human connection. And you also start to see the real beauty of a person when they help somebody less fortunate. A life of unselfish purpose, empathy, compassion, all those words that are excluded from the political and social ideologies of our times, suddenly become accessible through the most basic of human actions and behaviors.

BRAD EVANS: So why do you think, then, that we often act and behave against our better judgments? I am thinking here of our attraction to relationships and people we know to be detrimental and indeed toxic to our physical and emotional wellbeing?

RUSSELL BRAND: Possibly a misplaced sense of romanticism. What I mean by that is the individualistic notion that you can find fulfillment by being with some aspirational figure that comes from the desire to be with some deity or earthly goddess. I'll find salvation if I find the true one, like your own personal Jesus. This idea, I think, is highly prevalent. And yet, even more toxic than that is the commodification and objectification of all relationships. To view somebody like an object that can serve you, make you feel better, and improve your social status. Now I have to admit that, in my case, this happened all too easily. I have to work to not approach relationships in this indulgent way.

But these are just tendencies, and that's what a recovery program means to me. It is to learn to acknowledge and deal with these tendencies on a daily basis.

It's also important to recognize it's not the difference between having a program and no program. We are socially and culturally programmed to behave in certain ways, not least the program of vapid consumerism. And so, if you don't undo that program, decode yourself from the "I'll never be good enough unless I get my hand on that object," like somebody who is leaving an all-too-consuming cult, then that's the program which will come to shape your existence.

We have to learn to untangle the strands that bind us to materialism. We know the material world is an illusion that is transmitted into our consciousness through the senses. This is why personal crisis is important here. It gives us the opportunity to re-evaluate our lives and ask difficult questions.

BRAD EVANS: There is invariably a deep philosophical underpinning to this project. And that is the attempt to connect with something, which, in the most inexplicable but no less real ways, gives meaning to this all-too-fleeting life. Am I right in saying this is truly a search for the substantive over the superficial? Or, to put it another way: maybe it's an embrace of something irreducibly spiritual, which only comes from certain courage to the truth about your existence?

RUSSELL BRAND: What is substantial about the spiritual to me is its efficacy. I know it works. When I do these things, I feel better in ways I can't explain but know they are real. I don't require any science to tell me this. When I am kind, loving, and when I surrender, I know that I am becoming a better me. These things can't be measured. Nor can they be mechanized or monetized. They are, in fact, affective. They have a truth, which is different and difficult to legislate or iterate.

This brings up another deception of secular materialism. It teaches us to become suspicious of those feelings we know to be true. And then, it sells us solutions to our problems that come from living under these same false ideals of consumerism. This is how addictions take hold. They don't appear as problems but as solutions in our attempts at seeking some form of human connection. And this is why I think we are all somewhere on the addictive scale.

I know that I could lapse at any moment. I don't know what's around the corner. What unforeseen event might push me back into the depths of loneliness and despair? This is why I haven't written this book from a position of authority. It's written from a position of an experience I am still living. And it's when I actually think that *I* will take full control of this situation that the ego starts to reappear, armed with its desire, pleasure, and fear, to send me down the wrong path. So, the reason why the spiritual is important is that it is the only thing that can transcend the material and transcend passive consumerism.

BRAD EVANS: You talk in the book of the need to confide in others about your troubles. I would like to read out this particular segment, not only because it brought tears to my eyes, but also because I think it really addresses what's at stake here:

> Suddenly my fraught and freighted childhood became reasonable and soothed. "My mum was doing her best, so was my dad." Yes, people made mistakes, but that's what humans do, and I am under no obligation to hoard these errors and allow them to clutter my perception of the present. Yes, it is wrong that I was abused as a child, but there is no reason for me to relive it, consciously or unconsciously, in the way I conduct my adult relationships. My perceptions of reality, even my own memories, are not objective or absolute, they are a biased account, and they can be altered.

The moves here — from the deeply personal and tragic to the transformative — are powerful. And it no doubt takes a great deal of courage to put this onto paper. How do you hope these words can help in the healing of others who carry such difficult memories?

RUSSELL BRAND: As Jarvis Cocker once put it, "without people, we are nothing." Recovery and spirituality are collective and communal activities. They cannot be achieved by being stuck into a pod and shot into outer space. Primarily, it is about how you relate to yourself and how you relate to others as people. Just to clarify, the abuse you referred to in the passage happened outside of my family, and I feel it's important to remind us of the fact that it's possible to alter our perception of the past, and in doing so, we also alter our perception of the present. But you can't just say this to yourself stuck in some room. It has to be related.

BRAD EVANS: Let's now connect this more specifically to your earlier work on the War on Drugs. Historically, the drugs issue has often been neatly separated into war/law vs. development/health paradigms. Now, while the critique of the former is most welcome, too often the latter can reduce this to questions of individual pathology or deviance. It is simply the individual who screws up! How might we learn to better connect the social to the individual in this context?

RUSSELL BRAND: The criminalization of drugs is a useful social tool in the management of populations. And I agree with your critique of the health model as a determinate means for reducing what is a social issue to some individual pathology. Addiction can affect anybody, but it is certainly exacerbated by economic depravity. There are different forms of depravity too, like emotional depravity, so it's not like the poor simply have full ownership of this. Though it would be nice for them to have exclusive control of something! What I mean is that its effects are felt more there in terms of the experience, the treatments, whether you are criminalized or not, and often whether it takes your life.

A while back, I went on a police raid in West London. This was a very revelatory experience for me. They battered the door in of this "crack house" — which, in itself, is an interesting description for a deprived home — and what dwelt within was not monsters. It was like booting down the door of a leukemia ward. It was full of thin, emaciated, and broken people who were slumped and pale in chairs, denied sunlight of every variety — literal and spiritual.

These were people who were just holding their lives together. And what I realized here was that it's precisely those programs, which take you from the individual narcissism and nihilism to forms of social care and compassion, that are most needed here. If we have an inclusive, empathetic society, then, by definition, you don't abandon people to the fate of forces beyond their control. We need to help people so that they are not defined by problems, which are often social problems. If we have systems that emphasize the corollary and connection between us, then we will build a better society that is more inclusive.

BRAD EVANS: I want to push you a bit on this term "recovery," which is used for the title. The way you seem to use and deploy the term here is different from more simplistic understandings, which might refer to the rediscovering of some essential self that's been somehow trapped or frozen in time and just needs to be *re*discovered. And yet, this book seems to also be a critique of such perfectible lifestyles, arguing that to recover means accepting that sometimes it's actually okay not to be okay in life and that all of us struggle with our identities.

RUSSELL BRAND: This again is something I have only found in spiritual conversations. You accept fallibility as part of the human condition. And you don't punish yourself because of it. Humanity needs to relinquish the idea of perfectibility. Now, a natural bio-chemical entity like the human does have a code. It will grow a certain way if unimpeded by social, political, cultural forces. But we know those forces exist. So, when I use the term recovery, I am talking more about an intended path, which doesn't condemn us to live addicted lives and then succumb to the logics of passivity and false material prophets. We must be reborn from a world that sees us only as a statistic.

BRAD EVANS: To conclude, I'd like to end on the issue you begin with at the very start of the book — namely, the big impending "D," the death question. As you point out in the introduction, we don't like to talk about the reality of death individually, and it's certainly not something we like to talk about publicly. And yet, since Plato onwards, it has been appreciated that to philosophize is to learn how to die.

But I think this needs to be taken a stage further. As David Bowie put it: "Religion is for people who fear hell. Spirituality is for people who have been there." With this in mind, the questions your book leaves me asking are: How can we examine our life — to learn to appreciate its finitude and the impending death we all face by actually crossing over — and look at life from the perspective of death? How can we ask serious questions about our life, our present, and our hopes for the future while already knee deep in the mud of our tragic and yet still wondrous condition?

RUSSELL BRAND: This requires actually some rather simple shifts in acceptance and gratitude. To begin, on an all-too-human level, I relinquish the idea that I am not homeless, lying in a gutter and smacked up on crack because I am now somehow a superior being literally looking down. It's more because of some random set of coordinates and unforeseen events, which have deposited me into a comfortable life, and I'm really lucky and grateful So, I don't have a punitive attitude towards those people who, by chance, find themselves in desperate states.

I always find it a real honor that when I am amongst addicts, they will often just take me for who I am. They know my past and my fallibilities. And it's in these moments that I also realize we are all ultimately connected. We are all experiencing this thing called life together as part of a shared consciousness, for better and worse. And when I realize this, I know I am not on my own anymore. I am no longer afraid. I don't have these obligations to prop up some avatar of myself — some deification that people might love or give approval in order for me to ameliorate some inner sense of worthlessness and isolation.

When the self feels like its worthless or nothing, I feel we are searching for a deeper truth. How can we not be disconnected or divided, separate from, and, therefore, we are everything? Clearly, the retreat into individualism is more than self-defeating here. Because if we separate, we are condemning ourselves to nothingness! This is not about the annihilation of the self as in subjugation in a violent or destructive way. But the recognition that there is no need for fear because we are already one, and these things are not just philosophical tropes or empty mantras — they are things you can live by recognizing that your own suffering is an opportunity and call to break out from the imposed paradigm that reduces worthiness simply to what objects you accumulate. And this is what it means, I think, to find out the truth about ourselves.

Originally published in somewhat different form in the Los Angeles Review of Books.

Violence, Conflict &
the Art of the Political

Brad Evans

Friday, 10 November 2017

WE HUMANS ARE FOND of telling ourselves a particular fable about the history of the human condition. Often, it begins with a tale of two prehistoric hominids, who, becoming more vertical in their posture — hence, more humanlike due to their elevated modes of perception and ability to see the world from a different angle of vision — make the most necessary of discoveries: the creation of fire.

We often picture these pre-political and pre-philosophical beings dwelling in some dark, desolate, and dank cave, lonely, uncomfortable, huddled together in a way that is devoid of love, compassion, and the joys of existence while protecting themselves from the brutal outside environment and the odd marauding saber-toothed tiger lurking at the doors. Armed with fire, however, everything changes. Soon, the hominids become more confident and self-assured. They become hunter-gatherers and even have the time to entertain themselves by painting nice images on the cave's walls, just for art's sake. Thus begins what we might call a natural history of violence out of which humankind learns to deal with the insecure sediment of its existence.

The rest of the story is very familiar to the Western political and historical imagination. With this most precious of elements now at our mastery and effective disposal, or so we like to think, soon the human species develops iron, steel, and other technologies for earthly conquest, leading to centuries of battles and violence forged during "darker periods" of human evolution. Importantly, the darker periods here don't refer to the technologies these humans actually produced despite all their violent intents and purposes; they refer instead to the "darkness" of being human while still living in a state of nature, living as an unruly, ungoverned, disaggregated, and — to use the discursive language of the so-called "enlightenment" — savage mass.

Eventually came the English Civil War — ripping apart the still darkened serenity of the otherwise beautiful British countryside, which compelled an observant Thomas Hobbes to write that, left to this state of nature, "the life of man" was "solitary, poor, nasty, brutish, and short." With the Leviathan keeping a watchful eye over the increasingly deforested mountain tops while literally embodying the fate of all peoples, we begin the reign of modern sovereignty, which sets in place the notion that there is no politics without security and no security without the state, replacing the state of nature with a very real state of terror. Order was to be maintained and hierarchy naturalized through the force of law and the monopolization over the means of violence — supposedly to prevent any return to social disintegration and some chaotic state of anarchy.

Now, as is well documented, the subsequent shift from princely states to colonial appropriation, exploitation, and dissection of the planet and its peoples eventually gave rise to the emergence of the world of nations born of various secular dreams. Such dreams and phantasmal visions became known as "ideology." Displacing earlier theological forms of allegiance and disagreement, this period of human history also gave rise to the myth of nations and new claims of supremacy — something that was wonderfully captured by George Orwell, who noted, "by 'nationalism,' I mean first of all the habit of assuming that human beings can be classified like insects and that whole blocks of millions or tens of millions of people can be confidently labelled 'good' or 'bad.'"

This conception of nationalism and its increasingly materialized sovereign divisions and tensions was purposefully developed and rigorously articulated by the German theorist Carl Schmitt, who put forward his idea that sovereignty ultimately was nothing more than the ability to define who was the friend to be secured and who was the enemy to be vanquished. Sovereignty, as Schmitt maintained, was nothing more than the ability to decide upon the state of the exception, which was just as important in defining what and whom was to be included as opposed to what was to be abandoned. Schmitt started from the basic premise that humans were born into a violent state of nature, and this violence, in turn, required — to bring about internal peace — taming of the natural world and monopolization over the means of endangerment. The world was thus subjected to a state of permanent emergency, in which conflicting ideas about the good life — not to mention the desire to still appropriate what your neighbour possessed — resulted in a modern state theory full of entities constantly navigating a fraught political landscape of diplomacy and warfare.

The trouble with those who possessed ideology, however, was that they tended to have no respect for sovereign integrities and visions of internal peace. Thus, as the 20th century developed, the modern theory of sovereignty was accompanied by theories of resistance and revolution — which, tapping into the anger and sense of disillusionment some felt with the progressive order of things, introduced terms such as the vanguard, dialectics, and negation (indeed the negation of negation) into the political lexicon.

Much of the theory here was relatively straightforward. The historical architecture of the world benefitted certain elite groups, so, in order to bring about genuine revolutionary change, you needed a small, educated cadre of committed revolutionaries who were willing to throw their bodies on the line — well, actually the bodies of those they instructed. After all, some revolutionaries are more important than others since they were the ones exposing the masses to all that was wrong within this state of affairs. Resistance thus begins as a form of negation — a profound disavowal or disagreement with the existing order of things — and, like a fly caught on a web, left trapped and screaming out in the hope of bringing about, often through the means of more righteous violence, a better and more equitable future.

What we encountered here was a conflict between different logics of violence — one that was premised on the need to justify its instrumentality to maintain the peace forcefully wagered against a revolutionary other, who, in turn, argued that violence was justified in an emancipatory context in order to bring about more equitable ends for peoples. All the while this was unfolding, liberals kept reading and appropriating Carl Schmitt in order to try and vanquish this most formidable of enemies.

Fast forward to the 1990s. As the Berlin Wall fell and ideological con-flict was said by liberals to be condemned to the dustbin of history (and hence the modern theory of resistance and revolution, too), so liberals set out to defeat Schmitt and all such dogmatic political re-alists once and for all. Not all liberals disagreed with the reality being presented here; on the contrary, many understood that the world of individual sovereign entities operating in their own nationalistic in-terests was, in reality, dangerous and conceptually an affront to any universal predisposition.

Schmitt and his allies weren't, therefore, dangerous because they spoke untruthfully or deceitfully. They were dangerous because they embodied the truth of the times. Thus, with the question of ideologi-cal revolution largely settled — at least that's what Francis Fukuyama had us believe in *The End of History and the Last Man* — in order for the world to be at peace, what was needed was the creation of a new global architecture for rule, a system that allowed us to overcome un-natural divisions segregating humans into various enclaves around the world.

As the last two decades have shown, however, the more liberalism has proclaimed planetary peace, the more it has needed to declare and wage planetary war. The results have been devastating. We are now living in an age that is terrifyingly normal, one where wars are so natural and technologically determined they no longer even need to be declared, and where once familiar demarcations between notions of inside/outside, friends/enemies, times of war/times of peace have been put into political crisis. We are living in a state of dystopian real-ism where the future often appears as an endemic terrain of catastro-phe and crises.

So how might we conceptually rethink our way out of this? And should we even bother? After all, even the most positive voices out there now seem to tell us that we are all eventually fated to our own extinction. I'd like to suggest a purposeful way out of this quagmire is to rethink the political itself by producing an alternative reading of the history of the human condition — one where we bring into question the undoubted-ly crude conflation between violence, conflict, and resistance. To do this, I want to open up the discussion on the relationship between vio-lence and power by linking this to how we might see conflict and resis-tance in more affirmative and, indeed, more artistic terms. In doing so,

I am trying to reach for a different concept of the political — one based on empathy, love, and the imagination, one that doesn't follow the familiar trajectory from endangerment to enmity to outright extinction.

In Hannah Arendt's important 1969 essay, "Reflections on Violence," which was originally published in *The New York Review of Books*, Arendt wrote: "Power and violence are opposites; where the one rules absolutely, the other is absent. Violence appears where power is in jeopardy, but left to its own course, its end is the disappearance of power." What Arendt is suggesting here is the need to have a better conceptual understanding of power and violence as categories in the ordering of human affairs. Violence, she maintains, is actually a manifestation of political impotence. Those who demand recourse to violence effectively have inadequate power at their disposal. The violent man is the one who cannot command others through the power of his ideas or the nonviolent forcefulness of his means of seduction.

There are, of course, a whole number of conceptual issues this distinction raises — not least some of Arendt's crude essentializations and sometimes misplaced faith in the political agora — but I do think it is worth pursuing as a way to reclaim something out of the conceptual collapse. We owe a great deal to Michel Foucault for providing us with a more sophisticated understanding of power and its architectures, structures and its affects, beyond the reductiveness of material explanations — and power, as Foucault suggested, has never been totalising, nor can it be held like some possession, neatly boxed up and contained. Power has no essence at all. It is relational — always a power relation — which points to the forces that can affect the dominated and the dominating alike. Indeed, since power is relational, by definition, it holds the potential for reversals of fortune, for the subversion of its affects and its disintegration. Power, in other words, is wholly dependent upon the capacity for struggle, conflict, and resistance.

Without these qualities, there is no power relationship to speak of and, since there is no such thing as totalising power, what remains is the order of violence. There is, however, a number of qualifications that need to be made here.

1)   It is not simply the case that violence is negative and power is positive. Violence can be just as much bound up with progressive nar-

ratives as much as power can lead to forms of self-annihilation and political nihilism.

2)   Just because power is positive doesn't mean that all power is necessarily good. Indeed fascism, as Deleuze maintained, is all about the positive manipulation of human desires which emerge from a toxic combination of fear and emancipatory discourses and which, nevertheless, still ultimately represents a manic attack upon the political body.

3)   Just because a person struggles against power doesn't mean they will create the world anew. Too often, in fact, the impulse to resist either ends up mimicking the logic of the system so that there is merely a changing of the guard, or it is dominated by what Foucault called the "sad militants of theory" — who, caught in a dialectical bind, create nothing, as they are too busy negating everything.

But what this does mean is that conflict is an important quality not only in terms of thinking about empowerment — with disagreement itself being key to understanding freedom and liberty — but also in conceptualizing a theory of resistance, which, premised upon the affirmation of differences, takes us some way toward understanding the human desire to create and what this means in terms of the relations of power into which it's thrown.

As I say this, I can already here the various political grumblings and voices of discontent that would demand a return once again to the original question of violence. Is it not, after all, this vexed issue of "difference" that gives rise to violence and conflict in the first place? The idea that difference is the cause of many of the world's problems is present as a foundational truism of modern political thought. Indeed, it is fair to say that we still largely operate within the Kantian image of thinking, where difference is seen as the unnecessary and dangerous impediment to the universalization and inevitable unification of the human race — those of you who are familiar with the implicit and explicit racism of Kant's anthropological writings will note my irony here. But is it necessarily the case that difference — especially ontological difference — causes violence?

When dealing with this issue, I am often drawn to both René Girard's *Violence and the Sacred* and Frantz Fanon's *Wretched of the Earth*, along with various other literary texts. Girard's thesis offers a theory of violence that is exclusively bound to human tragedy and the ethos of competition over power and wealth. To develop this theory, Girard uses the classic Greek play by Sophocles, *Oedipus Rex*, which illustrates the relationship between tragic dispossession and violence. It is through the tale of Oedipus and his return to reclaim the realm from which he was abandoned that we uncover a genesis of sacrificial violence that is linked to some "past tragedy."

Oedipus thus epitomizes the motif of the lost prince whose modes of contestation can be understood through competing claims to the "same object of desire": when two uncompromising entities vie over the same object of desire, violence necessarily erupts. Through Girard's decoding of the Oedipus myth, what we therefore find is any attempt to repossess the object of desire necessarily requires the guilt of those currently in possession — a sacrificial victim. Thus, to overcome tragedy, one must come from the "outside" — a violently destined return that can only be justified by making a claim to the original sin, or what Girard terms a return to the "original scene." However, as Sophocles tells it, such violence is more than simply a reclamation of that which has been taken. The violence of the already dispossessed desires to re-establish the authentic order, which has been falsely appropriated — to re-establish the paradise lost.

Importantly, for Girard, such violence is not a relation of difference but is more defined by the logic of *mimesis*:

> At first, each of the protagonists believes that he can quell the violence; at the end, each succumbs to it. All are drawn unwittingly into a violent reciprocity — which they always think they are outside of because they all initially came from outside and mistake this positional and temporary advantage for a permanent and fundamental superiority.

Plunging into an opposition, which "reduces the protagonists into a uniform condition of violence," all claims to "difference" are effectively "eclipsed" by "a resurgence of reciprocity." This is, perhaps, what Jacques Derrida had in mind when he said: "the rapport of self-identity is always a rapport of violence with the other; so that the notions of property, appropriation, and self-presence, so central to metaphysics, are essentially dependent on an oppositional relation with otherness."

Or in Girard's words, "everybody" effectively becomes "the double" inasmuch as they become the "sole object of universal obsession and hatred."

It is precisely in these terms that Deleuze and Guattari would critique what has, in its Freudian usage, been termed the "Oedipus Complex." But unlike Girard, who sees the Oedipal tale as being the natural basis for human anthropology, Deleuze and Guattari argue that it is bound to an imperial logic. The Oedipus tragedy is not only reenacted every time there is a return to some authentic basis of obstacle and rivalry, but it is fully written into the progressive orientation of biopolitical drivers of modern political economy. This takes us to real tragedy, for regardless of how successful our enunciation becomes, we are forever engaged in the reproduction of an "internal colony" within which the oppressor and the oppressed remain categorically assured. Girard himself acknowledged this, adding that while the "roles alternate," there is "always a tyrant and always an oppressed."

Here, then, the strength of Fanon's text displays its full brutal glory. For what Fanon understood is that the violence of dispossession creates a mimetic situation in which both the "oppressors and oppressed" believe that "everything can be solved by force." What is more, as Fanon maintained, nonviolence appears like a gratuitous gift of violence, too, in that nonviolence can only be achieved by the absolute supremacy of a master whose monopoly over "legitimate" violence prevents any actual violent encounter. This is why we need to purposefully read Fanon's remarkable text not as a prophecy or call to arms but as a warning against repeating the violence of the past — a violence based upon establishing degrees of sameness to some authentic standard, which, in the process of a forced unification, sees difference as a problem to be solved.

I am now drawn here to Stellan Rye's silent horror movie *The Student from Prague,* which has inspired a number of compelling literary and cinematic classics. In this tragic tale of poverty and violence, the impoverished student, Balduin, makes a bargain with the Devil as he exchanges his reflection for more immediate compensations. Upon eventually seeing himself, however, the student is avenged by an angry double, which begins to wreak havoc as it seeks to revenge Balduin's betrayal. Following an eventual violent confrontation the student has with his double, Balduin shatters the mirror that is central to the plot and thus destroys the fantasy of endangerment, the source of his afflicted curse. Inevitably, however, since the double was an essential element of this Faustian agreement, in killing the violent double, so the student kills himself. Such is the order of political nihilism — which is precisely the will to nothingness.

Writing in the 19th century, Nietzsche argued that nothing was more deeply characteristic of the modern world than the power of nihilism. Nietzsche's intervention allowed us to move beyond the well-rehearsed attack upon Platonic reason or Christian faith to focus instead upon "the radical repudiation of value, meaning, and desirability." Nihilism, thus understood, referred to the triumph of *reactive thinking*. It was all about the negation of life, and it appeared to be incapable of affirming that which is properly and creatively different to human existence. Hence, for Nietzsche, nihilism was not simply reducible to some historical event in time — i.e., some exceptional moment in history — which could be shamefully written into annals of human suffering. Nihilism was the recurring *motor of history*, as the operation of power leads to a will to nothingness that strips life of any purposeful meaning. Crucially, as Nietzsche understood, this repudiation of the affirmative realm of experience is something *we create for ourselves*. Nihilism, in other words, is to be understood through a sophisticated manipulation of desires such that the individual subject depreciates itself to such an extent that it actively participates in a custom of political self-annihilation.

So, what does this all mean for the way we are to rethink effective resistance to the present? As I have already mentioned, while Hobbes argued that there can be no politics without security, and no security without the state, it was Kant who encouraged us to believe that there can be no security without universality and no universality without moral progress towards the unification of the species. However, if Kant inaugurated the modern age, it was with Hegel and his theory of dialectics, notably picked up by Marx and many others, where modernity's problematic inner workings became self-consciously theorized. Hegel is, therefore, for many the founder of the modern theory of *resistance*. Its advocates have seen dialectics as providing the escape plan from a world that is unjust. But dialectics has never been about difference but about what Deleuze highlights to be a "difference of contradiction." By internalizing all possible experience, as Fanon understood all too well, what the dialectician produces is a "negative style of thought," which ensures that we are only capable of revealing an identity that has already been conceived. Indeed, historically speaking, since the dialectical method has been implicit in recreating the master/slave dichotomy out of the ashes of liberation, inscribed into the fabric of its counter-hegemonic discourse has been a profound distaste for anything that differs from the orthodox Eurocentric schema. Or as Deleuze further argued, it is based upon "power as the object of a recognition, the content of a representation, the stake in a competition, and therefore making it depend, at the end of a fight, on a simple attribution of established values."

To explain what is politically at stake here in the present moment, I could do no better than turn to the example of Donald Trump in the United States. Trump has seemingly summoned a retreat back into 20th century paradigms for thinking. Armed with the mantra "great again," he invokes a direct appeal to the logics of sovereignty, and, in doing so, makes a naked appeal to what Walter Benjamin called mythical violence. Now, it's perhaps no coincidence the advent of Trump has also seen a resurgence in criticisms of theorists such as Foucault, where the shift towards post-truth is neatly conflated with a certain post-enlightenment disposition, devoid of the virtues of reason, rationality, and calm deliberation. Leaving aside the nonsensical notion that Foucault and others disavowed all notions of truth or concerns with the brutalizing violence of the enlightenment and its deeply racializing images, what has become interesting is the way orthodox thinkers recognize that Trump is a condition of possibility for marking out their own authentic and dogmatic positions. Indeed, not only have we seen a response to Trump, once again the world appears in neat sovereign territories and clear dialectical markers of notable political (in)distinction. Even if we put aside the recent history of liberal wars, this response to Trump retreats back into a liberal puritanicalism armed with its own version of unquestionable truth.

Trump has undoubtedly mobilized the politics of the visceral to devastating effect. It is, in fact, a textbook case of what Wilhelm Reich termed the mass psychology of fascism and the manipulation of petty fears and insecurities of the everyday in order to bring about the liberation of prejudice. Or as Spinoza might have said: so that is how the masses learned to desire their oppression as though it was their liberation! Trump has also mastered the art of distraction by inducing what Marxists would no doubt term a "false consciousness." Trump's false consciousness is consciously dialectical. The nature of his *faux* retreat demands it. Shifting the mode of perception in a retro-topic way back to times that never *were* great for the vast majority, he consciously invokes the terms "fake" to create a consciousness around traditional sovereign markers (i.e., state, media, political elites), which once appeared familiar, comforting, and secure in their knowledge production. In doing so, Trump can present himself as a familiar dialectical revolutionary, unapologetically mobilizing the anger and rage of the disenfranchised and socially downtrodden.

Such a dialectical move depends upon materializing power in the form of a reductive "state object" against which conflict can be waged. The conflictual nature of power in this regard is very site specific and even locatable on a map. To bring about a change in the nation's fortunes, there is a need to storm the palaces and bring about a material revolution in the halls of power. That the state might be fully immersed in complex networks of global political and financial rule beyond sovereign integrities is completely written out of the drama. The problem here is in the conceptualization of the theory of resistance. A dialectical account of resistance always lends itself to elitist vanguardism. There is always the revolutionary figure, who is always deeply compromised, who is always educated, more often white, most often male, who has the educational foresight to say enough is enough. Publicly armed with a giant "no" at his disposal, the revolutionary man parades through the streets as a courageous hero for the people, talking the good fight and promising to bring about a fundamental transformation in the system — all the while appealing to preexisting logics of power, justice, and violence in the name of those requiring his service.

What is clearly required here is a different concept of resistance, one that can bring about a fundamental transformation in human relations in a more affirming way. According to Deleuze, if we wish to outlive the terror of the modern, then it is imperative we begin to think differences of nature, independent of all forms of negation. The search for a non-dialectical theory of subjectivity and social relations is central to Deleuze's oeuvre. Conceiving that political subjectivity is not something that distinguishes itself from a preconceived original design (i.e., the blind trappings of an authentic and universal subject), the liberated subject emerges in the processes of *becoming* different — creatively so. Ontological priority therefore needs to be given to change, innovation, and difference, for if we accept that the political is the very capacity to become otherwise — to become different and imagine better worlds — then we can see that any style of thought that works within predetermined limits are fully complicit in the suffocation of political space. This brings me to two quotes by Deleuze that are worth repeating:

> The final word on power is that resistance comes first.

> To create is to resist.

Taken together, difference is shown to be ontologically celebrated to the extent that it is forced to *become resistive*. This has a remarkable bearing on our understanding: resistance is not a negative process but a positive and creative force — "to create is to resist." That is not to say that people forcefully resist before they are being dominated, but if we want to understand it, resistance must be ontologically situated in relation to the limitations and suffocations that are imposed upon the creative lines of difference. It is not resistance, then, which is forced to be creative; instead, through various technologies of incorporation, *that which is creative becomes resistive*. What is therefore seen to be the "no" is already an excess since it is already in the affirmative.

So where does this all leave us? The history of the modern subject, we are continually reminded, is one of survival against all the odds. Thrown into the world, as Martin Heidegger once proclaimed, it learned to adapt to whatever surroundings it found itself imperiled to inhabit — only to learn that the mastery of any given space was illusionary at best. The life of the subject upon this embattled terrain remained, as Nietzsche declared with more critical purchase than is often acknowledged, "all too human." To live has been a story of endurance unto the end. And any sense of progress amounts to a prolonging of human existence, making it possible to cheat death for as long as possible. All the while, of course, the modern subject remained sure that its existence would eventually end, albeit in some yet to be discerned event.

Are these narratives of human evolution and its accompanying stories of survival against all the odds satisfactory? Could it not actually be the case that there is *more to life* than this ongoing tale of survival? As Deleuze succinctly put it,

In every modernity and every novelty, you find conformity
and creativity; an insipid conformity, but also "a little new
music"; something in conformity with the time, but also
something untimely — separating the one from the other is
the task of those who know how to love, the real destroyers
and creators of our day.

What is at stake here is not simply the "aesthetics of existence" wherein
life conforms to some glorious representational standard of beauty.
Such constructed imaginaries always gray the magnificent colors of
the earth. What is demanded is the formulation of alternative modes
of existence that are not afraid to have reasons to believe in this world.

There are, however, some qualifications that need to be made here.
We cannot be content to see artistic production as something that fos-
ters a negative response to the realities of the world. Creativity must
precede any account of the dialectic. Nor must we confuse the art of
living with the conforming arts that merely perform a well-rehearsed
dance. Seeing life itself as a work of art is necessarily affirmative in the
sense that it appeals to the yet to be revealed. It has no taste for the
simulacrum. Neither is it content to accept the need to live dangerously such that we are forced to live with déjà vu all over again. The self is
to be actively produced as a non-stable subject that does not seek to
emulate some normative standard but, instead, forcefully challenges
the vulnerable ground, which it is said to occupy. Needless to say, this
art of living that finds political value in those poetic expressions that
remain irreducible to life — empathy, love, and imagination — stands
in marked contrast to the conformist arts, which seek to resemble the
world.

So, to offer some form of conclusion, I like to turn to arguably one of
the most brilliant, imaginative, and revolutionary political texts ever
written — Lewis Carroll's *Alice in Wonderland*. This narrative begins
with Alice chasing a white rabbit who has no time for anything. Could
there be a better metaphor for the contemporary moment than this?
In Caroll's *Wonderland*, the nonsensical is the rule, the exception has
become the norm. It's a place full of injustice where violence is arbitrary and power is unmediated. And let's consider the Queen: is there
a more fitting caricature of Donald Trump — she utters, therefore it's
true? But more important in this brilliantly crafted tale is Alice. She
continually learns to see things from different perspectives. Indeed,

this little girl is a real revolutionary subject in the most affirmative sense of the term. Alice doesn't negate the world; she brings out its wonder. Alice doesn't hide away; she resists what is patently intolerable. Alice doesn't judge the strange fellows she meets on her journey; she accepts people for their differences. And most importantly of all, Alice doesn't lament because she is armed with the greatest weapon of all — the power of imagination. Lewis Carroll once said, "You know what the issue is with this world? Everyone wants some magical solution to their problem and yet everyone refuses to believe in magic."

Originally delivered in slightly different form at the Conflict Matters *conference hosted by the Evens Foundation, London.*

Painting a State of Terror

Brad Evans

Saturday, 11 November 2017

SHE WAS YOUNG and terrified. Alone, she was led into the interrogation room. The smell of death was overbearing. Walls echoed the screams of tortured memories. Dark shadows became silent witness to many victims who had endured the most indescribable torment. Her violated body was already full of the penetrating scars inflicted by those who showed utter disregard for her life, her humanity, her right to exist on this planet. She was nothing in their eyes. Meaningless. Expendable. Yet another throwaway object, brutally cast aside on the scrap heap of a fateful history.

Her body was eventually found three weeks later. At least it offered some form of closure, they said. But what did it mean to find their daughter in such a ravaged state? Torn apart like a worthless piece of flesh. How the memory of suffering persists. Carried on in the countless nightmares and visions lasting a lifetime in the minds of others. Disappearance. Reappearance. There is no comfort in the absence or the recovery. Only the pain now that travels in thoughts, only tears and the tragically altered lives of those who will always carry her.

And what was her crime, they asked? Was she guilty of simply believing in the wrong ideas? Had she just happened to read the wrong book? Maybe she perished for standing up and fighting for a more equitable world? Then again, could it be something more arbitrary? Perhaps it was the darker color of her skin? Being seen in suspicious company? Maybe it was an overheard conversation? Or worse still, was it just a case of some mistaken identity? In truth, for her persecutors, it doesn't really matter. She was put on trial for her very existence.

But just as she is now yet another entry written into the brutal history of the human condition, the death doesn't end with her wretched body. Acquaintances, investigating journalists, human rights workers, concerned family and friends; soon are all caught in the ravaging crossfires of the violence. And the more the violence takes hold, the more it assumes a life of its own. Everything gets drawn into its orbit: bystanders, women and children all brutally consumed in an indiscriminate massacre of the innocents.

And so, we are compelled to search for answers. We get denial. Cover-ups. Miscommunication. We soon learn we are looking in the wrong places, that we are asking the State, but there is no such thing as the State. There is only its power and its violence. Its flags, parliament buildings, or border walls are mere facades. The State is always flesh and bone, its lineations tangled, consciously blurred, and overlaid with deception. A real Leviathan — the body politic — but instead of delivering happiness, hospitality, and hope, it revels in devastation, destruction, and death.

Such violence feels its way into existence. Trusting nobody, fearing everything. That's the real meaning of terror. There is an intimate reality to its appearance. Terror is not the fear of the unknown. It is the fear of something all too close, all too familiar. The home is no longer a sanctuary. Familiar streets are filled with vulnerability. Neighbors become enemies. Passing cars motor to the promise of potential abduction. And a simple walk alone is now the opportunity to imagine you may never return to see your loved ones again. How quickly it becomes normalized. Terror normality, abducting every feeling and thought in a ritualistic nightmare of the haunted mind.

But we cannot accept this violence, we need to refuse to normalize the wounds that tear apart the bodies of the living. And so, this world needs to remember. It needs to bring back the memory and life of those otherwise condemned to be forgotten. It needs those committed to justice to have the courage to speak truth to power. It needs the critical writers to explain the atrocious to not let every scar left upon the body of the victim become another weeping cut into the flesh of the earth. And it needs the artists to provide a visual testimony in this ongoing battle over the shattered landscapes of memory and all-too-human suffering.

The Mexican artist Chantal Meza's work takes us on a deeply moving and challenging journey through the intimate realities of the world's beauty and pain. Born into a family of local artisans in Tecali de Herrera, Puebla, Meza draws upon the history of local artisan techniques by using her hands as brushes. In doing so, her work captures the movements, feelings, and intensities of the raw realities of existence in all their complex and unsettling ways.

Finding initial expression in painting as a way to help deal with personal loss and heartbreak, Meza has more recently turned directly to the political problem of violence and, arguably, the ultimate challenge for artistic and philosophical interventions — the problem of human disappearance and displacement. Even when we confront the worst of the human condition — our capacity to inflict the most inhumane acts upon one another — political philosophy and aesthetics requires the presence of the disfigured and violated body for its rescue. But how might we respond when facing the absence of such presence? Perhaps this is where we find the true value and meaning of the arts as a form of political intervention and awakening. What is the purpose of aesthetics, after all, if not to make the invisible visible?

In her current *State of Terror* project, Meza counters the violence of disappearance by confronting directly the realities of the most intolerable conditions. Her state of terror is a state of mind — working in the name of those who have needlessly suffered. It is not abstract. It is intimate, and it's personal. The darkened spaces in her works point to penetrating wounds out of which the blood of life seeps. She enters into the world of the victim, the girl, alone in the room. Her work begins as a personal journey as much as it speaks to wider concerns. She opens her eyes to the violence, listens to the helpless screams of pain, immerses herself in the suffering to ask about her own position in this world.

And yet, there is a larger story here, for the same darkened spaces also appear like expanding black hole vortexes pulling everything into their nightmare vision. The artist paints pain, anguish, and despair of a people and its history — a history of continuously retelling stories of devastating loss and its aftermath. The bloodstained canvases populated by demons, monsters, and wretched souls testify to the worst of our capacity to inflict the most inhumane acts upon fellow humans.

Whatever the subject matter for art, comparisons will always be made with the work. The timelessness of violence, in particular, invites such conversations. Meza's intimate depth of color might be compared to Mark Rothko's deeply moving mindscapes, for instance; the engravings are stylistically comparable to Francisco Goya's *Disasters of War*; the disfigured movements reminiscent of a Francis Bacon scream; and the contorted bodies and lines remind one of Pablo Picasso's *Guernica*. But to make such comparisons, while legitimizing her by proxy, misses the point, and would be a grave injustice to the subject of violence and the importance of the work.

While all violence reveals historical continuities and traces in its ambitions, its claims, and its denials, violence needs to be dealt with in terms of its specificity in time and place. We are always confronting new demons, new monsters, and they require new conceptual language and new demands for justice. Each violation upon each unique individual is, after all, different. And each needs to be addressed with sensitive, ethical care and genuine compassion.

This is the real power of Chantal Meza's work. It provides an original aesthetic vocabulary and visual testimony. In the work, terror bleeds into memory, forgetting into public recognition, and most importantly, the nightmare into the dream of a better land for her people and its future. Meza's state — her Mexico — is not some place that objectively appears on a map. It is imagined, and it is all too real. And like the violence it confronts, its real depth is a field of emotion, feeling, sensation, desperation, and hope. Meza confronts wounds that have existed before her, to ask how we might outlive their unique repetitions.

We are still, it seems, incapable of answering the simple question: when is too much killing enough? The statistics keep accumulating, revealing the darker side of our infinite potential. *Everything is possible* means just that, which can be liberating and can be devastating. The statistics can mask the real horror of the violence. How many disappear without a trace? How many more women are victims of femicide? How many children's dreams are savagely cut short? It is not about the hundreds of thousands of lives being needlessly ripped apart. The totals are not the story. The story is always of one life — one life denied its very humanity countless times over.

Engaging with the problem at this all-too-human level, Meza's work is not, then, about some confession. The destruction of a life, which simply demands its right to life with freedom, integrity, and dignity is more than a juridical problem precisely because the right to exist is not a crime. Meza's work provides us with a new way to see and feel the thousands of wounds inflicted upon the bodies of innocent victims. It is a silent visual cry, which, demanding immersion and reflection, speaks louder than those who try to reason and justify away such abhorrent acts or to reduce them to an isolated evil motive. Violence is not a simple matter of crime and punishment. To confront violence requires not simply justice but to demand more of ourselves. I could therefore do no better than to end with the words of the artist herself:

> What art can reflect, at its best, is the awareness we have an enormous potential to transform without doing harm and that we have the real and tangible capacity to recreate this reality. Art can be the counterweight to violence. It is the poetry of nature.

Originally published in somewhat different form in Artlyst.

Works Cited

Adorno, Theodor W. "Aldous Huxley and Utopia." In *Prisms*, translated by Samuel Weber and Shierry Weber, 97-117. 9th ed. Cambridge, MA: MIT Press, 1997.

Arendt, Hannah. *The Origins of Totalitarianism*. New York, NY: Harcourt, 1973.

Aronowitz, Stanley. "Where Is the Outrage?" *Situations* V, no. 2 (2014): 9-48.

Badiou, Alain, and Nicolas Truong. *In Praise of Love*. New York, NY: New Press, 2012.

Bauman, Zygmunt. *Postmodernity and Its Discontents*. Cambridge, UK: Polity Press, 1997.

Bauman, Zygmunt. *This Is Not a Diary*. Cambridge, UK: Polity Press, 2012.

Bauman, Zygmunt. *Globalization: the Human Consequences*. New York, NY: Columbia University Press. 1998.

Bell, Colleen and Brad Evans. "Terrorism to Insurgency: Mapping the Post-Intervention Security Terrain." *Journal of Intervention and Statebuilding* 4, no. 4 (January 7, 2011): 371-90.

Benali, Abdelkader. "From Teenage Angst to Jihad." *The New York Times*, January 13, 2015.

Benjamin, Walter. *Illuminations: Essays and Reflections*. New York, NY: Schocken Books, 1968.

Biehl, João. *Vita: Life in Zones of Social Abandonment*. Los Angeles, CA: University of California Press, 2005.

Bobbitt, Philip. *Terror and Consent: The Wars for the Twenty-first Century*. New York, NY: Alfred A. Knopf, 2008.

Butler, Judith. "Letter from Paris, Saturday 14th November." *Verso* (November 16, 2015). https://www.versobooks.com/blogs/2337-mourning-becomes-the-law-judith-butler-from-paris

Butler, Judith. *Precarious Life: The Powers of Mourning and Violence*. New York, NY: Verso, 2004.

Butler, Judith. *Frames of War: When is Life Grievable?*. New York, NY: Verso, 2009.

Critchley, Simon, *Infinitely Demanding: Ethics of Commitment, Politics of Resistance*. London, UK: Verso, 2013.

Deleuze, Gilles. "Postscript on the Societies of Control." In *Negotiations, 1972-1990*, translated by Martin Joughin. New York, NY: Columbia University Press, 1997.

Deleuze, Gilles and Claire Parnet. *The Actual and the Virtual. Dialogues II*, translated by Hugh Tomlinson and Barbara Habberjam. New York, NY: Columbia University Press, 2007.

Derrida, Jacques. *The Beast and the Sovereign 1*, translated by Geoffrey Bennington. Chicago, IL: University of Chicago Press, 2009.

Dillon, Michael. "Governing Terror: The State of Emergency of Bio-political Emergence," *International Political Sociology* 1, no. 1 (February 12, 2007): 7–28.

Dillon, Michael and Julian Reid. *The Liberal Way of War: Killing to Make Life Live*. London, UK: Routledge, 2009.

Duffield, Mark. *Development, Security and Unending War: Governing the World of Peoples*. Cambridge, UK: Polity Press, 2007.

Duffield, Mark. "Getting Savages to Fight Barbarians: Development, Security and the Colonial Present." *Conflict, Security and Development* 5, no. 2 (2005): 141–59.

Duffield, Mark. "Global Civil War: The Non-Insured, International Containment and Post-interventionary Society." *Journal of Refugee Studies* 21, no. 2 (2008): 162.

Duffield, Mark and Brad Evans. "Biospheric Security: How the Merger between Development, Security and the Environment (DESENEX) Is Retrenching Fortress Europe." *A Threat against Europe? Security, Migration and Integration,* ed. J. Peter Burgess and Serge Gutwirth, Brussels, BE: ASP-VUB Press, 2012.

Evans, Brad. *Liberal Terror: Global Security, Divine Power and Emergency Rule.* London, UK: Routledge, 2014.

Evans, Brad. "Foucault's Legacy: Security, War and Violence in the 21st Century." *Security Dialogue* 41, no. 4 (2010): 413–33.

Evans, Brad and Julian Reid. (2013). "Dangerously Exposed: The Life and Death of the Resilient Subject." *Resilience: International Policies, Practices, and Discourses* 1, no. 2 (April 29, 2013): 83–98.

Evans, Brad and Julian Reid. *Resilient Life: The Art of Living Dangerously.* Cambridge, UK: Polity Press, 2014.

Fahrenthold, David A. and Jose A. DelReal. "'Rabid' Dogs and Closing Mosques: Anti-Islam Rhetoric Grows in GOP." *The Washington Post,* November 19, 2015.

Ferguson, Niall. "Paris and the Fall of Rome." *The Boston Globe,* November 16, 2015.

Fisk, Robert. "Isis Was Quick to Understand a Truth the West Must Now Confront." *The Independent,* November 19, 2015.

Flassbeck, Heiner. "The Attacks in Paris and Our Responsibility to Work Toward an Open and Tolerant Society." *Counterpunch.org,* November 18, 2015.

Floyd, Chris. "The Age of Despair: Reaping the Whirlwind of Western Support for Extremist Violence." *Counterpunch*.org, March 29, 2016.

Foucault, Michel. "On the Genealogy of Ethics: An Overview of Work in Progress." *The Foucault Reader,* edited by Paul Rabinow. NeW York, NY: Pantheon, 1984.

Foucault, Michel. *Society Must Be Defended*: *Lectures at the Collège de France, 1975–1976,* translated by David Macey. New York: Picador, 2003.

Foucault, Michel. *Security, Territory, Population*: *Lectures at the Collège de France, 1977– 1978,* translated by Graham Burchell. New York, NY: Macmillan, 2007.

Michel Foucault. *The Birth of Biopolitics: Lectures at the Collège de France 1978-1979.* New York, NY: Picador, 2010.

Foucault, Michel. "The Ethics of the Concern of the Self as a Practice of Freedom," *Ethics: Subjectivity and Truth,* edited by Paul Rabinow. New York, NY: The New Press, 1997.

Fulton, Deirdre. "Hysterical Corporate Media Fueling War Fervor, Xenophobia in 24/7 Cycle." *Common Dreams*, November 18, 2015.

Giroux, Henry A. "Between Orwell and Huxley: America's Plunge into Dystopia," *Tidal Basin Review*, 2015.

Giroux, Henry A. *Zombie Politics and Culture in the Age of Casino Capitalism,* no. 2. New York, NY: Peter Lang, 2014.

Giroux, Henry A. *Twilight of the Social*. London, UK: Routledge, 2010.

Giroux, Henry A. *Disposable Youth: Racialized Memories and the Culture of Cruelty*. London, UK: Routledge, 2012.

Gordon, Jane Anna and Lewis R Gordon. *Of Divine Warning: Reading Disaster in the Modern Age*. London, UK: Routledge, 2010.

Giroux, Henry A. *America's Education Deficit and the War on Youth*. New York, NY: Monthly Review Press, 2013.

Giroux, Henry A. "The Violence of Organized Forgetting." *Truthout*, July 22, 2013.

Graeber, David. *The Democracy Project: A History, A Crisis, A Movement*. New York, NY: Random House 2013

Grossberg, Lawrence. *Cultural Studies in the Future Tense*. Durham, NC: Duke University Press, 2010.

Hedges, Chris. "The Power of Imagination," *Truthout*, May 12, 2014.

Hobbes, Thomas. *Leviathan*. Cambridge, UK: Cambridge University Press, 1991.

Howard, Michael. *War and the Liberal Conscience*. New York, NY: Columbia University Press, 2008.

Human Security Report 2005: War and Peace in the 21st Century. Oxford, UK: Oxford University Press, 2006.

Ignatieff, Michael. *Empire Lite: Nation-building in Bosnia, Kosovo, Afghanistan.* London, UK: Vintage, 2003.

Jameson, Fredric. "Future City," *New Left Review,* 21, May-June, 2003.

Jimenez, Marina. "France Urged by Hard-Right Party to Annihilate Islamic Radicals." *The Star*, November 15, 2015.

Kaldor, Mary. "Why Another 'War on Terror' Won't Work." *The Nation*, November 17, 2015.

Kilcullen, David. *The Accidental Guerilla: Fighting Small Wars in the Midst of a Big One.* Oxford, UK: Oxford University Press, 2009.

Konno, Yuichi. "My Art is Not an Answer — It is a Question: Yuichi Konno Talks with Gottfried Helnwein." *Yaso*, Japan. September 5, 2003.

"Mass Surveillance Isn't the Answer to Fighting Terrorism." *The New York Times*. November 17, 2015.

Lee, Esther Yu-His. "State Lawmaker Supports Putting Muslim Refugees in 'Segregated' Camps." *ThinkProgress*, November 20, 2015.

Lerner, Rabbi Michael. "Paris: A World That Has Lost Its Ethical Direction and Spiritual Foundation and a Media that Cheerleads for Fear and Militarism." *The Nation*, November 16, 2015.

Levy, Bernard-Henri,. "Thinking the Unthinkable: This is War." *The Globe and Mail*, November 16, 2015.

Maher, Brendan. "Interview with Gottfried Helnwein." *Start Magazine*, Ireland. November 24, 2004.

Niles, Emma and Robert Reich. "Theorist Judith Butler Warns That France is on Way to Becoming an Extreme-Right Militarized State." *Truthdig,* November 19, 2015.

Obama, Barack H. "A Just and Lasting Peace." Nobel Prize Lecture. Oslo, Norway. December 10, 2009.

Packer, George. "The Other France." *The New Yorker,* August 31, 2015.

Pilger, John. "From Pol Pot to ISIS: The Blood Never Dried." *Counter-Punch*, November 17, 2015.

Pollock, Griselda. "Introduction." *Visual Politics of Psychoanalysis: Art in Post-Traumatic Cultures,* edited by Griselda Pollock. London, UK: I.B. Tauris, 2013.

Polya, Gideon, "Paris Atrocity Context: 27 Million Muslim Avoidable Deaths from Imposed Deprivation In 20 Countries Violated By US Alliance Since 9-11." *Countercurrents*, November 22, 2015.

Quiggin, John. *Zombie Economics: How Dead Ideas Still Walk Among Us*. Princeton, NJ: Princeton University Press, 2010.

Ramsey, Joseph G. "Against Moral Imposters: Mourning the Dead as a Part of the World." *CounterPunch*, November 13, 2015.

Rancière, Jacques. *Figures of History*. London, UK: Polity Press, 2014.

Rancière, Jacques. *The Emancipated Spectator*. New York, NY: Verso Books, 2009.

Rancière, Jacques. "Commentary on 'Theater of Images.'" *Alfredo Jaar: La Politique des Images.* Lausanne, Switzerland: JRP/Ringier, 2008.

Richman, Sheldon. "How to Respond to the Paris Attacks." *Counter-Punch*, November 17, 2015.

Standing, Guy. *The Precariat: The New Dangerous Class*. London, UK: Bloomsbury Academic, 2011.

Schmitt, Carl. *The Nomos of the Earth*. New York, NY: Telos Press, 2003.

Smith, Rupert. *The Utility of Force: The Art of War in the Modern World*. London, UK: Penguin, 2006.

Steiger, Kay. "Rubio Trumps Trump: Shut Down Any Place Muslims Gather to Be 'Inspired' — Not Just Mosques." *ThinkProgress*, November 20, 2015.

Taubes, Jacob. *Occidental Eschatology*. Stanford, CA: Stanford University Press, 2009.

Van Buren, Peter. "Paris: You Don't Want to Read This." *Common Dreams*, November 15, 2015.

Virilio, Paul. *Speed and Politics*. Los Angeles, CA: Semiotext(e), 2006.

Weinstein, Bret. "Let's Not Get It Wrong This Time: The Terrorists Won After 9/11 Because We Chose to Invade Iraq, Shred Our Constitution." *Common Dreams*, November 16, 2015.

Žižek, Slavoj. *Violence: Six Sideways Reflections*. New York, NY: Picador, 2008.